What a refreshing look at how one man dedicated his life to focusing on the most valuable resources we have—our children. Coach Ciccarello was able to form a positive outlook from his very difficult experiences as a child, and translate it into a long-lasting impact on thousands of young people in and around the State of New Mexico. Coach, Coach is a must-read for every coach and teacher working with young people.

Judge Stan Whitaker
Former Track Athlete

The true role of a coach and teacher could not better be illustrated than in Jim's book. It reminds us all of the tremendous, positive impact one dedicated, passionate person can have on a young person's life. Hats off to a man who bridged the generation gap, many times over, to reach out to kids through music, activity and character, to give them a window to the world and an opportunity to pursue any goal they wish. Coach Jim Ciccarello has made a difference with over 65,000 students and athletes, who in turn have passed on his positive philosophy to others. There is no way to measure his impact on New Mexican children.

Susan Craig
Executive Director, New Mexico Sports Inc.

Coach, Coach, Look at Me is a compelling story about how one coach took the time to look at every kid he coached, so that each could look inside himself, to find his potential to excel.

Marshall Bear
Hollywood Director/Producer

At first, years ago, it didn't make sense. But now everyday when I pick up that jump rope I know Coach Ciccarello's intentions were only to make me a better athlete.

Warrick Campbell
Highland HS, University of Alabama Track Athlete

Jim has made clear that life lessons can be learned in sports, from family to business. As he says, "If you can dream it, you can do it."

Karen Hudson
Real Estate Executive and Athlete

He chose the title, he says, because it reflects his desire to make every kid—regardless of his or her talent level—feel equally important and appreciated. The manuscript is autobiographical and his description of his impoverished upbringing in New Jersey is an eye opener.

Rick Wright
Sports Editor, **The Albuquerque Journal**

"Whittier Play Day! Such fun memories." '

Kiva Gresham
Athlete and Student

As my mind sprinted, jumped, and threw itself into his masculine-yet-intimate writing style, Jim's humor and memory of past athletes, coaches, and friendships was clear. What stands out in *Coach, Coach, Look at Me* is the passion, caring, and success that Jim brings out in the lives of the people he has worked with over the years. This book illustrates the positive approach Jim has used, whether teaching kids how to jump rope or coaching high school track and field. It's all about the dream!

Dr. David Helm
President-Emeritus, New Mexico Track and Cross Country Coaches Association

To KANWA

THIS IS A STORY OF
44 YEARS TEACHING
P.E. AND COACHING
TRACK & FIELD. THIS IS
TRUE AND NOT EMBELLISHED.

ENJOY,

[signature]

"COACH"

ACCOMPLISHMENTS

- 44 Years of Teaching & Coaching in NM
- 25 years of Teaching Jump-Rope Teams
- Seven NM State Championship Teams
- 200 Individual NM State Champions
- 24 Individual National Champions
- 20 District Team Championships
- Four Undefeated High School Teams
- Four Olympic Trials Athletes
- Named National Runner-Up Coach of The Year 2008
- Named National Region 8 Coach of the Year 2007
- Six-time NMHSTCCA Coach of the Year
- 2007 Albuquerque Sports Hall of Fame Coach of the Year
- 2011 Albuquerque/New Mexico Sports Hall of Fame Inductee

COACH, COACH, LOOK AT ME!

A memoir
of teaching and love

Jim Ciccarello

Coach, Coach, Look at Me!
© 2012 Jim Ciccarello
ISBN-13: 978-1480217041
ISBN-10: 1480217042

Book design: Adam Rubinstein, www.gourmetbookdesign.com
Back cover photo: Kim Jew, www.kimjew.com
All photos herein reprinted with permission

First Printing

Printed by CreateSpace, an Amazon Company.

CONTENTS

Foreword

CONTENTS

CONTENTS

FOREWORD

Roger Flaherty
Retired Educator, Counselor and Coach

It is with enthusiasm and humility that I introduce you to Jim Ciccarello. Jim has been my best friend and colleague since we met in 1977 and first began to formulate our philosophies for the technical and effective aspects of teaching and coaching.

I was fresh out of college, just married, teaching a self-contained multicultural eighth-grade class and coaching the Girls' Volleyball and Basketball Teams at the high school in Tombstone, Arizona when I met Jim. After taking my basketball team to consecutive state finals and semifinals, Jim talked me into taking my teaching and coaching skills to the big city of Albuquerque. He must have realized many years ago that he had a gift to help others. Over the years, he has discovered and developed many gifts, which he has shared with anyone who was interested. I am blessed to have been one of those.

Jim and I have always been close. I made the move and pursued my career, which eventually took me to Connecticut, where I acquired a double Master's Degree in School Counseling and Private Practice. I worked as a director, teacher, counselor and social worker, and developed a pilot program for a secondary alternative education school for 13 years. Although our geographical paths diverged, Jim and I frequently communicate and meet up for holidays and special events. We continue to trade ideas about teaching and coaching.

I have observed Jim in social settings all over the world, as well as in Albuquerque at track practice, track meets and in his elementary gymnasium, where he has been teaching 10–12 daily classes of PE for 44 years. In that time he has "recognized," with his exceptional personal attention skills, every single person in his life—no matter the age, race or gender—as a valued individual, pointing out his positive aspects and seeing him walk away, every time feeling better about himself. If there is only one, I hope this rare ability is the one Jim has passed on to his students and peers. This learning about and valuing others is the heart of his inspiring nature.

Having observed him during many track meets, I have marveled at his ability to see every detail, every angle, as he meanwhile orchestrates the win.

Jim has always taught that each person has something good to offer in this world. He has been successful because he relates to individuals and sees their relevance in their own terms, and in their own lives. His ability to teach everyone, regardless of their economic status, is noteworthy and exceptional. His skills in mediating, facilitating and delegating have made him one of the best problem-solvers I have ever known. Jim has a presence which is gentle, non-threatening—almost soft.

It's clear why his kids are so well-behaved. Jim begins each period by recognizing the "entire" class as a wonderful group of well-behaved and very smart individuals. Every child in every class starves for recognition and praise. Jim's technique for galvanizing and sustaining the students' attention is absolutely amazing. Once he has explained and demonstrated the activity or game, he readily observes and recognizes individual accomplishments, often calling attention to small but essential details. He deals with inappropriate behavior one-on-one.

Jim has also mentored hundreds of student-teachers and coaches in his career, many of whom I have met. All have expressed great admiration and appreciation for everything they learned from him, and applied to their own careers.

Part of Jim's success has been his insight into how to instill high energy and creativity into his athletic programs. One example of this is his jump-rope teams. He developed a team which travels locally and statewide to further enhance their skills, build confidence and display their great talent. One need only look into the eyes of these kids at the end of their performance to see the pride.

Inside Jim is a super-competitor. He is organized, disciplined and determined to maximize his own potential. As a basketball player he would want the ball for the last shot, even playing with Larry Bird. In golf he earned a single-digit handicap despite a degenerating spinal column and several major back operations. Jim reluctantly had to quit the game at 49 because of these troubles. To this day I know how much he misses it.

There have been so many individuals who have benefited from this man of integrity. He embodies the spirit of honesty and fairness. He accepts what he has to work with for himself and others. He then believes and gets others to believe that they are exceptional. His success is unsurprising. To this day Jim continues to discover new ways to help others. He has had to adapt to his age and limitations, and he has done so admirably.

At a time when our educational system is struggling to compete with many other countries, we must continue to draw valuable insight and wisdom from successful educators like Jim Ciccarello. In reading his memoir, we discover that he gives us not only a kaleidoscope of his selfless life, but glimpses of educational magic—times when his individual athletes, as role models, shined, and in the fireworks of their glory, rained down sparks of enthusiasm and work ethic to their team-mates. And we see Jim, the great magician and mentor; pass his wand to others—his students, his athletes, his student-teachers, assistant coaches, and parents—in a life-long pursuit of excellence to the finish line.

In the end, we discover just how he wins his incredible race.

RF August 2012

Dedication

For all the 65,000 students and athletes I have worked with....and you know who you are. If you believe in magic... the magic was in the time we spent together. You have enriched my life, as I hope I have yours. Thank you.

A Special Note

With a great deal of appreciation for others in our teaching and coaching profession, I would like to thank **all educators** for their contributions to the health of New Mexico's youth. Though this story is told autobiographically, I received input from **many** educators. Over 44 years I have met thousands of great teachers and administrators—we are so blessed with outstanding elementary, middle, and high school educators that there is not enough space to mention them all! In this book some have offered their observations; there are many more who have gone quietly about the business of educating and motivating young people. New Mexico is a special place. The relationship between our students and educators is as good as it gets, and all educators are part of this story. A special thank you to all of you.

This is the story of an elementary PE teacher, track & field coach, and jump rope instructor, not a professional writer. This is my voice, coming from the heart, and it is my sincere hope that you enjoy this telling of my journey, working with the young students of New Mexico.

Acknowledgements

Thank you Gary Chorré, Earl Lyon, Roger Flaherty, and especially Cheryl Flaherty, for your support and help in putting together this manuscript of my life-long career. Cheryl, I sincerely hope the hours and hours of editing have paid off. Adam, as the final editor I hope you are proud... I am!

A hundred years from now, it will not matter what my bank account

was, the sort of house I lived in, or the kind of car I drove… but the

world may be different because I was important in the life of a child.

Forest E. Witcraft

Coach, Coach, Look at Me!

THE BEGINNING

My education began May 7, 1942.

I was born in Jersey City, New Jersey to Ignacio and Helen Ciccarello. Mom was originally from Brooklyn, NY; Dad was born in Tampa, FL. They met at a party, one thing led to another, and with that came a new generation. They were both uneducated and hard-working. Dad worked several jobs, as a short-order cook at a restaurant and a laborer in the Brooklyn shipyards.

They had four children: Jim, Rose Marie, Frank, and Richard. Growing up in Jersey City was hard in the 1940s and this family had to struggle. Dad did not finish elementary school, and Mom did not finish high school. There was neither educational leadership nor economic help to raise the family. At times we were on Federal and New Jersey welfare.

Growing up in Jersey City for the Ciccarello family was a series of moves from apartment to apartment, trying to stay one step in front of the landlord. As young kids we did not understand this and just carried our things down the stairs and onto the street as we were told by our parents. We of course did not have a car, and carried belongings on foot and by bus, but we always stayed in Jersey City or a nearby town. The cities are back-to-back, and people did not recognize Jersey City from West New York, from Weehawken, or Bayonne. You could cross city lines crossing the street; outsiders never got it! One may have been proud to be a Bayonne kid, but not a Jersey City kid!

Jersey City is located just across the Hudson River from Manhattan. The Statue of Liberty was always in our back yard. There were probably nice parts of Jersey City, but we never saw them. We didn't know what middle class meant, but had to adjust to some trying situations in a ghetto environment. Most of our stops were with other minorities such as Italian-Americans, African-Americans, Puerto Ricans, and most low-income ethnic groups. We lived on welfare most of the time and in the "Projects," a series of red brick buildings with stairwells and broken elevators. The hallways were dirty and dimly lit. They were dangerous and dark, and desperate characters were always hanging out. The Marion Projects were the toughest part of Jersey City. The police department had a policy—if they had a call to respond to the Projects, and did not have four units—they did not go! We had many altercations, and the day we moved out was a godsend for us.

Our daily living was hard and we did not buy new clothes or eat a balanced meal. We ate mostly macaroni and cheese and tuna fish. Mom would say, "Tuna fish wiggle tonight"—I never got the wiggle part! Our food was always stored in the Ice Box, literally a box in the kitchen corner refilled with dry ice. The Ice Man sometimes had to lug that ice up three or four landings, and if he had a bad day he just wouldn't come. No ice meant peanut butter and jelly sandwiches for a week.

On Sunday our big meal was spaghetti and meatballs. Once in a while we had fried liver and onions, which I despised, and meatloaf. Clothes were mostly hand-me-downs from other relatives or friends, but they were always clean.

In this part of New Jersey there were so many schools they weren't even named. My first was Public School Number 35. I then switched to PS Number 23, and then to PS Number 17, on to PS Number 5, and finished elementary school at PS Number 6. I then attended Memorial High School in Weehawken, NJ for one semester before moving to Emerson High School in Union City, NJ for one year. There was no stability.

I was always behind in my classroom work. We were adjusting and making new friends. Names were a blur and teachers and other students I met were here one day, gone the next. So I became a quiet student and tried to get along with others. Many of us had the same problems and teachers had a hard time maintaining control. Most of the students in these school environments were behind in academics, and their mobility in the neighborhood affected their classroom performance.

From this environment came the beginnings of my own future as an educator! I was saved by a couple of Physical Educators at PS Number 23 and PS Number 17. Every day was hard in our family, and suddenly I found a bright moment, in a PE class. I always liked playing on the streets, in stick ball and stoop ball; competitive activities were outlets for me from the beginning. "Kick the Can," and "Ring a Lareo" were two of my favorite chase games. But at the elementary school, Mr. Lombardi, in a fourth grade PE class, introduced me to track and field. Here we were running relays in the basement and passing wooden sticks wrapped with athletic tape. We would compete against other schools and at the West Side Armory in Manhattan. A new world began to open for me.

I was never a gifted athlete, but I was a "player"—one who joined every game in the neighborhood. Touch football and basketball were two of my favorite team pickup games. We also were able to join the YMCA day camp and this allowed us to take bus trips over to Ebbits Field (home of the Brooklyn Dodgers) and Yankee Stadium. This is when I developed my first athletic hero and role model: Gil Hodges, number 14 and first baseman for the Dodgers. He was a gentleman and had a great attitude toward competition. He was a home-run hitter, a fan-favorite and my favorite. The Brooklyn Dodgers in the 1950s were one of the better teams in Major League baseball.

My personality developed with my athletic ability, as a result of playing ball in the streets, activities at the YMCA, participating in my PE classes, and joining any athletic team the schools sponsored. I can honestly say that when I was in the fourth grade I had a vision of becoming a PE teacher when I grew up. My elementary PE teachers were my biggest influence.

The kids in the neighborhood did not always share my attitude. Some of them were smoking, drinking, getting into trouble. Trouble included stealing, breaking and entering, fighting, hanging out on the street corner, playing pin ball in the candy store, cheating the machine with a magnet or tilting, breaking windows, roof climbing, trespassing, climbing the steel bridge, walking the railroad tracks, shoplifting, and general misbehaving. I did participate in some of this, but I realized early on it was not for me. Athletics was my passion and my way out of the Jersey City ghetto. Somehow I was strong enough to break away, and when I attended Memorial and Emerson High Schools, I embraced my opportunity.

I can unequivocally say that the discipline and success I learned from athletics carried over into the classroom. My own story demonstrates that teachers/coaches can help young people to find success. No matter what your early environment, you can raise your lifestyle. In our early years we were always on welfare. I was embarrassed and unsure of myself. Every day was a battle. We had rats, cockroaches, and bugs I can't even describe. If there was an elevator, it did not work. We always had to climb. We usually had the old-style dumbwaiter in the hallway:

you put your groceries on the scale and pulled it up to your floor with a rope. Most of the time in those buildings we had a bathroom outside in the hallway, which we shared with neighbors, or even worse, with strangers passing through. My first 15 years in this environment is a reality I will never forget—but because of athletics and education, I was able to recover.

For me it all started in Jersey City, NJ. The next "New" for me was in New Mexico. Everyone sometimes needs a fresh start. Whoever said "change is good" was thinking of families like ours, in 1958.

STARTING AGAIN

It's easy to pinpoint the start of my success. In the summer of 1958 my family was set to move again. I came home to a padlock on the door. This time we had nowhere to go and my mom was distraught and frustrated. My dad, a quiet man, never said a word.

My mom had a brother, Rick, in Albuquerque. He had landed there after World War II. He suggested we try a new beginning. This family has never been more than 10 miles from the NJ/NY Metro area in 15 years and this promised to be quite an adventure!

We packed all the belongings and we left our furniture on the sidewalk. To this day I do not know who paid for the tickets on that Continental Trailways bus. It took us three days to get to Albuquerque. My nose was plastered to the window all the way. For the first time in my life, I saw farms, cows, horses, rivers, and other natural wonders. I now know that city people who never get a chance to experience travel miss out on the beauty of our amazing country.

When we arrived in Albuquerque, we were immediately taken with the Sandia Mountains. In the high desert the pink and purple dazzled us as we arrived at sunset on a partly-cloudy day. Everything else was brown, and there were few trees. The East and the Midwest had seemed so green.

Uncle Rick lived in the North Valley on Green Valley Road. There was a chicken farm across the street and my dad was able to get work there, picking up eggs. Needless to say, we ate eggs three times a day, and Mom became an egg expert. We still ate "tuna fish wiggle" and spaghetti with meat balls on Sunday.

While I attended Valley High School from 1958 to 1961, the family moved about eight times. (Some things never change!) We lived all over the North Valley, and the only time we ventured to the Northeast Heights was when my basketball team played either Highland or Albuquerque High. Later on, Albuquerque Public Schools (APS) built Sandia and Manzano, which we considered a road trip. We never had a car until I bought one, a 1949 Buick, in my senior year, for $80. I had been saving money working on the Sims ranch, stacking hay.

EDUCATION AND ACTIVITIES FOR ALL

This move changed my life. I was an East Coast guy with a Jersey accent. On the first day of school, Mrs. Gonzales encouraged her students to share something personal as they read a small passage from an English literature book. At the time I was very shy and self-conscious. I sat at the back. When it was my turn to read, I had my head down trying to concentrate. As I read out loud, I could feel heat on my face and head. When I finished and looked up, everybody in the class was staring at me quizzically. Later I found out nobody understood a word I was saying, as my accent was too thick. James Airy, my classmate, told me later that it was the highlight of his first day to hear me speak. Kids in New Mexico were fascinated by that East Coast sound.

One of the first people I met at Valley High was Cal Guymon. He had also recently moved to the North Valley, from Colorado. We had a lot in common, and he was soon to be a great friend. We both loved basketball and team sports. He also had a great attitude and believed that education was important. Unlike the kids I hung out with in NJ, Cal had a sense of fair play and treated everyone with respect, regardless of their ethnic or religious background. And he didn't mind a guy with a thick Jersey accent!

Low-income Jersey City had left me behind in academics, and with a second chance to achieve, I diligently applied myself. At Valley I had opportunities in both the classroom and on the athletic field. I joined the debate team and met some very intelligent and dedicated students, including Willy Prior and Rodney Sievers. We bonded through athletics, despite our different backgrounds; they had been nurtured in academics while I was nurtured in street smarts.

Athletics and activities, such as music, performing arts, band, orchestra, dance, government clubs, and Future Farmers of America, bridge socioeconomic divides. If students are allowed to pursue their passions, they will learn self-worth, team-work, and peer-acceptance, all of which will spill into the classroom.

Sooner or later everyone is put in an unfamiliar position. I always remember being the new kid on the block. In my case it happened a lot. Never owning a car, our family took the city bus everywhere, and I always remember bus sickness from the fumes. Even though we never relocated more than a couple of miles away from our old address it was always a new situation, and adjustments had to be made. Hanging out with Cal Guymon and other athletes built up my confidence. Athletics was my ticket.

When I sat in the classroom and daydream, as all kids do, I would think about basketball practice with warm anticipation. When I knew that my next class was PE, I was wide-awake and could concentrate. Back in elementary school the whole day had revolved around recess and the next PE class. When I put things in perspective, I realize how important it was to have something to look forward to.

When I later taught PE, I saw how it made me a better student. I know that there are teachers out there who do not share this philosophy. They may have never experienced the value of total-body involvement.

The body is a complex system of nerves, muscles, and pathways. When we have total body movement we increase our mental and emotional capacity. Even today, as I enter my '70s, when I am not feeling right I pick up a basketball and just shoot hoops. In a few minutes I start feeling better, calming down. In athletics we call this a "zone," or a natural high. With better blood circulation and more adrenaline, we can tackle more complex mental tasks.

People who love music and the arts know this feeling. Runners get a "runner's high," a euphoria. At Whittier Elementary, my home school, we had a third grade teacher by the name of Art Barrett. At recess time when the kids went out to play Art would shut his classroom door and play the piano in solitude for 15 minutes. He then came back to his students greatly relaxed, with an improved attitude.

Group and individual physical activity motivated me to be a student every day. Later, I discovered that kids came to Whittier just so they could jump rope every day. I never forget my early years and the importance of that physical activity. To this day, especially when funding is scarce, I have to persuade educators who think otherwise to believe in fitness and in teamwork.

In high school I was a member of the Key Club, debate team, letterman's club, student council, and was an alternate to "Boy's State." These activities were exciting. They also helped my self-worth and belonging. In every activity a teacher or sponsor helped students to participate. When you are a member of a student organization, you look up to adult approval and leadership. Mr. Weathersby was a staff sponsor of the Key Club, a service club to the school. I would listen intently for ideas and approval from him. If I did something for the club and he noticed, I felt as if he was watching me individually. Twenty years later, I became a teacher and coach, and worked for him at Sandia High in Albuquerque. Some of what he taught me I used as a coach many years later.

Mrs. Hays was the Girls' Activity Director and PE teacher. I admired her outgoing attitude and that she knew everyone's name. Sometimes, I thought she was the focal point of the school. Marie Hays spent over 30 years at Valley, a fixture for many generations. When I performed well and she said my name, I wanted to do even better the next time!

Calling a person by name is an exceptional tool for an educator. Some teachers, because of their loving and helping personalities, are naturals at developing good relationships with students, and they have other tricks. My principal at Valley, Earnest Stapleton, was the grandmaster at motivating kids, using their names and knowing what they accomplished; he could remember *thousands* of names. To this day, 50 years later, Ernie Stapleton knows my name and what I am doing.

When you say a student's name you are recognizing him. Educators and administrators who do this show real concern.

BASKETBALL: A TRUE PASSION

In 1958 I went out for the varsity basketball team. I was a sophomore. I think it was because of East Coast basketball's reputation that the coaches gave me a chance. On a team with 10 gifted athletes at 5'9", all angling to play Guard, my size was not in my favor. Dedication to basketball became an obsession of mine. Being part of this team affected me everywhere. My teammates were very important to me:

Marty Andrade	Cliff Hays	Porfie Maestas
Adrian Armijo	Tom Higgins	Chano Martinez
Gary Boutz	Richard Heister	Eloy Martinez
Bob Burke	Orin Hall	Solomon Martinez
Norman Burns	Jim Hill	Chester Olson
Ronnie Case	Farrell Howell	Thurl Pope
Richard Casias	Gilbert Padilla	Clarance Starnes
Joe Gallegos	Jim Johnston	Jim Van Zant
Gilbert Griego	Joel Lampson	Matt Wacondo
Cal Guymon	Butch Macy	

I asked myself, "How am I going to get playing time among all this talent?"

I knew that I had to be a good shot and hit the outside jumper. My value to the team was in shooting, not so much rebounding or defense. I could fake and change pace better than most. I knew I had to show our coaches, Dick Fox and Charles Bernard, something to get into an actual game. That first year I was predominantly a JV player with a little varsity experience. When I was at practice I always made sure the coaches were watching when I took a shot. Years before, back in PS Number 23, I always stood by the coaches' office to shoot.

I wanted to make a basket, then receive an immediate positive verbal response. I would hold the ball for long periods waiting for the coach to look my way. As soon as I saw him look the ball would fly. If I made the shot and I heard the coach say, "Chic, nice shot," I was in Heaven. To me, this was the best part of my day: to hear an adult say I performed well. I realize now that by doing this, I was preparing myself to perform under pressure. This carried into my high school career. I was slow, and had no power, but could I shoot! I never forgot those moments. When I became a teacher and coach, it was automatic for me to give positive reinforcement to kids who did well. If you talk to any of my former students, I guarantee they will tell you, "Coach Ciccarello always tried to motivate me to do better." It all started in elementary school with a couple of coach-educators telling me I just did well! Coach, Coach, look at me!

I became a decent high school player, averaging 11 points-per-game. My best was 24 points against Rio Grande High. This was a big moment in my life. I received recognition from peers and others around New Mexico. That night I was also sick with the flu, running a fever of 102°. You might say I was on fire.

After the standoff with Rio Grande, other teams would guard me closer, and the games got harder. There were many other good shooters and I shared time with them. At the time, Valley was one of the top-ten basketball teams in New Mexico. At the District Championship game we played well but came up a bit short, losing to Albuquerque High by one point. John Dorn was their star and he played well that night. James Casias, a great defensive player at Albuquerque High, held me to eight points. This was devastating, as in order for us to advance to the State Championships we had to win at District. At least that Albuquerque High team went on to finish third at the State Championships.

I then played basketball with Cal Guymon and the Mormon Church of LDS. Although I was not a Mormon, each team was allowed one non-church member. This was very exciting; LDS had a highly-organized basketball league, and the competition was equal to what I knew from high school. We had a great team and went all the way to the regional finals, losing the championship game by one point. Had we not lost we would have advanced to Blanding, UT, earning a chance to compete nationally. I had almost won us the game with a last-second shot from the top of the key: it hit the back of the rim as the clock expired. I did receive individual honors that day, with the Most Valuable Player trophy. The award was nice, but the team victory was what I really wanted. We would have done well in Blanding.

The value of being part of a team and sharing life experiences was immeasurable. I believe that these competitions prepared me to become a caring and motivated educator. From my early years running track in New Jersey to basketball in the North Valley, and on to playing basketball with the LDS Mormon church, I was preparing to become a contributing educator to New Mexico students.

About this time in my life, I was about to go on a big journey. I first went to UNM in 1962, and majored in PE. At UNM we wore gray shirts with red lettering that said Physical Education Major. I was not comfortable wearing those shirts around campus. They identified us as "dumb jocks," which was far from the truth. We certainly had some PE Majors who had no classroom motivation, but many people would be surprised how sharp some of the PE students were. Some of my classmates went on to become FBI agents, lawyers, politicians, administrators and great teachers.

The PE program as a whole is not as easy as some would have you believe. There are elitists who argue that only high-IQ students have something to contribute. Of course, we need people in all areas of education to pass on the love of learning and aspire to excellence in their field. Is that not what higher education is about? Why should those who strictly attend academic classes be "holier than" we who study athletics? Why should they be recognized as more "important" than students who have chosen a physical-skill-based field of education?

When I was a student I saw this attitude every day. But this is also where I learned to appreciate and recognize other intelligences, like educating, and the arts.

THE UNITED STATES AIR FORCE

In 1962, during the Cuban Missile Crisis, Cal Guymon and I visited the Army and Air Force recruiters to see what special fields were available. We were promised the career field of our choice. Then, by chance, we met two guys from the army who had already gone through the process. Coming out of Johnson Gym one day they told us, "Don't do it, they lie. They will probably put you in infantry and send you off to war with a rifle in your hand." That had an effect and we both "chickened out."

I dropped out and joined the Air Force. As the armed forces go, it was a wise decision; it turned out that the Air Force offered an easier way to serve than others. There was less stress, and we would study for a career of our own choice. Cal went on a mission to Tennessee for the Mormon Church, and I went to boot camp. I always kid him that he got the easier road, but he did not share that opinion. Cal had to struggle in the South riding a bicycle on lonely roads in strange neighborhoods. I do agree that a missionary has a long road to travel, but I never let him forget that I signed up for military service, while he rode a bicycle.

I did my basic training at Lakeland Air Force Base in San Antonio, TX, and then travelled the world. In many respects the military was the foundation for my teaching success; I gained a lot of confidence meeting new people and developing new skills. I was sent to Morse Intercept School in Biloxi, MS. I learned a new language, but it was a limiting one. Six months of typing sounds onto a spreadsheet was my introduction to a career in the Air Force Security Service. If I had to do it over, I would have gone to cook's school or become a recreational specialist. At least then I could have fixed myself some good meals in my college years.

I could have gained valuable experience in the PE field. Listening to high-frequency noises constantly for four years damaged my hearing. Sometimes I hear but cannot distinguish the words: I will hear 'show' when someone actually said 'know.' I do have hearing aids but they do not correct the problem perfectly. I take pride that I have overcome my handicap.

Being stationed in Biloxi, MS was quite the experience for me. This is the "Deep South." I experienced more prejudice here in six months than anywhere I have ever been. This was 1962, and here I was a 20-year-old athlete, with friends of every color and ethnic mix. When I played basketball, it did not matter to me who I passed the ball to, as long as he caught it. Yet here, when I went downtown with some of my teammates and friends, there was a 'white section' and a 'colored section.' Drinking fountains were clearly marked; if you were Hispanic with dark skin you also had to drink from the colored fountain. Military guys as a whole better not look at the local girls—and gosh-forbid an African-American guy peek at a Southern white woman.

The culture in Biloxi, combined with the Southern drawl, was foreign to me. I had never tried grits and had never seen water snakes. I could not believe that snakes could swim! In New Jersey we had rats and German cockroaches; in New Mexico we had scorpions, rattlesnakes, and black widows. In Mississippi mosquitoes swarmed on us as we marched. The air was so thick that two showers a day were not enough to stay cool or clean. The winter was even colder than Jersey. Mississippi was the most distinct place I had ever been. But I did like the white sandy beaches!

I then went to Misawa, Japan for two years, as a radio intercept operator.

I have to say it was the most exciting time of my life. Traveling Japan and playing basketball for the Air Force still feels like yesterday. Being a pretty good player afforded me a chance to travel as a member of the base team at Misawa AFB. I met some great people and had my Morse intercept career while participating in the passion of my life at the time—basketball.

On the Air Force team I remember the coach watching me shoot. I would try harder. As I played with this team in Japan, the crowd helped me play better as I made long jump shots from outside the key.

Achievement meant recognition. After two years playing in Japan, I rotated to Trabzon, Turkey for one year of duty. While there I again played basketball with the base team. I met Capt. Dave Tucker and we hit it off immediately. I found out later that Dave had heard about my basketball career in Misawa and he made sure that I was assigned to his company.

Dave was a basketball junkie and he always knew about the arrival of new talent. He was a Russian linguist. I worked on his shift and copied Morse Code while he worked in the analytical interpretation of Russian military information He also was a motivator. I got so good at copying Morse Code I would put my head sets on my shoulder and the typewriter on my lap, lean back with my feet up and copy my assignments. A true "hot dog" I was! Dave recognized this advanced skill and was quick to give positive feedback. The whole room was filled with *dits, dots,* and *dashes,* and my motivation was to get better and copy despite all the sounds. Dave looked at me like a coach! So it was I got to know Dave on the basketball court and in the "War Room" both.

After leaving the Air Force in 1966 and returning to UNM, I lost contact with Dave for a while. He was on a 20-year career with the Air Force, while I had my sights on teaching and coaching. Morse Code was driving me crazy, and I was losing my hearing! There was no way I would make 20 years of *dits* and *dots.*

(Dave Tucker came back into my life in 1974. By that time I was coaching the Albuquerque Track Club (ATC). We had a great team and several outstanding athletes. I worked with a group of runners between ages seven and 14. We had a young seven-year-old sprinter, Jewel Baty, who was running some of the fastest times in the country in this age-group—*Ebony Magazine* did an article on her, which mentioned my name. Dave, back in the Washington DC area, happened to pick up a copy. We started to correspond by mail, and I was shocked to find that Dave was a "super" track fan. He followed it at every level. What shocked him, in turn, was the fact I was training athletes to compete nationally in track and field. He had always known basketball to be my main passion, and I likewise thought he was a basketball gym rat. We have connected on a regular basis now and he knows some of my athletes by name. Dave still motivates athletes. Even though he is retired, and sticks close to the Baltimore area, he still follows my coaching in New Mexico. It amazes me to this day that two guys who had a connection in track and field did not even know it at the time. Dave Tucker was certainly part of my "Coach, Coach, Look at Me!" approach.)

I did not enjoy the culture of the area where we were stationed. It was old and conservative; completely different than anything I had known. Americans were tolerated but not welcomed. The men sat in the marketplace drinking tea while the females hid behind closed doors, covered from head to toe. Some of the women worked the fields while the men drank tea.

This was a rural and undeveloped part of Turkey. The American soldiers had to be very careful that they did not offend the women by staring or talking to them. We were always on our guard, as we heard many a story of GIs who were attacked by locals who thought the solider was being disrespectful. A common sight was the open food market with fly-infested meat hanging from hooks. The rest rooms were small dirt-hole bomb shelters that looked dangerous and unsanitary. There was no tissue paper, only a running faucet. We were on an air base by the Black Sea and this was considered remote duty. (The only reprieve we had was a one-week furlough to Athens, Greece, after six months of Turkey.) The females still dressed in the black burqas from head to foot. This is in 1965 and Turkey was still catching up with the modern world.

Istanbul, through modern next to rural Turkey, still resembled more old Constantinople with its temples and mosques. It was at the opening of the Black Sea, a major shipping port. It was the largest city in Turkey and had a huge Muslim influence. Ankara, the capital, conversely was more Westernized. I had several Rest & Recuperation breaks to both Ankara and Istanbul and they were always interesting and exciting to visit.

We wanted to serve our tour and get home. Meeting Dave Tucker, a smart, educated man who loved basketball and athletics, was a highlight of that overseas experience. It was lonely there, except for the basketball games! Attending class had to be better than this. I was ready to sit down, listen, take notes, and learn to teach. In a way, a remote site near the Russian border with nothing to do but play basketball and think about my future turned into a profoundly motivational period for me.

In 1958 I thought New Mexico was brown and dusty, but in 1966, after one year in Trabzon, Turkey, Albuquerque was paradise. What a difference attitude makes! I could not wait for the Sandia Mountains and the 5000'+ altitude. The friendly people in Albuquerque were the right mix for me. These Southwesterners were a far cry from cold Northeastern personalities. Coming back from the Middle East and Turkey to the friendly wide-open spaces of New Mexico was a treat.

NEW MEXICO AND THE LOBOS

When I returned to New Mexico, I saw big changes in the American culture. In the mid-to-late '60s the Vietnam War was escalating and college students across the United States were protesting. People now had longer hair, and the "Hippy" look was in. Grungy clothes, unshaven faces, wild color T-shirts, drugs, heavy drinking, crazy heavy metal music, and liberal attitudes were now all part of the college atmosphere. I was shocked. People were protesting everywhere. All I wanted to do was become a PE teacher!

At UNM I was an older student, being a veteran now, and I had to adjust. I still wanted to teach and coach, which was still in the conservative stream in University life. When I was discharged, I still had short hair and a respect for higher authority, and I soon learned to challenge the thinking of our government leaders, and to express my own convictions of right and wrong. I never believed in the Vietnam War, but I was not a rebel. I was a college student who had returned from military duty overseas and I still had conservative values.

I was at UNM during the riots at Roosevelt Park and on Central across from the University. I saw the police and the National Guard try to maintain order. Students were breaking windows with rocks and burning cop cars. Friends of mine were involved and I watched. Fires were everywhere. At no time did I participate in the demonstrations other than as a spectator. I lived on Princeton, just two blocks from Central, and it was easy to see what was going on.

In this environment I was studying to become a teacher. While I was not a naturally academic student, I was a highly-motivated one. I was on the GI bill, a government program for veterans to help them get through school, and it behooved me to graduate. I did not get caught up in the disruptive things going on around me. While not being a goodie-boy type—I did party a little—I had a mind to keep moving toward that degree in education.

My experience in athletics had taught me to dedicate myself to higher and higher excellence. I came from a humble background in New Jersey; no one in my immediate family had graduated from high school, much less the University. I was on a mission. After I graduated and had taught for a while, several relatives followed me to college. My brother Frank and my cousin Jack both graduated to become accountants. I felt like a role model to them. I took the first step.

Classes were hard for me, especially Kinesiology and Abnormal Behavior Psychology. My good friend Cal Guymon was at UNM now, majoring in physical education. He too was struggling some; we had to study more than most students. We never cut class and learned that if we listened and took good notes we could pass the tests. Most college professors based their exams on their classroom lectures. The discipline I had learned in athletics helped me then. There were many students who started with us, but attrition was high. The student-athletes who thought they could get an easy degree did not even make it to student-teaching.

Two of my favorite instructors were Woody Clemens and Armond Seidler. They both told stories about teaching and coaching as they lectured. Woody, an old country boy with twang in his voice, always had a technique of facing the class and, with a piece of chalk in his hand, putting a check (like a Nike swoop) on the board for emphasis. It grabbed your attention and you wondered if he would misplace the check. Eye contact! Even today, I use some of his techniques. Woody was also a former basketball coach at UNM. He described everyone as "folks."

Dr. Seidler was from Illinois, a Mecca of physical education, and always had a long story to relate to athletics and student life. He would tell us stories of athletes and coaches from the 1920s and 1930s. At times, he would go off on a tangent and talk about things not even related to physical education. But both men held my attention with their stories. In their classes I learned that if you can get your students' attention, you can take them anywhere.

When I became a teacher, it was important that I made an impression on all students. My basic philosophy in teaching is that all students are important and we need to speak to all of them. If you do not have their attention, you are breaking the chain of learning. Unlike my role models, many teachers talk to students without eye contact, do not speak in a firm voice, do not reach all corners of the room, do not change their tempo, do not keep the topic interesting. I learned early that great teachers motivate regardless of their knowledge. You can compensate for a lack of expertise with great presentation; if you have both, you will be a most effective teacher.

My favorite professional basketball team was the Boston Celtics. I always liked Bob Cousy and Bill Russell, the mainstays of the early dynasty years. I would fantasize that I was Bill Russell and I would make a move in the paint and turn and hit a high arching hook shot. I could be alone shooting outside on a lighted court and in my mind I was Bob Cousy hitting a long outside shot to win the game, with three seconds left.

My favorite player was John Havlicek. He was a decent human being and one of my best role models. John Havlicek, Gil Hodges, whom I spoke of earlier, and Roger Staubach, were my all-time role models. They inspired me to love athletics and to practice good sportsmanship. I have never heard or seen anything derogatory of them. In all of sports there are athletes who don't care to be role models. I am of the opinion that young people look at everything we do for guidance. I think we should take pride in the act of role modeling.

In 1958 the Lobos were just an average team and they played in Johnson Gym on UNM campus. The games were never a sellout. My friends from Valley would love to go to a Lobo game and catch Claiborne Jones, Tom King, and Francis Grant as the Lobos played the University of Utah with Billy "The Hill" McGill. In 1962, when Bob King took over coaching the Lobos, they went to a new level. The basketball team became the dominant team at the University. Ira Harge helped take the NM Lobos to a top-20 team. In 1964 the Lobos went to the NIT in New York City and finished second. Lobo Basketball Mania was born. Because of that team's success, the Lobos are the top athletic show in Albuquerque even today.

Wherever I was, I followed Lobo basketball. I would check every news report for scores. When I left the service, I chose UNM over many other schools for Lobo hoops. (I did consider UCLA, as they were in sunny California and had the great UCLA Bruin teams to root for.) UNM was special to me, and they were building a new basketball arena. I was hanging out with Cal Guymon and Lee Hays (an ex-Highland High basketball player). We never missed a game in the new Pit. Our favorites then were Mel Daniels, Ron Nelson, and Ben Monroe. The Lobos were a top-10 team for several years and even had a chance for the final four.

The Pit became a legend then, and we were part of it. I was exposed to high-performing athletes and I had dreams of taking my students there, too. I would study why they were so good. I watched the legendary coach, Bob King, his motivational techniques. He cocked his head to one side, spoke with a squeaky inflection, had a stiff jaw, and he motivated his players to play defense. At times he was gruff! Coach King was very demanding and players had better learn to play defense. He slowed the game down and forced the other team to play his style of basketball.

He realized early that if they did this, and played a tough man-to-man defense, he could play with any team in the country. However, he had to have his players and his assistant coaches buy into his system. Sometimes the fans did not see it, and I would hear booing during a slow game. In the end, though, all was forgiven when the Lobos won. It took many a year for the fans to get Bob King's system. Eventually they did, and loved winning.

I've always studied other educators. To this day I still say, "Let me watch you work with young people for 30 minutes, and I will become a better teacher." I watch, listen, learn, memorize, modify, and adapt.

Watching the Lobo players, fans, and coaches made a big impact on my career. I was never big, fast or good enough to play for the Lobos. (As a freshman I went out for the team and got lost in the mix. I did not last a season.) I was soon playing in intramural leagues instead. I could have gone to a small college and played, but I was in love with Lobo basketball and if I could not play for them, I wanted still to be around them. Our intramural team was made up of ex-players from high schools around the state. We had a great team, went undefeated and captured intramural championships against the fraternities with all the big name players. We had Jack Olive (Gallup), Rick Schalk (Sandia), Rick Cheney (Highland), John Haaland (Manzano), Punky Garcia (Gallup Cathedral), Lee Hayes (Highland), and me. They were good players with great teamwork and a will to win. It was a great way to attend college, having fun and staying fit.

One big lesson I learned from intramural play was that you did not have to be a superstar or play in the big leagues to find success. Yes, the Lobos were getting national recognition and they were the big cheese in New Mexico. Our team, Bill's Bums—don't ask me where that came from—were the hot-shots on campus, and we had our 15 minutes of fame. We felt good about our skills and still have great memories of that team.

Athletics and PE are not just for the gifted, but for all who love the game. The value of fun, fitness, recognition, teamwork, commitment, dedication, and motivation are all products of any level of participation. A nine-year-old playing kickball is just as excited as the superstars in the Pit. Great teachers get excited for all kids that play the game, regardless of the level of play.

I knew this profession was for me when I was first teaching kids long jump-rope. They could not turn the rope. Something inside me said, "Ciccarello, teach them." I loved watching them learn it. It was easy for me to react positively, and I try to encourage all teachers to make this a part of their daily routine. Everyone should stop and think about a teacher or coach who took the time to look when you did something well: making a basketball shot, a fast time around the track, doing 10 pushups, mastering a dance step, or picking up trash to keep the playground clean. All of us know an educator who recognized us in the moment. It is especially motivating when the praise is immediate.

Back in Jersey City, at PS Number 23 I swam 10 laps in the pool without stopping. Mr. Lombardi raved about it. That was so good for my ego that every time I was in the pool, I tried to please him, and I became a better swimmer.

Why is it that all of us can look back and only recollect one or two adults who impacted our development? Why can't all adults have a goal of helping young people improve? Is it passion itself for the field that makes a difference between greatness and mediocrity? I think that's most of it, but also their desire to help others excel. The great teachers all seem to share this trait!

STUDENT-TEACHING

In UNM's the College of Education all students had to complete two semesters of student-teaching. The first semester was at a junior high or at a high school. To be licensed to teach at an elementary school a prospective teacher was required to student teach at that level. I first went to Jefferson Junior High, close to UNM. This was in a nice neighborhood and students fed from here to Highland High

School. (Twenty years later I would be coaching track and field at Highland.) It is one thing to try educational techniques on your peers and quite another to go before a class of 30 14-year-olds. Kids sometimes do not listen or follow directions. Still growing up, they have their own set of problems. They can put a student-teacher to the test, not realizing that they might be putting a career on the line.

Cal had preceded me at Jefferson and had had a great experience. Harold Cheeves, the cooperating teacher at Jefferson, also coached football and basketball. Harold was very knowledgeable in PE and had a great rapport with kids. I asked to serve under him to master teaching junior high kids, if *anyone* can master that age-group. Cal would say, "Chic, you need to go to Jefferson for student-teaching. The students are very athletic and very smart. Harold Cheeves will help you." This choice was a slam dunk for me. I worked with Jim Hart, Jim Dodds, Pete Espinosa, Jack Schooley, Mark Mahorich, and others who went on to became some of the best athletes in Albuquerque prep history. Pete Espinosa was the fastest student at Jefferson. He became an educator and eventually a principal at Kirtland Elementary. Through the years I met the rest of his family. They were all educators.

Harold and I had a very good relationship, and I studied hard under him. He went into administration and became a principal at Eldorado and La Cueva High Schools. Although he is retired, he still subs for me at Whittier Elementary. Even in his '70s he is a master of motivation. I hope he forgives me for mentioning his age, since he seems to defy aging in general. Harold is one of my role models as I enter my own '70s.

Critically, Harold taught me how to keep control of my class. "You can't teach if you don't reach," as the old adage goes. Back in the day, coaches would kick over chairs; grab kids by the shirt, paddle, push, and shove to get control. As we all know, that day is over! Paddle a kid today, your job is gone tomorrow.

When I watched Harold teach I noticed that he was tall and strong. He stood about 6'3," and when he wanted his students' attention, he would stand tall and stare at them. *That* got their attention. His kids knew he cared and wanted them to listen.

I was not as tall as Harold, but I was young and athletic. We often had basketball pickup games. The students loved to play with the coaches; when I was in high school I remember playing at noon with my PE teachers. This was a natural course for me at Jefferson. It helped to build rapport, since the students always want to test themselves against older guys. Over the years, this has not changed, except that the day comes when the aging head coaches have to bow out and let the young assistants take over. As we age, we learn to motivate differently.

I was blessed with great students at Jefferson… but my classroom management was not that good. The kids had good self-discipline and were self-motivated. All in all, Jefferson was an outstanding environment for a young student-teacher. The future for me was going to be a challenge. Even then I had a lot to learn.

In the spring of 1969 I was assigned to Cortez Elementary to complete the elementary section of student-teaching. It would be grades one–six, and my cooperating teacher was Dale Shelby. Years later Cortez Elementary became a magnet school called New Futures.

When I reported for duty at Cortez, I immediately knew things were different. Walking into the cafeteria to meet Mr. Shelby during the noon time lunch, 500 sets of eyes stopped. Cortez Elementary was close to UNM and it was a student-teaching center. The kids at this school were used to new student-teachers, and the environment was one of constant change. Being young and not confident yet with elementary kids, I was intimidated. The kids were saying, "We are watching to see what you will bring to the table."

Yet, as I looked back at those children it immediately triggered a vivid memory of the fourth grade, PS Number 23 in New Jersey. I remembered wanting to please. As I made eye contact around the room, I saw tenderness in those children. I still remember that moment. My brain was moving faster than my feet—and I had fast feet at the time!

Mr. Shelby walked me around the room to introduce me as the new student-teacher. The kids were polite and inquisitive. *What activities are you going to teach us coach? When do you start? Do you play for the Lobos?* The questions were endless and bounced off me like tennis balls on a wall. It was non-stop.

At this point in my career I had concluded that I would teach high school PE and coach boys' basketball. Was I ever wrong! For two weeks I observed Mr. Shelby teach class, taking notes and watching the kids. It did not matter what the activity was, the students were into it! Mr. Shelby would say, "Run two laps around the playground." They not only did it with no questions, they responded "Can we run extras?" The attitude of this age-group was completely different from the secondary students. The secondary students were great, but the little kids were more energized, and I gravitated toward them for their enthusiasm.

When I took over the classes it was easy to motivate and direct. At first I thought the kids would not cooperate as they did for Mr. Shelby. Wrong again. I started first with a gymnastics unit, as I had just finished a tumbling class with Rusty Mitchell at UNM. It went well. We covered beginning and intermediate tumbling skills. My next unit was track and field, with relays and individual running events. This went extremely well, and I had a mini-meet for them at the end. I called it the "Cortez Olympics." I put their names on the cafeteria wall, with their place and time. Their excitement was heartwarming.

Cortez was a turning point for me: I now knew I needed to teach at the elementary level. I made the connection with my own elementary PE class memories in Jersey City and how much fun it was to be involved in physical competition. There was no stopping me now, and the hunt was on to find a PE position in APS.

FIRST YEAR TEACHING

Everybody has to be first at something: first in line, first in a new job, first day out for track, first time buying a house or car, and of course, a first-year teacher! I remember 1969 like yesterday. My senior year at UNM, I lived on Princeton Drive, one block north of APS administrator Desi Baca.

Desi was a principal at Riverview Elementary in Albuquerque's South Valley, with a "million" years in APS. I got to know Desi because he owned the laundromat I used. He would be at the laundry giving out change and soap. Desi was my first APS boss. He hired me.

Back then all educators had to moonlight or hold a second job to pay the bills. In the '60s, teachers and administrators were not very high on the salary scale.

I myself had three jobs: I was a film processing delivery boy to Santa Fe, a referee in the Albuquerque Sports and Recreation league at Wells Park Community Center, and a Driver's Ed. Instructor, first with NM AAA and then with McGinnis School of Driving. I had to pay the bills!

My Uncle Rick had a film delivery service: we would pick up film and put it on a plane to Phoenix where it would be developed overnight. The next day I would take it back to Santa Fe. It paid my bills and afforded me a nice car.

Meanwhile, I met some great people refereeing. Bobbie Gibbs and Hank Sanchez were big names in the youth sports of Albuquerque. The Wells Park Basketball League was huge back then. Cal and I were always calling basketball games when we weren't playing in them. I learned that to be an excellent referee you had to "look" at the players. You always had to put yourself in position, running hard, to see everyone and the action. You had to focus. Players knew when you were lazy and made bad calls. They would let you know they knew, too. Basketball players liked fair and impartial referees. I took pride in becoming liked among the teams.

Driver's Ed. was no different. Of course, not all the moves were nice. Many a time the car would land on a lawn or sidewalk and I had to physically push their leg off the accelerator. If you said to turn too soon, they would turn immediately, instead of at the next light. So I always said, "When you get to the next light, please turn right." I had a brake on my side of the car, and so when they made a huge mistake, we had a backup.

Helping older women whose husbands had given up on them were my favorites. They were very appreciative and would sometimes thank me with chocolate cakes. My senior year of college I gained 15 pounds.

Teaching a person to drive a car was most rewarding. To this day, I have 50-year-olds come up to me and say, "Coach Ciccarello, you were my drivers' education instructor and I never forgot you." We teachers don't make a lot of money, but we make a huge impact.

One day Desi Baca said, "Jim, would you like to teach at a low-income school?" I said, "Sure, I grew up in a low-income neighborhood so it might work out well for me." I wanted to get into APS. I had never heard of Riverview Elementary and I figured it must be by a river. Albuquerque has the Rio Grande, and there was Riverview, just north of the South Valley, located in the Barelas neighborhood. I did not realize at the time it was in the oldest, lowest-income part of town. Most of the students were Hispanic, and some did not speak English. I could only speak English—with a Jersey accent. This was quite the combination with which to start a teaching career! I was young and I could adjust easily.

After I was hired, Desi relocated to the main office at APS, and Reginald Chavez became my first principal at Riverview. I also learned I was to teach PE at two schools. In the morning I would teach at Riverview, and in the afternoon at Lowell Elementary. Manny Smith was to be my principal there. Lowell drew most of its students from the Kirtland AFB Addition. This was a predominately African-American neighborhood. Here I was in my first year, teaching two completely different cultures. Both of these schools would test and mold me. I was ready.

I learned that Mondays I would only supervise showers. My first day of teaching, I wouldn't be teaching. I studied four years at UNM and my first class was supervising kids to take a shower.

Times were different in the '60s. The reason for the Monday shower was simple: the students in the South Barelas neighborhood did not have running hot water and the school did. It was a weekly tradition at Riverview, and I was now part of it. I learned to supervise the showers in a very professional way, even if I didn't like it. I think I had the cleanest kickball team in Albuquerque.

The kids at Riverview were Hispanic and I had a lot to learn. I had always been used to diversity, but a 100% Hispanic district was new to me. I knew with my motivation I could work these kids to a higher level. They'd had a new PE teacher every year, so they could handle one with a "Jersey" accent.

Lowell Elementary was a different situation. It was located in the Southeast Heights and the kids who attended that school had home situations that were different from those kids in the South Barelas neighborhood. Neither school had the economic advantages of students located in other areas.

The students at Lowell amazed me: they were super-motivated athletes. They lived close to UNM and were familiar with the Lobos, but they had never been to a game. They knew the players but had never seen them play. This brought me back to my roots. I knew I had a challenge at both schools, and I was determined to make a difference in their lives.

The students at Riverview were in dire need of attention. They never had an opportunity for after-school programs. If they did not get an extracurricular activity at school it might never happen in their lives. They were not developing the physical skills or social skills that more affluent kids did.

I believe the school system should step to the plate and offer opportunities to low-income students. I have seen money denied to low-income schools, while granted to others in wealthy neighborhoods. Parent groups who are more educated in the ways of raising funds are always volunteering in the schools their kids attended. Their children had better equipment and supplies, on the playing field and in the classroom. Riverview suffered a lack of parental support.

I quickly realized this was a battle that I might not win. To do my part, I tried to teach appreciation and sportsmanship. These kids were very receptive to my attention. Even if they could not hit a ball they wanted me to watch them swing!

For two years I worked diligently to try to get the Riverview kids ready for competition. Riverview had no history of inter-school competition. There was no parental support and most of the faculty was too busy to get involved. So as Harry Truman used to say, "the buck stops here;" I made up my mind to schedule a competition. At first the administration balked. But with constant pressure, they agreed to a game of basketball. I already had a natural tie-in with Lowell Elementary as I was teaching there, too. I thought, "Why not schedule a game between them?"

Meanwhile, at Lowell I was teaching kids physical skills. There was a big difference since the students at Lowell were more advanced in athletics. In their neighborhood the older kids were always organizing pickup games. The older Lincoln Junior High and Albuquerque High kids were always playing pickup games after school, and the kids at Lowell were able to plug into that.

The game did happen. I got a bus to take a group from Lowell to Riverview. Less than three miles apart, neither group had heard of the other. This reminded me of New Jersey—we never knew kids three miles away, either. Kids in low-income areas have a tendency not to stray far from neighborhood borders. My challenge was to get the kids to compete and respect each other. I worked with each school independently, planning to bring them together, without precedent.

The game was not as close as I had hoped. I refereed and tried to keep it close, but Lowell dominated. Do not schedule a competition in which one team is sure to win; no one likes to get drilled! In my enthusiasm I forgot that cardinal rule. On the way out of the parking lot the older kids from Riverview gave the Lowell kids a hard time, throwing rocks at the bus. I was able to mend fences at school the next day as the kids appreciated that I tried when no one else had. This was the beginning of my second year of teaching, on my way to 40+ more.

I found Lowell to be a very interesting and influential experience. In two years there I met some of the greatest athletes of the next 30 years:

Carolynn Adams	Angela Carruthers	Chris Hollis
Morris Aiken	Scott Carruthers	Kathy Jordan
Jewel Baty	Donna Corley	Gale Pennington
Marcie Baty	Mark Corley	Steve Rogers
Melanie Baty	Neil Corley	Virgil Stanley
Vince Baty	Kathy Donaldson	Bobby Sweet
Eugene Bell	Regina Flanders	Darrel Thronton
James Bell	Vivian Flanders	Jeanette Thronton
Val Boyer	Graylin Hightower	Alice Watson
Suzanne Brown	Yvette Hightower	
Eugene Burrell	Barbara Hobbs	

There were many other athletes who came out of Lowell and the Kirtland Addition (the "Kirk"). They had great careers in high school and college athletics, some at very high levels. Joe Powdrell comes to mind. He was a great pole vaulter and an influential member of the Kirk community.

My first day at Lowell was quite the experience. When I went out to the playground, I wanted to meet the kids. At 27, everything was new, and I wanted to see what I could do with my first recess duty. I saw a group looking for something to do. My first thought was to have them race each other. So I blew my whistle and said, "Anybody want to race?" Before I could get my whistle out of my mouth there had to be over 100 kids ready! "OK!" I said, "Run from here to the swings, around the basketball court, around the Tether-ball poles, around the backstop and back to me." They all took off as I directed. I thought they were running for a spot on an Olympic team. Val Boyer and James Bell finished first and second, two of Albuquerque's finest future athletes racing each other as little kids. Little did I know, this was the beginning of a long and exciting relationship!

One of the best teachers I have ever seen in my entire career was in my first year at Lowell. Mrs. Abby LeCesne, a sixth grade teacher (back then elementary school went from grades one to six) had a class of 40, with complete control over the classroom. Though she was an African-American woman teaching African-American kids, she could have taught any kid, regardless of background. She was a stern disciplinarian. She had a voice I could hear on the entire playground 400 yards away. As a first-year teacher, I was in awe of how she got these low-income kids to perform. Back then the kids had their chairs and tables in rows and she would walk around them, looking at each student with high expectations. Watching her raised *my* expectations! Abby had a tough love for all kids, and though she was hard on them verbally, she impacted all of them. They could read and they became great listeners—or the wrath of Abby was upon them!

While I was at Lowell, Abby was recognized by *The Albuquerque Tribune*, with its first distinguished teacher award. It was well-deserved; I learned a lot by watching her. She was one of those teachers who looked at all students and rewarded them with verbal praise. Abby could instill the fear of God kids with just her voice. Although the 1960s were a different time, with different teaching techniques, her approach was effective. I think it would work well today.

Manny Smith was the principal at Lowell. Until the late 1970s paddling was used daily. Though he paddled quite often, the kids seemed to respect him for his fairness. He also helped them to become better students. I would see him mentoring on the playground after administering a paddling.

While most kids who were paddled at Lowell changed their behavior immediately, there were several kids who were too tough to change. I could hear the *crack* from the playground. There were always tears after a visit with Mr. Smith. He would make attitude adjustments with one swing; very seldom did one return to the office for a behavior modification. One particular fifth-grader never cried and never said a word, even as he was paddled twice a week. When someone went to visit Mr. Smith, the kids always told me, "Coach, someone's going to get a licking today!" It was usually right after afternoon recess.

One day as I was teaching a sixth grade class the kids told me this student was in the office. I heard what sounded like a "boom," and I knew that Manny was trying to make a point. For the first time ever, the hardest and toughest student at Lowell cried out. I cringed! When I saw him in tears I knew that had to hurt! It hurt *me* to just look at him. He never said a word. By my recollection, he was never hit again. Within a year or two paddling was no longer allowed in APS.

My philosophy had always been to be firm, and when kids messed up, I would ask them to take a break, return when they had cooled off. In all my years of teaching, I could never paddle a student, though I knew other PE teachers who did. Mine was a softer approach. As the years passed, teachers and administrators followed my "time out" form of discipline. They would keep kids in from recess and make them spend time by themselves.

Just like being a parent, a teacher has to ad-lib discipline. In the absence of corporal punishment, teachers and administrators were left to develop motivational management in new ways. To find strategies that work with students most of the time is the essence of discipline; no strategy works all the time.

Some students come from homes that only know negative attention. These students see various school-approved disciplines as acceptable responses *because negative attention is still attention*. Today students take time away from the class and spend quiet time or in a special room called "detention." Classroom management is perhaps the hardest thing a teacher has to do, and yet it is the least-taught aspect of the educational training. Teachers arrive with unbelievable knowledge in their subject area, but often without any skills to motivate a misbehaving kid.

This is particularly true of the public schools. Private school can require students sign a contract that equates misbehavior with being expelled. Very seldom is a kid expelled from a public school. Classroom management is one of the biggest issues facing the future of public education.

I am a product of my total environment and everything that has happened to me. Attending school in the 1940s, I had teachers who would give me positive reinforcement immediately, which inspired me. Today, I take it one step further.

Why not give a student a positive remark, even before you start? You win the student to your side. As my class approaches me I tell them how good they look. If it is an individual who needs some kudos, I tell him to "give me a good look." Most people would be shocked to find that the student or group will transfer that positive attitude to the task at hand. It is all part of the "Coach, Coach, Look at Me" philosophy. In 1976 there was an African-American comedian on TV, *Freddie Prince*, who used to say, "Looking Good…" and though it was funny, it served a point: he was proud to look good. Compliments are a good way to "head them off at the pass." Get the students on your side, and you can take them anywhere.

Have you ever been with a team (or individual) that just put on a new uniform? They beam from head to foot. And they want someone to tell them they look good! When we purchased uniforms for the ATC in 1974, the team donned bright yellow tops with a red stripe down the arm. The warm-up bottoms were a bright red with a yellow stripe down the leg. They looked and felt like the USA Olympic Team. We had a photo session. We ran some of our best times on the track that year and the shiny new uniforms helped their self-esteem tremendously. When we would go to Arizona or California the other age-group teams would marvel at our "spiffy" uniforms. In New Mexico we were the "darlings" of the track fashion world. Looking good is inspiring!

Many years later, at Whittier Elementary in 1992, I bought 50 T-shirts for our beginning jump-rope team. We were preparing to show our skills to a school-wide recess. The money for this first batch was from my own billfold; I considered it an investment. (All teachers, at some time, donate their own money to help kids excel. The public does not know how much money a teacher will spend on his class to make it through the year. I never hesitated to pull out some cash to "get the job done.") When the recess bell rang the kids were wearing their shirts all over the playground and proud as peacocks! It was infectious— teachers and students alike asked how they could get one of those shirts.

All administrators have a discretionary fund of some kind. I try to encourage administrators to help the kids by spending on new gear. I feel they must grasp this concept as one that pays off handsomely in future positive student performance.

COACHING AND EXTRACURRICULAR ACTIVITIES

Even though I was first and foremost a physical educator, I believe in extracurricular activities. If you want to make school exciting and a fun place to be, offer the kids something to do at the end of the day. I will never forget sitting in a third-floor classroom looking out the window in the fourth grade at PS Number 23 as kids played basketball. I remember thinking in about 45 minutes I would be joining them, practicing relay handoffs. I could not wait for the bell to ring and run down those stairs. I could be part of the team and compete against other schools. I used to think, "Get your academic work done and go to practice." Our school and our team became important to me.

I am here to tell you that in a low-income neighborhood, if the schools do not provide activities after school, there will be none. Too often we get caught up in our own dreams for our children and forget to stop and ask, "What about those economically disadvantaged students? Do they get to play?" After-school activities—band, chess, dance, karate, newspaper, drama, and any organized program in which adults lead kids to bigger and better things—are for all children, not just for the privileged few.

In 1969 I received a phone call from Richard Herrera and John Haaland, two track coaches in the far Northeast Heights of Albuquerque. They, along with Tony Sandoval, John Baker, and Pat Cox were starting an age-group track team called the Duke City Dashers (DCD). They knew I had some fast kids at Lowell and asked for my help recruiting. That phone call changed my career.

I had a plan to teach elementary school PE, and then move to high school to coach basketball. Cal Guymon was the head basketball coach at my alma mater. I had visions of joining him on the coaching staff at Valley. Basketball was my first love and the one sport in which I excelled.

I already knew that Val Boyer and James Bell were fast. Students kept telling me to check out Donna Gill. Check her out—heck; I couldn't even find her! She was very shy, and as I later found out, her full name was Donna Gill Corley. The first time I saw Donna she was standing over by the swings at recess watching the kids race. She was a nine-year-old, but had an athletic look, strong and bigger than the other girls in her grade. I coaxed her into racing a few kids; she blew them off the track! After timing and racing many kids at recess, I came up with about 100 fast runners, 50 girls and about 50 boys, almost 1/4 the total students at Lowell. Students there had natural talent for racing. It was a special moment as I realized I already had a pretty good track team.

Richard and John invited them to a local track meet at Milne Stadium. It was about a mile from Lowell and I had a hard time getting them to attend: most kids from low-income areas do not have the funds or transportation for after-school events. You will not believe how many kids I piled into my two-door 1971 Catalina Pontiac. I am again proud to be one who stuck his neck out.

The results at the local meets were amazing. The kids from Lowell dominated the sprint events. Donna Gill Corley was an instant success in the age-group program and started running times that put her on a regional and national level, and she immediately won gold medals at local and state competitions. James Bell and Val Boyer also did well, but no one could catch up with Donna. The Duke City Dashers became renowned. In 1970 we took a 400m relay team to UCLA to run in the USA National Age-Group Invitational. They not only won a gold medal but ran one of the fastest times ever recorded for a Nine-and-Under Division team. The team was Laurie Downs, Tanya Meadows, Lois Adams, and Donna Corley running the anchor leg.

The Duke City Dashers represented many areas of Albuquerque. We were split up in neighborhoods and the coaches generally worked with the kids in their own schools, coming together only for the meets. My neighborhood was the Southeast

Heights, which included most of the kids from the Kirk—primarily underprivileged African-American students. The other neighborhoods were in the more affluent far Northeast Heights. Some of the runners from that group included:

Sally Balderston	Laurie Gilliland	Dine Norerro
Ann Dehart	Lisa Gilliland	Linda Stecker
Therese Dorwart	Kathy Hart	Susie Vigil
Carrie Gilliland	Cheryl Newton	Linda Yount

There were many other quality athletes. This arrangement worked for a couple of years, but eventually we split apart, due to socioeconomic differences. Out of this humble beginning would develop the Albuquerque Track Club.

One day at after-school practice at Lowell, I saw a tall African-American girl by the fence watching us. She had to be at least 5'10"; she looked like a high school kid. One of my students said, "Coach, that's Alice Watson, and she's *fast*." She was just watching. Of course I had to talk to her. Intimating as Alice looked, she was quiet, and very nice. I found out she had graduated from Lowell a couple years before and was now 13, attending Lincoln Junior High. Growing up she had always been fast but never had a chance to compete. I hoped to change that.

She had heard of this new young coach and the team he was starting up. I convinced her to come and run with us. She ran undefeated in track meets in New Mexico and Colorado. Tony Sandoval told me, "Ciccarello, she is the fastest girl I have seen in Albuquerque ever." No boy could beat her and no girl came close. In 1971 we went to Bakersfield, California for the National Age-Group Invitational and we entered Alice in the open 220 (the US was still measuring by yards then). Dan Dehart, the president of the DCD at the time, said, "Coach, I think she has a chance." Dan was one of the most knowledgeable track fans I have ever met, and in my opinion, Albuquerque's best track official of all time.

Being a young, energetic coach then, but not knowing all the rules and protocol for coaches at national track meets, I was down on the infield at the beginning of the Girls' 220. As the starting gun went off I saw Alice blaze out to a lead coming off the curve. I myself sprinted across the track toward the finish line. When Alice hit the finish line in first place, I was right there to congratulate her.

Dan later told me, "Chic, the only time faster than Alice that day was your race to the finish line." I later found out that she was in danger of being disqualified for her coach being on the field. (I have not done it since.) Alice Watson, an African-American 13-year-old from the Kirk, had just won the Duke City Dashers' first gold medal individual championship at a national track meet. A former Lowell elementary student was now on one of the highest podiums ever. Forgive me for my youthful exuberance!

The following year, in 1972, after winning the 100m dash at the Age-Group Nationals, Alice went to the USA Olympic trials in Eugene, OR, and competed on her biggest stage to date. The USA athletes were *very* good, and she did not place beyond the preliminaries. Alice later went on to run for the ATC, and UNM, where she earned an athletic scholarship. To this day I have a great relationship with Alice, now in her mid-50s and living in Denver with her family. All she wanted was a coach to "look at her;" and to give her a chance. She ran age-group track, in national and college competition, and graduated from UNM. Her success speaks for itself.

THE ALBUQUERQUE TRACK CLUB

In 1972 a new track club for boys and girls was born. It was a combination of athletes from the DCD and the Heights Track Club. Barry Rodrigue and I were the two founding coaches. Later on we were joined by Lee Hays, Lou Granados, Earl Lyon, John Alfaro, and Jeff La Bowe. This club was to become a major player in the age-group track and field world.

Track and field age-group hit its peak in the '70s. The Albuquerque Olympette Club, (a track and field team for girls), had been running for several years since the mid-'60s, and competition for girls and women had always been limited to private clubs. Title IX passed in the USA Congress in 1972. This legislation gave females the right to equal competition in the education system across the nation.

Prior to Title IX, many clubs had produced great track and field athletes. The Amateur Athletic Union (AAU) system had provided opportunities for females to advance to the Olympics and compete on the world stage. Males were developed not only in the club system, but also in high school and college athletic programs.

At the time, track and field was huge in the AAU system. Private clubs were not organized in soccer, volleyball, and basketball as they are today. Athletes stuck to one sport, and it was easier to find kids who wanted to compete in track and field. Albuquerque in the '70s had a huge participation and competition in age-group track and field. In addition to the Albuquerque Olympette Club, we had the ATC, the Supremes Track Club, the Police Athletic League, and the Boca Grande Track Club from Roswell. The Duke City Dashers and many smaller track teams from around New Mexico were also in that group. The competitions started in a local community, moved to a district site, and then on to an age-group meet at the national level. This was an exciting time for a kid to be a track and field athlete.

Many of the coaches were teachers, former athletes, or parents. The competition was hot and heavy on the track as well as in the recruitment of athletes. Uniforms had to be bought and entry fees had to be paid. Travel expenses were huge. Many of these athletes went on in later years to compete for their local high schools.

Barry Rodrigue and I were on the same page. He also loved all age-groupers, regardless of background. We agreed that the kids did not have to work every day, all year long; they needed to experience other interests as well. For lower-income athletes, we provided a more forgiving system to keep them involved. This team was the biggest and best family of athletes I have ever experienced, and it produced the best age-group team in Albuquerque history. The statistics don't lie.

Many athletes came to the forefront running with the ATC. From the very beginning the dominant female athlete was Val Boyer: this skinny little African-American girl running around the Lowell playground developed into something special. I could write a book just about her and her accomplishments. Margaret Metcalf was another great track athlete. Sandy Beach, a member of one of the more pronounced athletic families in state history, became our first age-group national champion in cross country at age nine. This was 1972, still just our first year.

I had just left the Duke City Dashers when Sandy's father Joe came to me at a park with his little girl. I knew the first day there was something special about Sandy Beach. Barry said he had never seen a young athlete with that kind of heart. Heck, we even loved her catchy name! In her first year of running, she went undefeated and won the NM State title, the regional title, and the national title at the age-group Cross Country nationals. Her mother, Gloria, so proud of her, told me "Coach, she's going to win nationals." This was held in Long Beach, California, and the competition was stiff. I said, "Gloria I hope you are right, but those girls from the Rialto Road Runners and Southern California Cheetahs look tough to beat." Moms are often right, and Sandy dominated the field. Not only did Sandy win, but the ATC won the Nine-and-Under team championship. We were on our way to greater victories, and Sandy on her way to being a great high school and college athlete, at Valley High and Arizona State. Eventually she taught and coached with me at La Cueva High School.

At one competition Sandy was running in California. It was a big meet. She always wore pigtails pass her shoulders. As she came around the far curve, the girl behind her, who could hardly keep up, grabbed one of them and pulled as she passed. Sandy immediately reached out and pulled the girl back with a yank on her long hair until they were even again! Sandy got so far in front this girl had no shot. After that, she switched to a ponytail. No one ever pulled her hair again.

Christine Brockhoff is one of the best all-around athletes with whom I have ever worked. She came to us with Barry Rodrigue from the old Heights Track Club. There was no event that Chris could not master. Her best was the long jump. She could high jump, run hurdles, the 400m, and throw the shot put. Her new event was the Pentathlon.

In today's track language track people would say she was in the "Multis." Coaches love these kinds of athletes because they are so valuable to the team. In 1973 Christine Brockhoff became our first national age-group individual champion in the pentathlon. I have rarely seen an athlete more proud than Chris on the podium. If you looked at her, she jumped higher and ran faster. She was easy to motivate, with the talent to back it up.

On a road trip to Irvine, California, Chris locked the keys to my car in the trunk. Back in 1973 it cost a couple of hundred bucks to get a locksmith to open your car. Chris was very humble in informing me about the keys… but she made up for it by "kicking rear" on the track! Chris went on to Manzano and had a stellar career as a jumper and hurdler. She now teaches in APS. She sent me this touching letter:

> Coach Ciccarello, whereas many of your students have gone on to become educators, the mark of an exceptional educator is one's ability to make a difference in a student or athlete's life from the perspective as an adult. When I was blessed to stand on the victory stand as a 13-year-old, the true victory came as an adult in recognizing what that moment did for me in a life time. It changed who I became by instilling a true work ethic, confidence, and most of all, the recognition that someone was willing to give up part of his life to make mine better. In the long run, victory is the shaping of a human being who is able to contribute to society and give back to others in any endeavor of their choosing. That sets the exceptional educator apart from the crowd. You fall into that category."
>
> Sincerely,
> **Christine Brockhoff**

I could write volumes on the ATC athletes, but there is limited space in this book. Leo Archuleta came to us with his three daughters: Dolores, Debbie, and Donna. Without a doubt, Dolores Archuleta is the smartest and toughest athlete I have ever coached! Her parents supported her to the hilt. She briefly competed with us as a Duke City Dasher, ran cross country, became a multi-event athlete, and was one of the original ATC athletes. She could run anything from a 50-yard dash to a two mile run. She was short by athlete's standards, about 5'4," but she could high jump over her head. She was running over 30" hurdles as if they were sticks on the ground! I once saw Dolores in an age-group meet hit a hurdle, fall down, get up and win the race. She lived by Yogi Berra's creed, "It's over when it's over."

In her entire career she never gave up and people who underestimated her were soon to discover that was a big mistake. Dolores was so smart that we coaches would go to her and ask Dolores, "What do you think about these entries for the coming meet?" She would always have the answer. Any kind of word or memory game was hers to win. Dolores wanted to improve with each meet. Even though she was a talker, she was also a great listener and very coachable, and I think that is why she was able to beat bigger and faster athletes.

Delightfully, Dolores also came to coach with me at La Cueva High School. She used her expertise in track and field, and her passion to achieve in education to help athletes rise. Athletes always listened to her. I enlisted her help to converse with some of the parents. She became a very valuable assistant coach.

Elmer Baty and his family—Shirley, Jewel, Marcie, Meloney, and Vincent—had moved to Albuquerque from Clarksville, Texas in 1958, the same year my family had moved from New Jersey. His wife, Shirley, became one of the top moms and supporters in the ATC. Elmer encouraged all his children to run track and field. This was a super-athletic family who came out of humble beginnings in the Kirk. Elmer told me one day, "Coach, I want my kids to run track and learn discipline from you. I want them to go on to get an education." These girls were some of the fastest kids to run with ATC. They were never a discipline problem and the whole Baty family was one of the most inspired to come out of that neighborhood. Every one of them, with family support, went on to get a good education and become an important part of their community. They gave back to the Southeast Heights by being the perfect role models. As adults, they also coached age-group kids in track and field.

Elmer and Shirley helped to raise money, organize trips, and take care of uniforms. They did whatever was needed to help the athletes of the ATC. Elmer was also a track timer and official. Greg Papp, the Albuquerque High School girls' basketball coach said to me, "Coach, Elmer Baty is a *saint* among parents of kids in athletics… he is one of the most appreciative and hard-working parents I have ever seen." He helped his kids and left the coaching to us.

Greg had Elmer's children in his classroom as well as on the basketball court. Marcie was a great quarter-miler while Jewel was a super-sprinter. In the mid-'70s,

Jewel, as a seven-year-old was one of the top rated sprinters in the US. She was featured in a story in *Ebony Magazine*. She brought great recognition to herself, her family, the ATC, Lowell Elementary, Kirtland Elementary, and brought national publicity to Albuquerque. Runners and coaches from across the USA read about her. One day in competition at Milne Stadium, she won the 100m dash, 10m ahead of her nearest competitor. In 1974 Jewel was voted the Athlete of the Meet in Phoenix, AZ at the Valle Del Sol Invitational. In that meet she won the 100m and the 200m, and ran on a leg on the winning 400m relay team.

At 14, Marcie ran on an indoor mile relay that broke the NM State Record. This was the first time the ATC had beaten the more established Albuquerque Olympette Club (with their great runner, Carol Hudson). When I went to my first age-group meet in 1969, I saw a then 14-year-old Carol running a mile relay: one of Albuquerque's best runners of all time. She took a perfect handoff; it was a work of art. I remember thinking, "I hope someday I have a runner that good." Who would have guessed that dream would be fulfilled many times over! Jewel and Marcie went on to lead Albuquerque HS to great victories. Eventually, they became parents and coached their own kids, who ran for the ATC. Marcie's daughter, Amber Battle, daughter of former Lobo basketball great Bruce Battle, became the New Mexico State Champion, running for Cibola High School and broke the State Record in the 100m dash. The Baty family is a multi-generation story that continues to surprise and inspire.

The ATC was special first because of the great and diverse athletes we coached. Bobbi Gallegos was a little nine-year-old whose parents came here from Mexico. We never knew if she was in the US, ready to run, or if across the border visiting family. I first met Bobbi when I started at Whittier Elementary, in the Southeast Heights. At recess I would ask, "Who would like to run the big race?" She would be the first one at the wall ready to go. It was just a simple little race around the dirt field, but she was the first one back at the end. She became a great distance runner in the age-group divisions and as a nine-year-old, broke NM state records in the 800m and the mile run. She also was a State Champion in cross country and was on a National Championship nine-and-under cross country team.

In 1971 when I went to Whittier, where I still teach, we recruited new athletes. Mary Lynn Griffin was the first athlete to join our team when we were still associated with the Dashers. Her mother Joann discovered us and brought Mary Lynn to a practice at UNM soccer practice fields. She came in the back way, and I always remember her climbing under a hole in the chain link fence to reach us.

Mary Lynn was the first Whittier girl to join our team. She was never intimated by the kids from the Kirk; she was assimilated immediately and became a great runner. In 1973, she was on a 10–11 Medley Relay that won and set a national record in Irvine, California. She went on to become one of the best hurdlers in New Mexico. I used to carry bricks and bamboo sticks in the trunk of my car. We would go to a park and run "hurdles" by raising the bamboo sticks with the red bricks. The athletes would kid me, saying, "Coach you look like you drive a low-rider." Back in the early '70s we had no equipment or a track, so we improvised, and practiced at city parks.

Glenda Padilla, also a Whittier student, became a high jumper/middle distance runner. She ran on that nine-and-under national cross country championship team. I also taught her siblings Gary and Kim. I would put the foam pits on the roof of my car and the high jump bar would stick out the back window. The kids were in the car and I would take back roads to the parks, as it was illegal to carry all the track equipment sticking out the windows and tied to the roof of the car. We did whatever was necessary to get the job done.

LaDonna Omori, a Hawaiian of Japanese descent, joined our team in 1972 and was an outstanding high jumper. Her sister Holly was also a distance runner. La Donna would come to Whittier to practice high jump on the grass in front of the principal's office. The principal and the secretary would stare out the window in amazement as we had this kid high jump. In February 1972 La Donna went undefeated and was voted the AAU Indoor Athlete of the Month. She was also selected by *Sports Illustrated* as the athlete of the month, and appeared in "Faces in the Crowd." She also competed in the 400m and won that event at the Region 10 indoor championships.

Cheryl Thompson was a 400m runner who went on to take honors at every level. Her mom was a teacher at Lowell. Cheryl ran the 400m on the 10–11 Medley Relay that won the National Championship in 1973. Cheryl eventually became a high school star at Manzano and at West Mesa. She was a State Champion in the 100m, 200m, and the 400m.

Carolynn Adams, also a Lowell student, started running when she was an eight-year-old. She was a sprinter and ran relays. In 1978 she was on an 800m relay that broke the NM State Record and she earned her nickname "Lightning." I find it interesting that Carolynn "Lightning" Adams had that nickname long before Usain 'Lightning' Bolt, "the fastest man alive," was born. We put her at the second position and she would open up a lead no school could catch. She would take off after receiving the stick, in an incredible burst. When she handed the baton to the third runner the race was just about over. She was a team player, and liked by all of her teammates. She was a joy to be around.

Mary Sedal was a good friend of Sandy Beach's. Because Mary was tall, we developed her in the hurdles, high jump, and the 400m run. Mary developed a phobia about high jump bars and hurdles; she was so strong that if she came up to a bar that was not right, she either ran through it or climbed over it! Mary developed into one of our better quarter-milers and ran on relay teams. Her brother John was the number-one-ranked shot put thrower in New Mexico, and like Mary, was very strong. Mary, after many years with ATC, went to Valley HS and competed with Sandy on some outstanding Viking teams. Mary, like many of ATC's runners, became a teacher. In 2012 the jump rope team went to her school Mission Elementary and performed.

Crystal and Mary Grace Lemaster were sisters who came over from the old Heights Track Club. They were middle distance- and sprinter-type athletes. Both ran on relays in track and field and on cross country teams in CO and AZ. Their dad, Jack Lemaster, was our parent athletic trainer who helped prepare athletes for their upcoming event. Val Boyer told me once, "Coach, if Mr. Lemaster doesn't get here soon and give me a rub down for warm-up, I don't think I can run that 100m final." This great sprinter was adamant about his value to her track performance. This was our chemistry. We were a family on the track.

Our club cared about our athletes' health and performance. We were special in that way. We bonded, supported, and respected one another, and the sport. The coaches gave verbal reinforcement for good work. I often quoted Benjamin Franklin: "No gain without pain." They responded to that quote every day.

ATC parents supported both athletes and coaches, even in their unbelievably hard workouts; the athletes worked harder than any team I have ever coached. Leo Archuleta, Joe Beach, and Jack Lemaster wanted their kids to excel. They knew hard work meant a bit of discomfort. I can't say that about today's parents, who often appear to be more skeptical of hard work. Today's parents over-emphasize health issues. Some parents do not want their own children pushed too hard. To be good, an athlete must have natural talent and must work hard. You need both!

Also joining us were two more sisters from the old Heights Track Club: Alice Nunley and Gretta Nunley, who fit into our program perfectly. They were dedicated individuals whose parents supported everything they did. Alice was a 400m runner and a thrower. Gretta was a thrower. Both of these girls grew up and joined the Albuquerque Police Department. Today they are retired with full benefits.

Always appreciative of their coaches, Alice and Gretta kept in contact. That contact sometimes came on the streets of Albuquerque when once in a while I would be driving in Nob Hill only to see a cop car behind me with lights flashing. Invariable it would be one of the Nunley girls giving me a hard time about my driving. I always had a good laugh and evaded a ticket. Until I knew who was pulling me over, it scared the Dickens out of me! I always thought of it as payback for all those workouts. I mended my driving habits while in Nob Hill.

Christine Roybal is yet another athlete in a special category. She was a young 800m runner and a high jumper who also ran cross country. Chris could compete locally, regionally, and nationally with ease. She was on our National 10–11 age-group championship team. She ran on many winning relay teams. Not only did I coach Christine, but many years later her daughter Alex Darling ran for me at La Cueva High School. Alex was the high-point champion at the NM High School State Meet. Years later I began to coach successive generations of athletes on my teams.

Other ATC athletes who ran for us were:

Rhonda Adams

Lynn Allen

Joyce Anderson

Ruth Anderson

Debbie Archuleta

Donna Archuleta

Denise Bailey

Deidra Barker

Margie Bernard

Mary Bolton

Loretta Brockhoff

Patricia Brockwell

Susanne Brown

Deann Burright

Stephanie Carter

Rhonda Dawson

Mary Jane Deflice

Kathy Donaldson

Nicole Earing

Regina Flanders

Vivian Flanders

Paula Frakes

ZZ Fritz

Karen Gleason

Kathy Gleason

Brenda Goble

Cindy Goodwin

Kathy Governale

Terri Green

Lindy Griggers

Patricia Hankins

Holly Haskew

Barbara Hobbs

Kathy Jordan

Lori Keel

Stephanie Keel

Tera Lewis

Patricia Lujan

Juanita McKeller

Jenny Monceballez

Lori Monceballez

Cindy Monceballez

Holli Omori

Tracy Parsons

Leslie Pimental

Linda Portasik

Janice Quintana

Linda Rettinger

Ann Schmidt

Liz Scott

Rose Sparks

Celeste Thoma

Carol Thompson

Diana Thompson

Regina Thronton

Wannita Williams

Yevette Yepa

These athletes and others were all part of the ATC family. At one time the ATC had 200 girls and 200 boys in competition, from all across the Albuquerque area.

The family was important to all of these kids who found it important to wear those red and gold uniforms. While our numbers were high, the problems were low. Many of these athletes were with the club for 10 years, and it was an important part of their development into adulthood.

Athletes become good students for many reasons. They learn the value of commitment and dedication at an early age. They deal with pressure in a competitive environment and keep moving forward. When you make friendships with other student-athletes, you strive to perform at the same level as those friends. I have always said, "Show me who you hang out with and I will tell you who you are."

Many of these athletes started in the age-group program, and learned their work ethic at an early age.

If you start people early in life on the path to success they have a better chance to achieve it. When a child becomes a teenager she has many distractions: the media; new hormones; peer pressure; and the pressure to make mature decisions. As parents start letting kids go on their own, teens have to make tough choices. This process begins for many around the time they turn 13.

It is not necessarily the easy thing to do. I have observed many parents back off kids at this age. It is important to make an impression on kids before they reach these years. While the practice of allowing them to fly on their own is not 100% foolproof, I believe it is more effective than not in encouraging future success.

The ATC athletes joined the team for the most part at about age nine, which I think was critical to their future success. I can document how many of them turned out. I always told them, "You can be whatever you want to be." And they did. They became teachers, lawyers, judges, doctors, administrators, police officers, engineers, college professors, professionals of all kinds. Used to hard work, most finished high school and went to college—some against the odds. And as great student-athletes, they became fantastic role models for their successors.

Today's kids are blessed with advanced knowledge and vastly improved nutrition. For one, they have the best training facilities and equipment I have ever seen! In my earlier days, we used to cut broom sticks and tape them for relay batons. We used old clothesline for jump-ropes. The kids ran on dirt tracks with white dust marking the lanes. Some ran in old sneakers. We would practice in a city park and hope we did not step in dog waste! The high jump was a group of net bags full of foam. There was no pole vault pit and sometimes the long jump pit was filled with sawdust or dirt. The uniform in the early years was a T-shirt and an athlete's choice for running shorts. Hurdles were anything you could put together. There were no athletic trainers available to treat injuries and the coaches did all the taping. Most times we did not have tape. When we practiced relay handoffs, we used sticks on the ground to mark the hand-off zones. Starting blocks were a luxury and many times kids showed up to a meet without block practice. At a meet, if we needed track officials we would pull parents from the stands. There were no digital timers and no one had even heard of an electric timer. Fully Automatic Timer (FAT) was for the Nationals and the Olympics. A camera at the finish line did not exist.

What mattered was that kids got to experience competition and teamwork. They made the best of what they had; by yesterday's standards the athletes of today are spoiled. To win a ribbon in an age-group meet was something special. To win a *medal* was like money in the bank. An individual trophy was Olympic.

The excitement of waiting heat after heat until your turn was infectious. You would wait hours to run. To go on a road trip was the biggest event in your life. You made lifetime friends. The ATC kids were having the time of their young lives—and may not have even known it. Now, years later, after these athletes have matured, I receive testimonials of their time together and how important it was to them. Most of them tell me, one way or another, "Coach, being part of that team helped me in later life." Regardless of their finish, I keep hearing that the club, competition, practice sessions, dedication, commitment, teamwork, sacrifice, and fitness were hugely influential for these kids. What a testament—especially in today's world!

WHITTIER ELEMENTARY, 1971

I have been at Whittier well over 42 years. The first 20 were completely different from the latter. The one constant, though, has been what the kids want: nurturing. Imagine if you will, instructing in six decades. In 1971 I transferred to Whittier so I could teach at one school. Not many teachers I know ever stayed in one place for so long. Whittier has been my longest educational adventure.

I watched the changes in the school community. Many occurred in the student population, the school administration, and education everywhere. In the passage of an era, there have been changes both good and bad. This story is one that will mostly touch on the favorable side.

Whittier is located about two miles east of Lowell, in the Southeast Heights. At this time it was solidly middle class. The climate was completely different then Lowell and Riverview—90% Caucasian, with very few Hispanic students— though this Hispanic population was middle class and fit in neatly. There were few African-Americans and Native Americans.

I was not completely aware of that when I signed on. Here I was coming from two of the most disadvantaged schools in the Albuquerque system, into one of the most advantaged. This designation is always made by test scores. Testing has been standard in APS for many years, a practice in place before I arrived in 1969.

In my entire career test scores never mattered to me. I had come from a poor neighborhood in New Jersey, and our scores were low. In APS I soon realized that the scores were determining social migration. That migration invariably creates an uneven field for most students in the system. Over a long period, we see neighborhoods change so much so that some "abandoned" schools are "known to be bad" schools. Of course, they can have great teachers, administrators, and support staff. I have seen some of the best teachers in APS come out of these so called "bad schools," and outstanding students and athletes develop from less-affluent neighborhoods. In 1971, when I left Riverview and Lowell, these two were at the bottom of the test scores, but were not lacking for teachers who cared.

Today Whittier is considered struggling. The community has changed, as have the boundaries for enrollment. We have gone through several periods of probation. But the teachers are still excellent! The administration is hard-working and dedicated to helping students excel. Equipment and facilities at the school are the best they have ever been.

My first day was most interesting. I was "super-prepared." I did not want any problems. My dress was perfect: a professional look, with a new hat, PE shorts, and PE shirt. I even had a fancy whistle on my neck. My clipboard was filled with the best lesson plans imaginable. I was going to be tough and avoid every discipline problem under the sun. Jim Ciccarello was on top of his game, ready to keep those kids in line.

Well, to my great surprise, as the bell rang and the sixth-graders marched out to class for the first time, I was shocked. Back then Whittier had a dirt playground with a slab of cement in the middle. As I stood at attention on my teaching station, two straight lines walked silently toward me: one line of boys and one of girls. The boys sat down in front of me, the girls standing behind them in a straight line waiting for instruction. That moment is as clear today as then. I checked my pulse—was I in Heaven? All teachers, regardless of era, want their students to be in self-control. Here I was prepared to jump on these students to get their attention, and I had it without asking. In 1971, the Whittier students were a dream to teach.

They were good listeners, respectful, non-violent, and cooperative, excited about learning, and generally ready. Their parents were just like them. These children at Whittier were being nurtured at home, read to, expected to perform academically, and above all, were taught to respect their teachers. Teachers not only earned respect from the students, they were afforded it the minute kids stepped into the classroom.

After my initial shock, it was time to get to work. The students were dressed in proper PE gear and ready to exercise. We ran, galloped, skipped, and moved all over that cement slab. The kids got their heart rates up and we started work on upper body and large leg-strength exercises. We then played a kickball game. Before you knew it, our 30 minutes was over and they went back to class. I had ten classes that day, and each one was a mirror of the last. That Monday I knew I had found home.

In elementary school the only time comparable to a PE class is recess. My first day at Whittier, I stayed out to see what the kids would do. As the bell rang hundreds of kids ran out and organized playground games. They headed for the Tether-balls, the backstop, and the open football field. I walked over to a dirt football field and watched something I had never seen: a young lady, about 10 years old was organizing a touch-football game. She was the quarterback and set all these fourth- and fifth-grade boys on the line of scrimmage. She would yell signals and the boys would go out for a pass when she said, "Hut." No one argued with her. I was floored to see such leadership. This was my first look at Nicole Earing, a student-athlete who liked football. In Jersey City, at Lowell and at Riverview, I had never seen a girl take control of a game like that. This was before Title IX. Nicole was definitely ahead of her time!

Nicole was far from the only athletic student at Whittier. There were 600 kids, and most played some type of sport. Eric Ramey, a sixth-grader, was bigger than I and he could play some football. Danny Lamar was almost as big as Eric, and a year younger. Scott East was one of the fastest kids on the playground. When he became a student at Highland, Scott became a State Champion in the low hurdles. He always told me it was the motivation of running at Whittier that started his track career. Phil Romero, not big in stature, was a big man on campus. He knew everybody. Glenda Padilla and Mary Lynn Griffin were the fastest girls in the school. Eddie Wheeler was so fast he was a legend while still in the sixth grade! I was surrounded by athletes of all kinds.

They could run, play football, participate in gymnastics. Valery Lamar could do cartwheels and back handsprings across the entire playground, and play baseball and softball. The Whittier kids liked to play soccer. Mary Bolton, Linda Rettinger and Liz Scott were in both track and gymnastics. Here I was, a 28-year-old PE teacher, surrounded by kids who wanted to play ball. Unless I forget, they were all excellent students, too. As I gave these kids my full attention, I began to realize if I would just "look at them" they would take that energy, and shine.

So a recess never went by that I did not go out, watch or organize some athletic activity for and with them. I also conducted many after-school athletic activities. Track and field, soccer, gymnastics, softball, and basketball were just a few.

We would compete against our neighbor-school Bandelier Elementary. My good friend Lee Hays taught PE there, followed by Carl Brand. We continued to compete against Bandelier in soccer and Blast Ball for several more years, even as Lee left teaching to open a movie theater in Arizona.

The early '70s were special years at Whittier. I immediately added athletes to the ATC. I had about 50 boys and 30 girls who ran in an after-school program, and participated in track and field. Mr. Frank Monceballez, a sixth-grade teacher, helped me organize them. He had a son John, and three daughters Cindy, Lori and Jenny, all part of the program. It was a natural activity for Frank as his own kids ran and he helped raise money for the club.

Frank was also one of the most effective classroom teachers I have ever seen. You could literally hear a pin drop in his classroom. His son John had a friend—Al

Unser Jr.—whom he would bring to practice at Roosevelt Park. I knew immediately that "Little Al" could run. He did not like to lose. Little did I know that he would win the Indianapolis Five Hundred 15 years later. Little Al in his first NM State Cross Country Championship meet won the nine-and-under division at Roosevelt Park. If he had continued running as he got older he would have been an outstanding high school runner and college runner. But Al Unser Jr. was on a mission, and instead became one of the greatest race car drivers of all time.

Around this time, my brother Richard and I had a Limousine Company. We would drive all the rock music groups who came to town from the airport to the concert gigs. We drove Elvis Presley, Sonny & Cher, Jefferson Airplane, Ginger Rodgers, Elton John, the Pointer Sisters, Neil Diamond, and many other groups. So I always had a big black Limousine that I would park in the faculty lot at Whittier. Once in a while I would drive the kids to practice in a limo. One day Frank Monceballez, a kid at heart himself, put on a chauffeur's uniform and drove to Roosevelt Park with a couple of age-group kids from Whittier and Lowell. He parked the car, opened the doors and helped them out, and they ran around the park a couple times. They then put their sweats back on, and Frank helped them into the limo. People in the park were astonished and could not figure out who these running stars were. The kids would remember this day forever!

By working with these kids, and having fun along the way, they would do any workout we gave them. At the time we would outwork any high school and UNM track teams. We would also beat them in competition, even though we were age-groupers. Our ATC kids ran against UNM with four 14-year-olds in a 4x4 relay race and beat them 3:49 to 3:59.

One of our workouts at Roosevelt Park was whistle fartlek up and down hills for 45 minutes. This workout is so hard that athletes could not even carry on conservation while running with their teammates as they had to conserve energy. Adults and high school athletes could not do it. I would watch them and give verbal reinforcement as they attacked the hills. Talk to your athletes while they run. As George Patton once said, "If a man has done his best, what else is there?" I have always said, "It is the athletes' effort that counts, even more so than the result." Usually, though, if you give the effort you get the performance!

Back at Whittier the kids were studying and performing in athleti
est level. We had a phenomenal teaching staff and supportive a
The Whittier Parent Teacher Association (PTA) was so strong that we couiu ..
fit all the attendees into the cafeteria for our meetings. We sometimes had to go
in grade-level shifts. At Whittier we always had money for school supplies and
bus trips, and all teachers were awarded a stipend from the PTA of $100 for each
classroom to use in any way the teacher saw fit.

Our principal in the early part of the decade was Mrs. Dora Clark. She ran a
tight ship and parents supported her. Dora came right at the end of APS's corporal
punishment policy and swung a mean paddle herself. In fact, Tom Gentry, the
son of Highland HS football coach Bill Gentry, told me, "Coach, I was paddled
only once in my entire time as a student at Whittier. Mrs. Clark hit me a good one
and I never needed a paddling again."

Whittier had few problems with discipline while Mrs. Clark presided, and Mr.
Doug Carmichael replaced her in 1976. He used a paddle but he was not that
tough, and things began to relax for both students and teachers. Mr. Carmichael
paddled kids only two more years. He was a very social administrator and believed in teamwork for both staff and students. He supported the PE program and
even got involved with after-school activities. He would travel with us to UNM
and help carry our gymnastics mats in his pickup truck, and go to Bandelier for
a soccer match.

There were several outstanding teachers at Whittier in the early '70s. Mrs. Rob-
erts and Mrs. Wiff both taught third grade, and their students were bright, eager
to learn, and self-disciplined. Then Mrs. Montoya and Steve Clapper took the
fourth grade to another high level. At the sixth grade level Mr. Monceballez and
Earl Lyon were amazing teachers, with great control of their classrooms. As the
late '70s became the early '80s, kids became harder to control and teachers had
to imagine better classroom management. Each succeeding decade discipline was
changing. In many respects teaching is harder today than it was in 1980.

In 1972, when I first saw Valery Lamar doing gymnastics on the playground, I
wanted to expand it to include other children. We started to practice at recess and
in our PE classes. I had taken gymnastics and tumbling with Rusty Mitchell at

UNM as an undergraduate student; while not very proficient myself, I did learn the basics. I figured if I could have a student demonstrate, the class could follow.

It worked. Val demonstrated a forward roll to perfection and everyone else got excited to try. Soon I had everybody doing advanced gymnastics stunts and rolls. As long as I was watching them, they tried even harder. Because of the safety factor, I never left them alone, and I made sure they knew when they accomplished something difficult. If you can't do it, find someone who can.

We got so good that I started hosting gymnastics shows for the Whittier PTA and other schools. The Whittier gymnastics team sent more students to the Albuquerque Gymnastics School and Gold Cup Gymnastics to compete than any other public school program in New Mexico. John Charzuk, with whom I attended college with at UNM, was the head coach at AGS, and he marveled at our little elementary PE kids' abilities. His assistant coach, José Camacho, a middle school PE teacher, stayed in touch. Years later, José told me, "Coach, the kids in those early years were the hardest workers to earn their place on the team. Later on the kids that followed had a different attitude. The '70s kids worked to earn their positions, while the kids in the 2000s felt entitled to them."

Looking back myself I do see the change. The kids back in the '70s did not have the distractions of today. The kids today are involved with too many activities at the same time, in a hurry to reach the top. In 1972 my students just wanted to have fun and put on a show.

Around that time I got a bright idea. The Boys Club used to play basketball at Lobo halftime shows with little kids. I thought, "Why not a gymnastics halftime show?" I secured a date. We lugged mats to and from the game, and performed setup. I had plenty of help in Mr. Carmichael, Mr. Lyon and Mr. Clapper from Whittier as the years went on.

I cannot express enough how important that halftime show was. A Lobo basketball game meant 17,000 people in attendance. Our exposure was tremendous and the self-esteem boost for the students was enormous. We did these shows for about 15 years. They helped our PE program grow, as people from all over New Mexico saw us in action. We became known as a "Gymnastics School."

Of course, I knew better. At Whittier we had gymnastics, track, soccer, baseball, and much more. One of my favorite statements is, "You are my 'everything' kid." In my career I had thousands of students who could do everything. I tried to encourage students to try it all. All they had to do was to keep trying! All we had to do was encourage them!

I had my first physical setback in 1971. I have always played basketball, and in my late 20s I still liked to play. We would go to Johnson gym on the UNM campus and play most nights. Sunday afternoon was the best. We played in pickup games, in which anybody who was somebody in the Albuquerque basketball community participated. Having been a "gym rat" my entire life, I fit in perfectly.

One Sunday afternoon after I went up for a rebound, I hit the floor with a stabbing pain in my lower back. The pain never went away. It was declared spinal stenosis. After many doctors, physical and massage therapy, acupuncture, ultrasound, and other methods, I went for a spinal fusion. It was a tough decision. My back was to be fused at the L-5 level to limit movement, a piece of bone from my hip to complete the fusion. I wanted to heal and get back to the court. I hoped to start teaching PE again. I thought about something Theodore Roosevelt once said: "In any moment of decision, the best thing you can do is the right thing, the next best thing is the wrong thing, the worst thing you can do is nothing."

In December of 1972, I scheduled the operation for Christmas break. This was my first major surgery, and I was confused and in pain. The nurses would roll me over in my bed sheets every four hours to control bed scores. Morphine was the choice of pain control, and it worked, but I did not like the prospect of using it for an extended period of time. One week after the surgery I went home to recover. Exactly six weeks after surgery, I returned to Whittier and began teaching again.

Being young and strong I knew I would recover quickly. I could have taken the rest of the year off; my doctor offered to excuse me for a year of recovery. I chose instead to return to work. I limited my activity but still taught gymnastics. Several parents and teachers assisted me in spotting and helping students. I would sit in a chair and give verbal feedback. It was important that I would look at them as they did their forward rolls and stunts; they always looked for my approval.

In fact, because I was there recovering from a serious back operation, I believe the kids tried *harder* to please me. In today's world it would have been hard to manage students while in serious recovery, but the students of 1972 were more forgiving than their own children 20 years later. As I continued to recover, I became more involved. I wanted to be the best PE teacher I could be.

In the '70s and the '80s we took our gymnastics show to Highland High School, Wilson Middle School, UNM and other elementary schools. We held an APS district-wide seminar for gymnastics, and always had a PTA show. Some names that were involved at this time were:

Valery Lamar	Shannon Taylor	Molly Roach
Jennifer Monfiletto	Marnie Elliot	Liz Roach
Val Mueller,	Sarah Kovach	Carla Williams
Tammy Hatch	Leisha Rupert	Mary Lynn Griffin
Donnie Martin	Tynae Abrams	Sharon Griffin
Kelly O'Brien	Amanda Crumbly	Jana Hays
Susan Ballinger	Judy Green	Claudia Gonzales
Kathy Shaw	Kelly Lopez	Cordy Gonzales
Mary Jane Deflice	Francesca Lopez	Carol Gonzales
Kelly Taylor	Anne Roach	

The list is endless! There were others. One year we took 75 kids to do a half-time show at a Lobo game. This was the same night that Marvin Johnson set a UNM record, scoring 50 points, helping the Lobos to win the conference title. The crowd was crazy and our little elementary kids were part of the big show.

I had Donnie Martin walk on his hands from one baseline to the other and the crown went wild. Henry Tafoya and Keith Griffith were broadcasting the game on TV and they told me they received numerous phone calls about our Whittier students. In our own way, the Whittier kids helped the Lobos excel that night. We pumped the crowd up!

But all good things must come to an end, and as the '90s approached, we started to tone it down. Administrators cut gymnastics in high schools and at UNM. Liabilities started to appear, and kids began to lose their self-discipline. A student at

Eldorado High school had a serious accident on a trampoline. At UNM they cut our halftime show to six minutes (from 15). It took us six minutes just to get the mats out on the floor! You might say gymnastics was gone with the wind. (It does get windy here. I have had the mats literally blown away as we unloaded them.)

Whittier was a special place for families in the '70s. They watched out for one another. The entire family of the athletes would come to watch everyone else. The Roache family would ask me over for spaghetti dinners and talk about their kid's involvement in athletics. Jim Roache sent me a letter as an adult:

> Coach Ciccarello, I remember in a Blast Ball game, you telling me I could do it (hitting the ball) against Tom Potter (a super-athlete) and when I hit a long one and cleared the bases you again said, "See, I told you that you could do it." Thanks, for you were right.

His sisters were on my gymnastics team and always gave thanks for the opportunity to compete. Jimmy Spinello, younger brother of Janet, sent me a letter that said, "Coach, thanks for all the Play Days and all the running around the Whittier playground...." The kids and families at Whittier never forgot!

I bought a house in the Whittier neighborhood in the early '70s. My next-door neighbors were the Rodriguezes. Emma, the mom, was on the New Mexico School Board of Education. Dad was on faculty at Highlands University. My first year at Whittier, Ray was a sixth-grader while his brother Matt was in fourth. I still played basketball, and would shoot hoops with Ray on the playground.

Even at a young age I could see Ray's talent. He eventually became a great player for the Highland Hornets. Later, he coached there, moved to Washington State to coach basketball, and returned years later to coach basketball at Cibola High School. Ray is one of the most respected coaches in New Mexico. Matt, now in his adult years, buys and sells cars. I am always asking his advice, as I buy and sell them myself as a hobby. Matt and Ray always remember Play Day and the ribbons I gave out. Matt told me one day, "Coach, on the first day of school we would start picking our relay teams for Play Day—even though it was nine months away."

Meanwhile, back on the track, the Whittier and ATC athletes were performing at a high level. The Club would go to an age-group cross country meet and win every age division, both boys and girls. We were traveling to Colorado, Arizona, California, Florida, Nebraska, Ohio, and Texas. Every trip cost money. The parents were supporting us and we solicited funds from the local business community. We hosted car washes, spaghetti dinners, raffles, movie nights, fireworks sales, bake sales, and other fundraisers. The more we did together the more we became a family.

The Club parents were amazing. There are several families that need mention. The Beach family never missed a meet, even with nine kids. The Baty family had four kids and went on every trip. The Archuleta family always drove wherever their three girls needed to go. The Frakes did the same for their three girls. Mr. and Mrs. Roybal never missed a meet. Other parents were:

Mrs. Anderson	Mrs. Lopez
Mr. and Mrs. Brockwell	Mr. and Mrs. Monceballez
Mrs. Hankins	Mr. and Mrs. Nunley
Mr. and Mrs. Keel	Mr. and Mrs. Omori
Mr. and Mrs. Fritz	Mr. and Mrs. Quintana
Mr. and Mrs. Lemaster	Mrs. Sedal

We had many other parents involved. When you are talking about something as huge as we were, you had to have adult support. Anytime kids have adults and leadership in their lives, they are much more likely to become successful. Again, all kids want teachers, parents, and coaches to, support them.

Give them your time. They will shine.

VAL BOYER, MARGARET METCALF AND CURTIS BEACH

These are three names that deserve special attention. I signal out these three because they have gone on to wear the uniform of the USA.

First and foremost: Val Boyer. I could write a book on Val alone. Someday I hope that she will find the time to write her own story. Phil Casaus, an Albuquerque sports writer in 1989, had this to say this about Val: "She is ATC's guiding light and would always be the team's alpha and omega." I love all my students and athletes but I have to comment on our role models.

I first met Val at Lowell in 1969. She was a skinny little fourth-grader, unassuming and just a little bit inquisitive. As a first-year teacher, I was full of vinegar and energy. Standing on the playground looking at kids was new to me. I blew the whistle and asked, "Is anybody ready to race?" Val was among the first to show. This was just a simple race around the Tether-ball poles and the backstop. Even then she had that competitive look. There were others there too, like James Bell, who wanted to race and show the new coach how fast he was. Needless to say, when I blew the whistle, Val took off with James in pursuit and a mob of kids behind them. Val won, James in second, and both were cool about it, as if they knew that was the way it was supposed to be.

Who would have guessed a little bitty fourth-grader would become a superstar? And what about James Bell? He went on to become one of Albuquerque High's greatest football players, and later a star in the Canadian Football League.

Both of these young students were a product of the Kirk; their lifestyle was tough from the very beginning. Remarkably, though, out of this neighborhood have come some of Albuquerque's finest athletes. Today when I think of being a young rookie coach, and working with these Kirtland Addition athletes, I realize they gave to me as much as I gave to them. I may have been paying their entry fees, training them, driving them to meets, motivating them to run and study, but they blessed me with their presence. I had the incredible gift when I first started out to work with great talent. They returned the energy I gave them.

Realizing I had some quality athletic talent at this school, I connected with the Duke City Dashers. I started to train these kids during recess, and for a couple days after school. Val Boyer was not the fastest girl there; Donna Gill Corley and Alice Watson had her beat. When we met as a city-wide team Val was not even fast enough to make a relay team. But Val had an ace up her sleeve: she never gave up and her attitude was the best of anyone's. She also appreciated my help, which she showed by working hard and doing what was asked of her, win or lose. Until now, she had never gotten this kind of attention, and she was ready to relish it.

In PE class she was a model student and I realized early she was very smart, and very motivated. Val always asked me about everyday life, and how it had been traveling the world. I told her stories of living in New York and New Jersey. I told her about my US Air Force years and she listened to everything. One day I mentioned girls' college scholarships and noticed a spark in her eye. I used to call it "Val Boyer Eyes." I said, "Val, if you study hard and get good grades, you might be able to go to college for free." I think that statement set the stage for the student-athlete she was about to become.

Nobody, and I mean *nobody*, has worked harder than Val Boyer. She earned everything. Countless repeats, whistle fartlek, sprints, and even cross country workouts were the order of the day. She would go down on the grass with cramps and I would ask her to get up and do another repeat. She always did.

Other girls would head for water or hide behind trees—not Val. If athletes did not want to do the workout she would do it alone. I have coached 65,000 students or athletes and never seen the equal of Valery Lynn Boyer. Val epitomized the perfect response to encouragement.

From 9–13, she could not even make our sprint relay team. She was running 800m's and cross country, trying to build endurance and strength. I used to tell her "practice makes perfect," and each year we noticed she was getting faster and faster. Just before she turned 14, she beat Alice Watson for the first time, and from then forward, she never lost a race to another New Mexico female. She went undefeated in high school. While at Manzano High School she was the leading scorer in state track and field history; the only races she ever lost were on the national- or world-stage. Her true competition was now Olympians the like of Evelyn Ashford, Brenda Moorhead, Chandra Cheesbourgh, and Florence Griffin Joiner. When she was 16 she ran in the Olympic Trials in Eugene, OR. At 17 she made the USA-USSR team and won the 100m and anchored the USA's 4 x 1 relay to victory, and was voted the most valuable athlete on that team. The following year at the World Cup, she was a member of the World Record-setting USA 4 x 1 relay. At the next Olympic trials in 1980, she tried again and made semifinals in the 100m and the 200. Turning on the television and watching her wear that USA uniform brought a spark to my soul. Often I think back about that skinny little girl on the playground running around the backstop, racing James Bell.

Val was a straight-A student at Hayes Middle School and Manzano. She went to ASU, where she was an All-American in track and field and graduated with honors. And indeed, Val received a paid education, courtesy of the sweat on the track. She majored in criminal justice, and upon graduation was accepted into law school. After graduating again with honors, she accepted a position as the Prosecuting Attorney for the city of Mesa, AZ. She was appointed to the bench in Chandler. Her years of goal-targeting paid off. It all started on the elementary school playground.

Val was inducted into the New Mexico Hall Of Fame in 2003. I introduced her to the audience, in a very proud moment for both of us. Val is now married to Roger Wells, with four children and several grand kids. They live in Paradise Valley, AZ, and are productive members of their church and community. Sandy Beach, one of her teammates, said of Val, "She always has been a role model to everybody: being a great student, becoming a lawyer, being a wife, supporting her family, becoming a mother, and being a friend to all her teammates."

After all these years, Val, now in her 50s, still calls me "Coach."

I called and asked her some questions for this book. Below is our interview:

What made you want to run track?

Track and field was the vehicle that changed my life. I am the sixth of seven children to a single mom. My mom did the best she could, even worked her way off of state assistance over the years. However, as a child growing up, college was for other people who could afford it. But, when I was 10 years old my PE teacher/track coach told me that if I ran fast enough I could get a scholarship to go to college for free. All I had to do was run!

That was a huge incentive for me. There was no way my mom could pay for my college education. I decided that I would run, run fast, and run right on to a college education. My goal, at a tender young age, was to be the first person in my family to graduate from high school, the first to graduate from college, and the first to graduate from law school. Running was to be the vehicle that would take me to those lofty goals.

Has success on the track helped you in your adult life?

You bet! I remember a workout where we had to do about 10 200m dashes, all timed. By the fourth one I'm calling "earl!" (You know the sound you make when you're throwing up? Yeah… that earl!) Well, after calling "earl" I would still have to get it on the line and finish the other six 200m's. I reflected on that time when I was in law school. It was late and I still had a few more cases to brief for class. I felt like calling "earl" and going to bed. But I had learned that you get on the line and finish what you start. I finished briefing the cases. You just suck it up and do what you have to do, no matter what the task.

How have athletics activities impacted your life?

Running track and field changed my life. The Following is a list of some of those impact changes. I learned to set goals. My focus was always on evaluating my goals along the way. I needed to stay focused and not stray from my ultimate goal to earn a college scholarship

1. I learned to work hard and be diligent, realizing nothing comes easy.

2. I established a work ethic. Running track and being a world-class athlete requires dedication and a standard of excellence. So does life.

3. I learned that with disciple comes success. As an athlete growing up, that meant attending all practices, eating a proper diet, no drugs, no alcohol, no sexual relations, no criminal activities, I had to commit to academics, I needed to choose my friends wisely. As a teenager there would be many distractions and I needed to stay on course to become that wife, mom, lawyer, and judge that I hoped to be.

4. I learned a lesson from my coach. "No gain without pain!" It did not always feel good when you were working hard towards a goal. It hurt to practice hard. But being successful because of that hard work felt good.

How many friends, family, and lifetime associates have you developed being an athlete?

Lots! The girls I ran track with as an age-grouper I am still friends with. We get excited watching our children compete in track. I am still friends with athletes I met in college and international competition.

Also, I got my first job as an attorney with the Maricopa County Prosecutor's Office as Deputy County Attorney because I had been a world-class athlete. The Assistant County Attorney who hired me said that to compete at that level, I must have an excellent work ethic and be a hard worker. He knew I would apply that same standard as a lawyer for the state of Arizona. I am a City of Mesa Judge today because everything I learned from running track. I am now over 30-years-married to the same man because of what track taught me. I am highly motivated. My adult life is a success because of track.

What do you consider your greatest moment in sports?

Some might think that my greatest moment was when I represented the USA in the USA-USSR dual meet championships in Virginia. In that meet I was selected by the Russians as the Most Valuable USA Athlete. Some might think my greatest moment was being on the USA World Cup team. Some might say it was the night I was voted into the Albuquerque/New Mexico Sports Hall of Fame. All of those moments were great. But for me, the greatest moment was in 1977 at the New Mexico State Track and Field Championships.

Manzano was my high school team and we were in a battle for the team State Championship. As we lined up for the mile relay (4 x 4) I had a pep talk with my other three relay members. I asked all members to leave everything they had on the track. I asked them to not hold back anything. Each of my teammates ran their personal best that night. We were up against some very good New Mexico teams. I remember getting the baton in last place. It was like everything I had learned about setting a goal and going after it was being put to the test. Each girl in front of me was mine to catch and pass. I did not think about how tired I was. I did not think about pacing the back straightaway. I did not think about the monkey that usually hops on your back for a ride at the 300 mark. I did not even think about the major cramping that takes place when you sprint the entire 400. I only though about each runner I needed to pass. I could hear a "whoooooo" coming from the crowd. Each time I passed a girl it got louder. I was picking them off one by one. I felt no pain. I remember giving Sally Marquez the baton in first place and her bringing home the baton for a gold medal and the State Championship. I think it was the most gratifying moment because it took all four girls to accomplish that goal. It took the entire team to win the team title. The mile relay and the new State Record was a great way to end the 1977 New Mexico State Championship.

This was a team that I helped start in 1976 when Title IX was allowing girls to have sports at the high schools just like the boys. In 1976 the number of athletes on our team was low. Even then we placed third at the State Meet. In 1977, because of the other girls that joined, I was able to lead us team to our victory. We were a team… a family… and we were champions! For me, that moment with my high school teammates was the greatest moment in sports.

What advice do you have for young athletes?

Always have goals. Goals make you think about every decision. Every decision has a consequence. It will get you closer to your goal, take you further away from it, or delay your achieving it. Choose wisely my child.

How many teachers, coaches, professors, became part of your development to reach your goals and the point in your adult life today?

It does not matter how many contribute to that development. All you need is one to make a difference. The one who speaks into your life, the one who tells you you can do what everyone else says you can't, the one who is willing to give you his time. The one committed to your success! The one who takes every experience (good or bad) and makes it a life lesson. All you need is one person that will be your biggest fan, your loudest cheerleader. All you need to know is one Coach Jim Ciccarello. Thanks, Coach, for being my "1."

Next is Margaret Metcalf-Watson. I also received this letter from her recently:

As I child, I grew up in a family of seven. My dad was in the Air Force so most of my childhood was spent on bases both in and out of the country. Regardless of where we lived though, I always had someone to play with. We always enjoyed running around and playing outdoors.

One of my first memories of the beginning of my running career was in the 6th grade at Dakota Elementary (1971–1972) at Minot AFB., ND. I always loved PE and participating in any athletic activity. During the track and field unit at school, I was selected by the PE teacher to participate in the city elementary-aged meet. I remember practicing a lot of baton passing for the 4 x 100m relay. I recall the meet seeming to be huge and having so many people everywhere! I competed in the 4 x 100m relay and the long jump. I remember grabbing the baton as the anchor for the relay and sprinting as fast as I could. I'm not sure how we placed, but we got a ribbon for participating. As for my long jump, it was a lot of fast and uncontrolled sprinting that resulted in the comment, "She runs like a spider!" I wasn't sure what that meant, but it didn't matter, because I had fun running and got another ribbon!

My family then moved to Aviano AFB., Italy where I finished junior high school and one year of high school. Since the high school wasn't built until my ninth-grade year (1974–1975), I wasn't involved much with organized athletics. My sisters and I did have a great time running around our neighborhood in Dardago, Italy. Ninth grade with the Aviano Saints gave me the opportunity to play basketball and run track, which was definitely a great learning experience. My running went to the next level with a 400m meter personal best of 60 seconds. I also attempted the high jump and had some success at 4'8".

My father took his final assignment with the Air Force in Albuquerque. I attended Highland High School for my sophomore year (1975–1976) and did not get involved in any sports because there was no track team. However, in 1976, we moved off-base and into Manzano's district. The summer before my junior year, I started running again at Manzano's dirt track. The 1976–1977 year turned out to be an epic one athletically. I decided to try basketball again. It turned out to be a terrific season, and I discovered that I really loved jumping for rebounds and playing defense. I also went out for track in the spring. It turned out to be an amazing team with awesome coaches who were able to motivate and pull the best out of each athlete. I remember some really tough workouts courtesy of Coach Ciccarello both on the track and at the parks. All of the hard work paid off with inspiring wins at the District and State Meets. As for my teammates, running with some of the best talent in the state was both awe-inspiring and humbling. Ciccarello's expectations and motivation brought Manzano's track team to a level that culminated in personal bests and talent that was prepared for national competition.

My next experience was to run club for Ciccarello and the Albuquerque Track Club the summer before my senior year. This time was filled with more hard work and making new friends in the running community. Attending track and field Nationals in Los Angeles that summer was an eye-opener! I tried my hand at the 400m meter sprint and high jump. My placement in both events wasn't anything to write home about. I was too star-struck with people like Wilt Chamberlain moving the high-jump bar!

My senior year at Manzano (1977–1978) started off with another great season of basketball that took us to state playoffs. Consequently, I got a late start to the track season. Early defeats in the 400m cut into my confidence, but Coach Ciccarello saw the bigger picture and believed in me. With my wonderful teammates, we ended up winning District and State again. I tried my hand at the 800m, and to my chagrin, I had to compete against my friend and ATC teammate, Sandy Beach. I had better luck with the high jump and set a personal and State Record at 5'8". It was an amazing feeling to jump so well and to end my senior year on a positive note.

That summer, I went with Coach Ciccarello and my ATC teammates to Junior Nationals in Indianapolis, Indiana. My two events were the 4 x 400m relay and the high jump. The relay was, as most relays are for me, the most fun. Our race didn't bring us any medals, but I redeemed myself by jumping my all-time best of 5'11". Since I placed second, I was able to make the Junior National Team and compete in Russia and Germany. This was the most remarkable and proud experience of my track and field career, and I am so grateful that I got to represent my country.

My time with Coach Ciccarello seemed all too short as I began college at UNM. My running career blossomed under Ciccarello's coaching, and I will be forever grateful that I had those experiences at Manzano and the ATC. Running has opened doors for me and given me opportunities that I never thought possible. A new-found confidence and outgoing attitude are two qualities that influenced my college running career and ultimately carried into my teaching. My proudest accomplishment outside of athletics was becoming a mother to my daughters, Shawn and Kelly. Passing along my love of athletics and sports to my precious girls is the ultimate accomplishment.

Margaret Metcalf-Watson

July 31, 2012

Margaret's memory of track and her teammates is precious. She was always a team player, even as she performed admirably in individual events. She was quiet and unassuming, and always gave credit to her teammates and her coaches. Tall and stately with a long stride, she ran like a deer (more than a spider). We were very proud to see her wear the USA uniform. I am also proud that she would mention in her letter that she passed on the love of athletics and sports to her children.

Margaret Metcalf is perhaps the most gifted athlete I have ever coached. In 1977, she transferred into Manzano. I had never heard of her. She had been lost in the shuffle at Highland. That was about to change. I am not accustomed to girls being so tall. Margaret was about 5'10". I already was thinking high jump when I saw her. She had all the tools to be a great track athlete: size, power, and speed.

Margaret was also very shy, and at first I was not sure she would become the competitor I expected. She was so nice, I did not think she wanted to hurt someone's feelings by beating them in competition. She loved her teammates and would do anything for them; I realized if I put her in the spotlight where her teammates needed her, she would shine. So I immediately put her on a couple of relay teams for her to bond. She had a lot of respect for Val Boyer and I knew if she ran with Val, I could expect 100%. When I put those two girls on the same relay with just about anybody else, it was an automatic gold medal. They set and broke the NM

State Record in the mile relay several times that season, which required breaking the record *at the State Meet itself.* (Back then records were in yards instead of meters, so tragically, all records set by those two girls have been wiped off the books.)

The first day of practice I noticed that Margaret had some pretty good speed, and a long stride. She might have a shot at a good 400m (quarter mile). Margaret never had trouble with any of our workouts. As I continued to watch and test her, I realized that she also had good endurance. Now, every coach I know would love to have a kid who could sprint on the relays and run the open quarter (400m). What made this even more special is that Margaret Metcalf could also run the half (800m). As the season progressed, I realized that Margaret could run (and win) the 100m, the 200m, the 400m, and the 800m. She could also run all of the four relays on the schedule. A high school athlete in New Mexico is limited to five events only. Only four of them could be on the track. Margaret was already maxed-out. She could do one more field event. This was a coach's dream. Whatever event I put Margaret in, she scored points.

As I tried to develop her other abilities, I never let go of the high jump. We would go to the high jump pits and at first she would clear 4'10". This is good, but she was sitting going over the bar, which indicated she could go a lot higher. We worked on her technique weekly. We needed her to do the "Fosbury Flop" and go over the bar backwards. As she started to arch her back, she went higher. I also noticed that as she ran faster on the track, she jumped higher in the pit. So we ran her in four events every meet to strengthen her legs. It worked, and by the end of the season, Margaret was ranked first in New Mexico in three events (the high jump, 400m, and 800m). At the NM State Meet she won all three as she ran a 58.60 (400m), and a 2:18 (800m), and high-jumped 5'6".

Bear in mind she won all of these while a junior in high school. Val Boyer was the senior on that team. Val was having a great year, undefeated. We could actually go to the State Meet and win the team title with just those two girls! But we had other athletes on that team, who were also good, and who also deserved time on the track. We scored 98 points to win the team championship. The nearest team, Roswell, trailed with 56 points. Val was the high-scorer and Margaret was second.

That summer Margaret joined up with the ATC and started running and jumping in AAU meets. She ran on some championship relay teams and went 5–8 in the high jump that summer. She became good friends with Dolores Archuleta and Sandy Beach.

Margaret did the assigned task without complaining, and responded to positive input from her coaches. So we would always compliment her on her effort. When she ran whistle fartlek with Sandy and Dolores we would call out their names so all teammates could hear. It worked, as everyone fell in line and did the workout. When kids do a hard workout they want the coach to acknowledge it.

In her senior year, Margaret went undefeated. She teamed with Christine Brockhoff, our hurdle champion, to lead Manzano as they again won the State Meet. Margaret was the high-point leader at the New Mexico State Meet in 1978. She won the high jump, 400m, 800m, and ran on two winning gold medal relays.

That summer we took her to a couple of AAU track meets with the ATC. What happened in competition that summer was outstanding. Margaret was mature and highly motivated now. The summer before, Val had made a USA international team and Margaret used her as a role model. We took her to a big AAU qualifying meet in California, and at that meet Margaret Metcalf high jumped 5'11". She was now on the USA Junior Team, on her way to Moscow for the biggest stage ever. She had also become the number-two ranked high jumper in the United States. She finished second in that international meet.

I remember going to the airport to greet her when she came back from Russia. Her whole family was there and many friends to congratulate her. I gave her a big hug and saw a pride in her she could not hide. Margaret was shy and not used to so much attention. That day at the Sunport the love for her was apparent. She was greeted by family, friends, teammates, and the local media. She smiled proudly.

Margaret received a full scholarship from UNM. She was also an outstanding student, and majored in education. She ran four years for the Lobos and specialized in the 800m run. She had a solid college career, but nothing that rivaled the accomplishments in the summer of 1978; and eventually she taught kindergarten at Acoma Elementary. Years later, I took my jump-rope team to Acoma. At the school-wide assembly it was a proud moment when I pointed out she was one of

New Mexico's great, historic track athletes. Margaret, quiet as she was, had never mentioned it. I was happy to have told them all.

Now let's take a detour to 2001, to Curtis Beach. He is the third athlete I have coached to make an international team. Given my focus thus far, you may think I only coach girls, but I started coaching boys my first year at Lowell, late 1969. I had 100 boys running for the Duke City Dashers, and later, more than 100 running for the ATC. Of all the boys I have coached, Curtis Beach is in a special category. He is Sandy Beach's nephew (sometimes people think he's her son) and they help form one of the most athletic families I have ever met.

While coaching the La Cueva Girls' Track Team, Sandy was an assistant on my staff. I had come down with prostate cancer the year before (2000). Sandy Beach Warfield (Sandy was now married to Steve Warfield) agreed to cover for me as I recovered from surgery. When I made my comeback in the spring of 2001, Sandy brought a young age-grouper to see me on the track at La Cueva: her very enthusiastic nephew, Curtis. I remember as if it were yesterday. He came across the track to my hurdle station to question me about running. We talked about the 800m run (Sandy had run the 800m many years before) and he wanted some "coaching tips." After giving him a few, I introduced him to the hurdles. "Why not, I'll give it a try," the young Beach said. The hurdles introduced him to the multi-events. They were the beginning of something special in Curtis's career.

He had started to run as a seven-year-old for the ATC. He had always been an active little boy, and his mom, Jeana, told me he liked to chase horses on their ranch. That sounds like a born runner to me. He knew about Sandy's history of running, but had never seen her run. He read the newspaper clippings and talked to the old timers about her accomplishments on the track. He was a Beach, and he wanted to show folks that he could run, too.

When I first looked at Curtis, I noticed his long legs. Then as he warmed up, and it was clear he had a long stride, and he was on his toes. This indicates a possible sprinter and jumper. I said, "Curtis come over to this hurdle. I want you to try a couple of drills." He had no trouble with the drills, and in fact, on his first day, he mastered some drills my high school athletes had been learning for months. After coaching thousands of athletes over 30 years, I knew immediately Curtis had a lot of natural physical talent.

What I did not know at the time was his drive. He soaked up every drill I showed him, and ran with my high school girls, who had five or six years on him. Even as a 10–11 year old, Curtis could outrun them. This was a win-win, as Curtis was running in front of the girls and the girls were trying their hardest to keep up with the young boy. I still say, "Curtis helped the La Cueva girls win a State Championship by his work ethic." No 17-year-old girl will give in to an 11-year-old boy. I had one drill in which Curtis was a rabbit and the girls were foxes, and had to chase him; they never caught him! He responded to the Coach's approval as I would warn him, "The foxes are coming—pick it up, Curtis!" This is a great whistle fartlek drill for speed and endurance. Sandy and I would stand in the middle and marvel at how hard Curtis ran.

I started Curtis in the high jump right away as I knew he was going to be a multi-event athlete. He loved it. Even after all the running and the hurdling, at the end of practice he would want to practice high jump. The sun would be going down and Curtis would say, "One more jump, Coach." The problem was everyone else had gone home and Curtis and I had to bring in the pits, which was hard on my back. I always knew Curtis could run, but the way he improved in the high jump and the hurdles was phenomenal. Early on, he started jumping about 4' 6." He always set goals for himself. I used to measure the high jump with a folding tape measure. One day I told Curtis, "If you jump 6', I will give you the tape measure." I had already realized if Curtis was challenged, he would chase the goal. He was the perfect example of a kid who responded to motivation. To be honest, he was nearly the most self-motivated athlete I ever worked with, second only to Val Boyer. The day Curtis sailed over 6', I immediately received a phone call: "Coach, that tape measure belongs to me." I was all too happy to hand it over; this was both an intrinsic and an extrinsic reward. I not only "looked" at Curtis—I challenged *and* rewarded him. His response was always, "Mission Accomplished!"

Each week he kept getting better in the hurdles. His three-step running pattern between hurdles came quickly. (Some athletes take years to get a three-step pattern.) With his work ethic, his inner drive, and his opportunity to compete in the hurdles, Curtis not only got his three steps down, but he also became the best hurdler in the state. And he dominated as he aged. Curtis not only won the short hurdles (110m), he also became the best in the long hurdles (200m and 300m). He would eventually dominate in the 400m hurdles, also.

As I hinted, Curtis fell in love with the multi-events. He too could have excelled in the 800m or the 400m hurdles at the state and national level, but he was on a mission to compete in the decathlon someday. He was a multi-event athlete in the age-group meets and sometimes there were five events, sometimes seven. At the local and Southwest Regional Meets he would win easily. We took him to Miami, FL to compete in a national age-group meet. He finished in the top five and was standing on the podium. I think that was when he realized he could compete on a national level. Curtis from that point on assumed a mind-set of the national level. The local competition would help him reach those goals.

Curtis was also wonderfully energetic and versatile. All the time he was training in track and field, he was also on the jump-rope team I had started with the Whittier/Bandelier Elementary Schools (more on that story later). He would come to practice at both and give back. And when Curtis attended the students responded. They loved for him to jump rope with them. Many a time Curtis jumped at the Lobo basketball games for a halftime show. I would hear people say, "There's Curtis, the great track athlete jumping rope!" At one game he dunked the rope through the basket and the crowd went wild! Honestly, Curtis became so good at jump-rope, he would intimidate other athletes warming up at a track meet. Some of them even tried to copy him, but to no avail. They would wrap the rope around their necks.

There was a defining moment in his age-group competition. We were in Knoxville, at UT, for a national age-group competition. The competition was outstanding and Curtis was ranked fourth. With one event to go (the 1500m), I wondered how strong he would finish. This was his best event of the day. When the announcer on the public address system introduced the leaders, he did not even mention Curtis Beach. As the race went on, that soon changed. Curtis picked up the pace and passed each runner, opening his lead substantially. By the end of the race, the public announcer was asking people next to him, "Who's that kid from Albuquerque?" Curtis won that race by such a large margin he leapt from fourth to first and took gold! A future decathlon athlete was born.

As a youth, he made his first "USA" international team, went to Ostrava in the Czech Republic and competed in the World Youth multi-event. He finished fourth in the world. I saw that look in his eye at the end of the multi-event in Ostrava. Fourth was not what he trained for, and he would come back on the international stage again and go for the gold medal. That was Curtis Beach.

He became dominant at the Albuquerque Academy, leading his team to multiple state titles. His coach at the high school level was Adam Kedge. Adam was instrumental in steering Curtis in the right direction. He set many State Records at the Academy. He was voted the "Gatorade National Track Athlete of The Year." He competed in and won the "Great Southwest Track Classic." He competed twice as a junior, and again as a senior, setting a national high school record in the decathlon. He then won the USA Junior Championships and went on to represent the USA in Trinidad & Tobago for the Pam Am Games. Curtis loved to compete on the national and international stage.

Curtis sought help from many coaches and teachers in his career. George Provolt helped him in the pole vault. Bill Frangos worked with him in the throwing events. His Academy teachers got him ready for college; at one time he was struggling with music and Spanish, and almost returned to a public school (Eldorado). But to know Curtis was to know his dedication. It may start on the practice field, but discipline follows us into the rest of our lives.

His mom, Jeana, once told me, "Coach Ciccarello, it takes a village to raise a child." In the case of her son, Curtis Beach, it sounds like she knew what she was talking about. I know the Beach family well and I can tell you that Jeana captained that team. She pushed Curtis and surrounded him with quality people. David, his father, a tech expert, helped Curtis research paths to improvement. David was always aware of changes in track and field. He knew how Curtis ranked in every age-group he'd ever competed in. These were parents who helped without interfering with his coaching, which is always an asset for both coach and athlete. The cost of competing at a state and national level was never an issue. In fact, his grandmother and grandfather, his aunts and uncles, his cousins and many other relatives would always find a way to attend his track meets. Curtis had many educators and coaches in his life. The future looks bright for this young man.

Currently, Curtis is an outstanding student and track athlete at Duke University. His new college coach is Shawn Wilbourn. He had offers from some of the best track colleges, but he chose Duke, a private school (like his high school), and it seems like the best fit for him. He has already achieved a Conference Championship and qualified for the Olympic Trials. He has also placed second in the outdoor 2011 NCAA Championships and won the gold medal at the 2012 NCAA Indoor Championships. Curtis has set his goal to become an Olympian for the USA. I, for one, would never count him out as they once did in Knoxville.

I asked Curtis Beach to send me a good memory of running track. Expecting a story about his current run at the 2012 Olympic Trials, I received this:

> Coach,
>
> Towards the end of elementary school, I became a second-generation Coach Chic athlete, following in the footsteps of my aunt Sandy, the first of my family to be coached by him. At that point, I was a distance junkie—running everything from the 800m to the 10k, with my only field event being the long jump. Coach expanded my horizons, introducing me to the hurdles, high jump, sprints, and the throws. There was no end-goal established when trying these events; we simply pursued them just to see what I could accomplish. Four years later, we arrived in Tennessee with a chance to win a national championship in the decathlon.
>
> With nine of 10 events completed in that Tennessee competition, I was in a position that would become relatively common: way back in the decathlon standings, needing a record time for the final event to take the overall title. Fortunately, it was the event Coach and I hold closest at heart: the distance one. 4:27 later, Coach Ciccarello could chalk up yet another athlete he has developed into a national champion.
>
> We explored the Smoky Mountains to soak up the experience, but it was only a couple days later, when we were back in the UT stands, when we began planning ways to improve. Coach selected an older competitor for me to focus on in the 400m hurdles. His name was David Klech—a multi-athlete, like me (and a token white guy in the competition, like me). Coach

had his stopwatch in hand; timing splits from hurdle to hurdle while scribbling the times on a wrinkled piece of paper. As David won the national title, Coach showed me his splits and firmly stated that I could do the same in two years. The very next season, we were back at it, consistently referring to the scrawled out splits, trying to "out work em" as he would always tell me.

Coach Ciccarello made it clear through this experience (and many more) how to work hard for self-improvement, soak up the great times, recover from mistakes, and blend those qualities into the rest of your life. Then take it a step further to teach others how to do it too. I never achieved those goals written on that wrinkled piece of paper, but I feel like I acquired exactly what he wanted me to in the pursuit.

Curtis Beach

When I talk about the Beach family I must include the Kings. Don King, his grandfather, would fly to every major meet in the country when Curtis was an age-grouper. Dorothy, his grandmother, always supported him financially. Ray King, his cousin, and Steve and Rene Beach also attended those trips, the latter from California, and many times I bunked with them. If more kids had the support he had it would be amazing what young people could excel at. The "it takes a village" mentality is evident in the Beach family legacy.

These three athletes, Val Boyer, Margaret Metcalf, and Curtis Beach took their talent to the highest levels possible. All three responded to positive verbal motivation; they loved to show the coach how much they improved. All are amazing, not only as athletes but also as role models for countless other aspiring student-athletes. I feel lucky to have worked with them. They may have reached the highest level of all the athletes I have coached, in my career; but of course all 65,000 of my students and athletes are equally important to me.

Another interesting sidelight to this coaching and teaching story is the fact that many of the track kids I coached went on to become educators themselves. They are teaching in APS.

Sandy Beach	Mary Lynn Griffin	Mary Sedall
Christine Brockhoff	Kathy Guerin	
Therese Dorwart	Margaret Metcalfe	

There are others who are currently teaching right here in Albuquerque or in other communities in New Mexico. Some are teaching in other states. I have received letters from former students now teaching who tell me that teaching started for them when they were motivated in athletics. If you talk with any educator who has been doing her job for a long time I will bet you will hear the same story. There are many teachers out there who inspire their students to go into education.

I have always asked the kids to give back. Older athletes and students are perfect role models for the young. When Curtis Beach would come back to Whittier to teach jump-rope or just race the kids, it was always a special day. These young people may decide they want to make teaching or coaching a profession, to give back to their communities. I had many special athletes who came back to Whittier to work with the students. Curtis Beach, Julia Foster, Grace Rich, Kiva Gresham, Kip Koeich, An Nuygen, Christine Ostler, Mackenzie Kerr, Aubrey Hererra, Jason Richardson, Rachel D'arcangelis, Allie Snell, Reece Cuddy, Mariah Rast, Kaylin Martin, Christina Clark, Chad Clark and Stephanie Brener are just a few that came and gave back to the next generation of Whittier students.

WHITTIER ELEMENTARY, 1980

The classroom climate continued to evolve as my career progressed. At Whittier the climate changed dramatically in the early '80s. With the abolition of corporal punishment and more freedom of choice, student behavior began to change. There were more federal programs like special education classes in the curriculum. Teachers' responsibilities and class sizes began to increase. The elementary schools now ranged from kindergarten–fifth grade. Junior Highs were now called Middle Schools, with grades 6–8. The High Schools were now 9–12. All APS teachers had to adjust, and for some it was hard. At Whittier we now had five-year-olds, who seemed very immature. Personally, kindergarten is my favorite. The sooner you work with young children, the better chance you will have to mold them. They respond to recognition immediately and they want to please their teachers. As students age, their peer group's opinions eclipse their teachers'.

In the '80s I had many outstanding students. Chris Montgomery and his sister Darcy loved PE. Chris told me many years later, "Coach, I remember you teaching us 'Planet of the Apes' and 'Pie Soccer.' Those were two games I made up and gave catchy names to grab their imagination. In my whole career I tried to use common up-to-date movies and songs to help appeal to the children. Students have an incredible imagination and I was determined to tap into it.

I use quotes so often because it invites students to stop and think. When we played "Blast Ball," I would say, "Nickel for a pickle." This meant that the student that caught the high fly ball I hit would win a nickel. Chris Montgomery was always there, trying to win that imaginary nickel.

Our new principal was Dr. Nell New, an experienced administrator with many years in APS. When she came to Whittier, the school system redistricted and we now had students being bussed in from a low-income side of town. The dynamics of Whittier changed drastically. We also added several behavior-disorder classes. We immediately had behavior problems on the playground, and Dr. New started forming committees to design a safer school climate. Our test scores started to drop. Teachers started transferring to other schools. A group of teachers took an early retirement. The change in our school was dramatic.

Student and teacher dress relaxed. Male teachers hung up their coats and ties, opting for dress pants and open-collared shirts. Female teachers left their dresses behind for pants suits. Levi's became the rage. Students dressed down also, as we gradually lost some classroom control. The administration saw the school slipping away. The neighborhood was changing, and with it, the school we knew. We changed our nickname and mascot from the Whippersnappers to the Lions because a counselor thought a new name would inspire pride. I did not agree, but I was in the minority. The Whippersnappers was a cool name and the only school in Albuquerque with it. We did get new T-shirts with the new mascot. Kids did not buy them. They could not afford them.

Remember that demographics were also changing. When I went to Valley in the '50s and early '60s, the Southeast Heights was the up side of town. We loved to drive up around Highland HS and see the latest fashion of the "Heights" kids. Highland was winning most of the State Championships and scoring high academically—and Whittier fed into Highland. Sandia was built, as were Manzano, Del Norte, Eldorado, and La Cueva, to accommodate the shift toward the north. This same 'economic flight' was happening all over the country, but it was very dramatic in Albuquerque in the early '80s. I myself lived in the Southeast Heights for 35 years and watched firsthand as the neighborhoods deteriorated. Whittier shared a boundary with Bandelier Elementary, which was shifted to funnel the higher-income kids to Bandelier. Later, I spent five years at Bandelier: the parents were more involved; the students showed more self-discipline. I do not believe this was a coincidence. Bandelier parents wanted to keep their school high-achieving.

At Whittier, my PE program was changing. These kids were not as self-disciplined as their older siblings, and they were not as physically skilled, as their parents did not have them enrolled in after-school programs. My task became harder, as I still wanted kids to achieve on the playing field and hoped it would transfer to the classroom.

Administration told me our funds were low and I did not have the equipment to facilitate a proper class. The PTA was not as active and little by little we had fewer funds to support the teachers and PE program. All that said, I still had soccer and basketball activities for the kids. Track and field was huge and throughout the '80s, I did continue with the ATC after school with the students.

Our biggest day of the year was Play Day. We would have track and field events all day long. Kids had to be in good academic standing to participate in Play Day. Can you imagine sitting in a classroom looking out the window while other kids raced? I have had many kids return years later and say, "Coach, Play Day was the most important day of the entire school year."

My Play Day was organized to eliminate financial concerns. Some years I would make ribbons. If I could raise some money, I would buy cheap ribbons with

"Whittier Play Day" emblazed on the ribbon. We prepared in our PE classes for two months. Kids practiced the 50-yard dash, relay handoffs, the three-legged race, tug-of-war, shuttle relay, and worked toward their best physical shape for the big day!

I always had a bull horn to make it loud and exciting. At times residents in the neighborhood would call the office and say, "What is all that loud noise over at Whittier today? Tell the coach to hold it down." Sorry, I did not hold it down. It was the biggest day of the year, and a memory to last forever!

I always liked to line the field with marble dust. I would make straight lines (most of the time) so each kid would have her own lane. Our playground was a big dirt field, so it was easy to make a track. The whole school was out there, and it felt Olympic. My judges were former Whittier students, now at Wilson Mid-School or Highland High. We were still a family and the Whittier kids always had pride.

Through the years I have observed that students always defend their school and its programs. Our kids who left Whittier and returned years later always remarked how much they loved physical education, Play Day, the ribbons, and all the activities. Every kid who participated in Play Day received a ribbon. They would run home with their newly-won ribbons to show their parents and put them in their scrapbooks. The pride of a 10¢ ribbon is unbelievable on a child's face. I always think back to when I won a ribbon at PS Number 23. I wanted to continue that tradition here—1800 miles away and 40 years later.

In the 1970s and 1980s we had many solid families at Whittier. The Brito family was a special one. They had several children at Whittier: Antonio, Ramon, and Alicia were outstanding students. The mother, Jeanette, was always on campus volunteering wherever she was needed. She even became a teacher's aide and the school secretary over the years. When one of her children developed a kidney problem, she donated one of hers to help him. Her kids were always involved in running and gymnastics. Jeanette's daughter, Alicia, became a photographer in the US Marine Corps. Alicia was so good at her job that she became the official White House photographer. She always worked hard in physical activities. I asked her to comment about how Whittier PE classes influenced her life:

Coach,

I am doing well and have an AWESOME three-year-old daughter. I am a Gy. Sgt. in the Marine Corps stationed in Washington DC.

Elementary PE definitely led me to my career as a Marine. It helped me focus on always wanting to stay physically fit. Being one of the smaller—or should I say, the smallest—kid on the gymnastics group also taught me to never quit once I started something. This is something that transfers to being a Marine. Size does not matter. Also, teamwork is very important. That is something that we learned from doing our gymnastic routines. This was taught to enlisted men and officers alike in the Marine Corps. We all had our role and without us doing our part we could not function as a team. Our field days at Whittier taught me to try my hardest to achieve a goal. No matter what the task, how big or little our job was, such as being deployed to Iraq, we made sure we could come back alive. This was our mission and our discipline. I'm now a mother and I find that I need discipline in that endeavor, also.

Alicia

This experience at Whittier is just another example of the need to give kids—all kids—reasons to shine. Support your child on the athletic field, and she will perform for you in the classroom. Do not let our children fall between the cracks.

MANZANO HIGH SCHOOL, 1976

While I was teaching at Whittier and running the ATC, an opportunity opened for me to coach high school track and field. Title IX was opening girls' sports at higher levels. Val Boyer was a junior at Manzano, and the administration asked if she knew a coach who could start a program. She immediately called, we hatched a plan, and I was accepted as the new head coach.

There was no money yet for the program, but I was able to find T-shirts that cost us $5 each; they could wear their own shorts. This cheap, hastily-bought uniform would come back to haunt us. We had no equipment and no practice field, so we went to a nearby park. I borrowed some equipment from the ATC, and we got by.

That first year at Manzano there were not many girls in athletics. Norma Simms, the athletic director, had first choice of girls for her drill team. But I had Val Boyer. I planned to develop a team around Val; we had about 25 girls out for track that first year. I asked Earl Lyon (from Whittier) and Lou Granados to be assistant coaches. Later on, Sam C. de Baca and Carol Barnitz joined the Manzano coaching staff. With Val dominating her events we had a good team heading into the NM State Meet our very first year.

We were a new team. We had qualified first in the 400m relay that year, and Val did the same in her individual events. Del Norte and Belen had started in track a couple years earlier, and had an edge. The State Meet that year was held in Artesia, New Mexico. To qualify you had to finish first or second in your district—which of course meant there wasn't much room for mistakes. I was about to greet one of the biggest disappointments of my coaching career.

Since we had a new track program with no budget for uniforms, we wore T-shirts—with athletes in their own personal shorts. All year we wore that particular uniform without disqualifications or warnings of any kind. At the District 2 meet, after we won the 400m relay, and beat the State Record, the announcer called me down to the track. Two coaches were there with a protest in-hand. They objected to Val Boyer's white shorts, rather than purple, like the rest of her teammates. They pointed out in a rule book that the Manzano team should be disqualified because of the difference in color—it being harder for other teams to distinguish team members. I argued that as a first-year team with a non-existent budget, we did not have an official uniform. The protest was upheld and we were disqualified. That meant our relay would not run in the NM State Meet the following week. The same coaches who filed that protest had run against us all year, and never said a word. Years later, when I saw another young coach make the same mistake, I advised her of the illegal uniform before the competition. She corrected it and no harm was done. May the best *team* win—not the best-dressed.

Our 400m relay did not run at State the following week, but Val Boyer did, and won every event she entered. Manzano finished in third place with the points that Val scored all by herself. If we had been allowed to run—and won the relay—we would have won the State Championship that year. We were disappointed to say the least, but galvanized for the coming season. We had something to prove. We did not need to make any mistakes. The girls knew they were the best team in New Mexico. 1977 came with brand-new spiffy uniforms and a killer attitude.

We added some new quality athletes to the track program that year, too. Christine Brockhoff and Margaret Metcalf were super sprinters and class hurdlers. From the ATC we also had Carolynn Adams and Cheryl Thompson. Sally Marquez, a former Olympette Club runner who had just finished volleyball and basketball, decided to run for us again. Our mission was to make a statement. We had brand-new purple and white uniforms and we were "Looking Gooood."

That year we became the first undefeated major school in the AA girls division in New Mexico, with an unbelievable year on the track. We won all four relays at the State Track Meet. Val Boyer won the 50m, 100m and the 200m. It was a windy night and though she beat all the State Records, it was discounted because of the wind. Margaret Metcalf won the 400m, 800m and the high jump, breaking the State Record. Sally Marquez was second in the long jump. The mile relay was the special race of the night. Before the race started, Val called her teammates together in a huddle. I *had* to hear that pep talk: "Ladies, we already have enough points to win this meet. But remember last year and let's give folks something to talk about. If you keep it close, I promise to run the race of my life!"

We were not running our fastest girls because we had used them in other events, and we were limited in the number of events in which we could participate. But we saved Boyer and Marquez for this race. Lindy Griggers ran a 65.5 second, first 400m; Kathy Guerin ran second and ran a 67.0 400m. When Val received the stick, she was in last place, almost 100 yards behind, chasing Belen, Farmington, Del Norte and Los Lunas.

This was the most amazing race I have seen in my coaching career. Val took off like a bullet. By the middle of the first curve she had already passed two teams and was eyeing the next two, who she passed on the straight-away. People in the stands were going wild—they were witness to track history. I heard other coaches say, "No way, is she going to die? She'll hit the brick wall." Instead, she broke through the "brick wall" and passed the last runner on the last turn, and handed the baton to Sally Marquez with a 50-yard lead. Sally easily "brought home the bacon."

The Manzano girls' mile relay had just shattered the New Mexico State Record with a 3:57 time. Ladies and gentleman, Val Boyer had just run a 52.0 split for her 400m. If she had run that in the Olympics, she would have been on the podium! Imagine what this team would have done if Christine Brockhoff, our number-two athlete, had not broken her foot running earlier that season. (She came back in her senior year and made up for it in very big way!)

Some people say the 1977 Manzano Girls' Track Team is the greatest in New Mexico history. They might be right. But 1978 brought a team to rival '77. The 1978 team, also undefeated, was led by Margaret Metcalf and Christine Brockhoff. Boyer and Marquez were gone, but Cheryl Thompson was at her peak. Christine Brockhoff won the long jump, and both hurdles, (80- and 100-yard hurdles) in State Record time. Margaret Metcalf won the 400m, 800m, and the high jump (5'8" was a new State Record). Viola "Raisins" Sanchez won the 1600m. (She ate raisins before every meet.) Cheryl Thompson won the 100m and the 200m. This team scored 107 points at the New Mexico State Meet, an unheard-of score. This group of girls bought into hard work and goal setting. I am very proud of their accomplishments and have particularly fond memories from that period.

I thought 1979 would carry that energy forward, too. But Cheryl Thompson moved to Albuquerque's West Side and enrolled at West Mesa HS. Her new coach, Sheryl Clemmer, helped Thompson to a great season. We ranked in the top five, but it turned out to be a rebuilding year. Our kids were nice and worked hard. We finished sixth at the State Meet.

That summer I went to Honolulu, HI to attend school at the state university. While there, I received a letter from the athletic director saying I was being replaced: they wanted an on-campus teacher to recruit more athletes. Of course I was devastated, and without recourse. APS signs coaches to one-year contracts only.

When I investigated, I realized another person on campus wanted my job and he was connected. The news media wanted to make a big deal of it. It would have been a big black eye for local track and field, so I let it ride and moved forward. At the time I was still coaching my ATC athletes in the summer and they were a blessing. Going to AAU track meets in the summer were fun and productive. It meant more time with Sandy Beach, Val Boyer, and the other ATC greats.

GOLF, BASKETBALL, FUN AND MOTIVATION

About this time I took up golf. When I was not coaching track and field I was on the golf course. In the late '70s when the Albuquerque Track Club would go to an out-of-town meet I would try to get on the course.

Lee Hayes had been playing for a number of years, and became my role model. In 1977 he introduced me to Roger Flaherty, a teacher and basketball coach in Bisbee, AZ. Roger and I developed a great friendship. There were times when we would putt on a green at 2:00 a.m., with only the lights from the club house. We were fanatical. We paired up in tournaments and played in some really big matches. While Roger was a big hitter, I had a great short game. Over the years Roger turned out to be a one-handicap player while I became a five-handicap player. I was still coaching track and teaching physical education.

My friends can attest that I'm a "practice animal." I did as I preached: "practice makes perfect." I would get up at 5:00 a.m. and head to the driving range as the sun came up. My first class at Whittier Elementary was at 8:00, and I would pull up to the playground at 7:45, ready to teach. My social life was limited to golf, track, and teaching. As I'm fond of saying, "If I had talent, I could have been somebody." I would never let another athlete out-work me. Later on in my coaching career I would tell my athletes to "out-work" their opponents. I developed an excellent short game, which included putting and chipping.

In basketball I would beat former Lobos like Hunter Green and Alvin Brossard in HORSE. I could shoot equally well with my left and right hands. Opposing players were distracted by the crazy shots I came up with; my favorites were off the wall or the ceiling. One time at the Midtown Athletic Club I was playing against someone from the University of Tennessee. I sunk the ball off the air conditioner (near the roof); he looked at this old man and said, "Is this what I've got to look forward to as I get older?" I never played these young players one-on-one, as I knew that would be a disaster. I had no speed and no jumping skills. But for a time, I was on top of the world shooting a basketball.

When some of my track athletes saw me play basketball or golf they would realize I could also teach them something in track: how important practice was. I would play Horse with Curtis Beach for hours. He would die to beat me. Little known to him (until now!), I once lost on purpose just to motivate him.

Someone once said, "you can always beat better talent when better talent does not work hard." I would take Val Boyer on a golf cart and hit a ball so far she could not see it hit the ground. This so impressed her that she would run harder at track practice to show me that she could also do something impressive. Mission accomplished!

I thank Cal Guymon, Lee Hayes, and Roger Flaherty for putting up with me on the court and the green. Because of their passion for the games I became a better teacher and coach. There were many times when I would give swinging or shooting lessons to athletes to help them improve. I learned better how to coach by playing, watching, participating, and observing.

Sadly, in 2001 after a prostate cancer operation, I also came down with severe arthritis. My hands hurt so much that I had to give up both golf and baskets. My physical fitness activity has now been limited to riding a stationary bike at the gym. This has not changed my attitude, though! Do what you can do—and keep moving forward.

SANDIA HIGH SCHOOL, 1980

Lo and behold, that fall I got a call from an administrator at Sandia. Joe Williams, the girls' track coach, had just resigned. They offered the job on the spot. I knew the principal, Keith Whethersby—he taught at Valley when I was a student there in 1961. Jim Ottman was the athletic director, and I knew him from my UNM years. I had a lot of respect for Jim and Keith. I went for it!

Here I was at Sandia High School in 1980, starting over with a group of athletes I did not know. I have never been afraid of a challenge. Little did I know what a nice, and motivated, group I was about to meet. They had never had a great team and were so hungry to win I hardly had to get them to buy into hard work.

Immediately we had a good team. Shannon Ryan, just a freshman, was a former Duke City Dasher in the age-group program. Shannon could run just about any event on the track, and long jump. Ann Bernitsky, a senior, turned out to be a great 400m runner. Teddy Sue Hogsett, also a freshman, could run a fast quarter mile. Allison Clower was at first hard to win over, but once I convinced her we were going to have a good team, she applied herself and became the most team-oriented athlete I have ever coached. Within the first month I knew I had a good team and the makings of a great mile relay (4 x 4).

I loved the mile relay. It is always the last event. If you are in a close meet, you had better have a good mile relay. It has always been one of my major focuses.

Sandia High School is mostly middle class and located in the center of the city. The parents involved themselves. They were hard workers and goal-setters. From day one I knew these athletes would excel. It was also a very diverse ethnic population, with middle class white kids, African-American and Hispanic students.

Coaching and teaching is not what people think it is. Not every child comes to you highly motivated and says, "Please, or thank you." Teachers have to use every trick they know to get, and hold, the students' attention. This team did not need many tricks from me to motivate them. When they showed up at practice, they were ready to go!

People think that coaches have their best years when they win State Championships. Have you ever asked an athlete with a lot of natural talent to do something and they took the easy way out? What if the highly talented kid did not want to work, but instead just showed up for the competition? Teachers are frustrated when a gifted student under-performs; we know they can succeed with just a bit more effort. Coaches want the gifted athlete to lead just as the classroom teacher wants the gifted student to lead. The 1980 Sandia team was ready to perform.

What separates a good teacher from an average one is the ability to draw talent from an unmotivated kid. We teach students at all levels. Some athletes will achieve more through extra effort. There are athletes who show up and win only because they are blessed with extraordinary talent. Almost anyone can work with the superstar, but who can draw the best out of the less-talented kid, or turn the unmotivated, highly-talented kid into something special? There is a reason why some coaches seem to win most of the time. They develop their athletes' latent abilities. (It is true that some educators sometimes never get to work with talented individuals. They have a particularly hard job, but generally, I still think they can develop a good program. They must look for leaders and role models.)

My time spent with this Sandia team was rewarding and they were appreciative. Their parents taught them respect for their teachers and they bought into our system of hard work, dedication, and preparation. Our discipline problems were very few. Sandia would remember this season for a very long time.

Lisa Henry (formerly Lisa Chivario), a great Albuquerque Olympette Club runner, was my assistant coach. Lisa and I put together a nice training program and were developing the team to peak at the State Meet. Each week we offered the girls positive reinforcement, and each week we saw improvement. I was lucky to have Lisa on staff, as she also had a few years of head coaching experience at Cibola HS. Lisa had married Matt Henry, another track coach, was now busy raising three boys, and did not want a full-time head coaching position.

Matt and I had been good friends for a long time, as he had done his student-teaching at Whittier. Cibola's loss was our gain, as Lisa was not only a perfect role model, but she could inspire athletes. We did many workouts at Montgomery Park, Lisa and I standing at different points and encouraging the athletes to run hard. Lisa and I both liked to see athletes raise their game. Lisa also believed in the "Coach, Coach, Look at Me" model. Lisa was a motivator.

I knew right away that we had a pretty good mile relay. I did not know about our sprint relay or our field events. It was an awesome year for track and field. Highland had the great Lynne Warren, who was untouchable in the 100m, 200m, and the long jump. They had a number-one athlete, Sue Qualls, in the shot and discus, and two great short relays. Two of my former ATC athletes, Mary Lynn Griffin and Glenda Padilla, were on their team. We had Shannon Ryan, Allison Clower, and Ann Bernitsky and some athletes who were up and coming.

Most of the season was a battle between Sandia and Highland. They had more speed, and usually came in first, us just a few points behind. As we entered the State Meet, they were the favorites. We were picked for third as one of the Southern schools (Hobbs) looked good for second. We had a plan, but even the best drawn plans sometimes do not work.

Highland led in the early part of the meet as Lynne Warren won the 100m and Highland won the 400m relay. We made a comeback as Shannon Ryan won the 100m hurdles and, in a big upset, Sandia's Christie Best won the high jump.

Now, it's important to note that I had told Christie, who was ranked fifth going in, if she won the high jump, I would let her drive my convertible MGB Sports car for the weekend. Can you imagine the yell coming from the high jump area when Christie cleared 5'5" and won the event? She came ripping across the field screaming over and over, "I've got the car!" People in the stands were saying, "What? When did they stop giving medals?" I made that promise, at practice, for motivation, not thinking she would really win. Another lesson learned: don't underestimate your athletes. Christie got the keys!

After the high jump, and after Allison Clower scored points in the open 400m, suddenly we were in first place. I added up the potential points left and figured we could win this championship. Highland's head coach (Glenn Lucero) came up to me in shock and asked, "How did you get that Christie Best kid to win the high jump?" I did not want to give him any new ideas, so I coyly said, "That kid just had a good day." Glenn was also a former student-teacher at Whittier under me. We were friends, but we both wanted that title.

But something was about to happen. Lisa Henry and I loved the Sandia High Girls Track Team and wanted to share this championship with them. They were the hardest-working high school team I had ever coached, and the most respectful. It would be the first in Sandia's history. With just three events to go, we had the lead and our best two events were coming up. And as Yogi Berra used to say, "It's not over till it's over."

Shannon Ryan, our number-one athlete and a kid who was the New Mexico State Record-setter in the preliminaries of the hurdles, was about to run the 80m hurdles. In the prelims she had won this race by almost 10 meters. All eyes were glued on the starter's pistol. Shannon was in lane four, Dolores Archuleta, a former ATC girl representing Cibola, was in lane five, while Mary Lynn Griffin, (another former ATC girl) representing Highland, was in lane six. You could hear a pin drop. Everyone knew this was the key race for the State Championship. Shannon was the odds-on favorite.

As the gun went off, all eyes were on Shannon as she sprinted to the first hurdle with an early lead. She hit the hurdle and hit the ground! By the time she recovered, the hurdle field had jumped out in front of her, and there was no way for her to catch up. Dolores Archuleta had won and Mary Lynn Griffin came in second. Highland picked up five points; Sandia had none. If we won the mile relay we would finish three points behind Highland for the team championship. It was a defining moment .

Shannon was not hurt, but it was a long walk in front of those stands and back up to the press box. Again every eye was on the Sandia team, and the coaches. We told her it was okay, we were glad she was not hurt and we wanted her to run that mile relay. It is moments like these that teach you about sportsmanship and the rigors of competition. "The thrill of victory and the agony of defeat," comes to mind. We were hurting inside, but the girls still had to run.

Highland did not have to worry about the mile relay now, as they had enough points to win regardless of the outcome. Our time smashed the State Record, running a 3:57, as Shannon Ryan ran a 55.7 split for her 400m. Ann Bernitsky, Teddie Sue Hogsett, and Allison Clower were also on that relay. At no time were we in second place after the start of the race. Our "Cinderella Season" closed with a State Record, but we finished three points behind Highland for the championship. That was a hard pill to swallow! And Christy Best brought my sports car back to me on Monday with an empty tank and mud all over!

There was also the irony that the two hurdlers who scored the points that beat us were Mary Lynn Griffin and Dolores Archuleta, two ATC athletes I had taught to hurdle in a grassy park as age-groupers-using bricks and bamboo sticks.

The following year, 1981, was even stranger. The Sandia Girls were hot on the track. Each week we were setting records and preparing for State. Our number-one rival that year was the Alamogordo Tigers. And they were *good*! Early on in the season, we went to the Alamogordo Invitational with all the Southern track powers and won a very close meet. Lisa Valle ran on that Alamogordo team. She was the best distance runner in New Mexico. Marilyn Sepulveda, the track coach at Alamogordo, was a tough coach with tough teams. Whenever we ran Alamo, we knew the sparks would fly! Marilyn told me, "When we start the season, the first team we look at is Sandia, to see what you got going." It was a healthy rivalry, and one I did not take lightly.

Our principle athlete was sophomore Shannon Ryan. Allison Clower developed into one of the best sprinter quarter-milers in New Mexico. She also became a great leader in workouts and was the best team person I had coached to this point. Allison, simply, just wanted Sandia to win the state team championship. When I looked at Allison in practice, she blossomed. She led practice with her work ethic. No practice was too hard for her. As a great high school role model, she fit the job perfectly. Teamwork and team performance were important to her.

Once, in a city meet, Allison had to race the NM State Champion, Reator Golston, in a 400m on the mile relay. Allison had a slight lead when she got the stick, and, when the relay was over, she had widened it! Her time was a 56.87. If she had done this at state in the open 400m, it would have been a new State Record. We also had Debbie Kidd, Julie Nichols, Cheryl Mathis, Teddie Sue Hogesett, and Christie Best back. Lisa Longerot was one of the top throwers in the state. Our expectations were high going into the next season.

Years later, I received this letter from Allison Clower Adams:

> The impact you made on my life alone is tremendous! I went from hating track my sophomore year to loving it when you were my coach. Those two years at Sandia with you on the track and watching you teach and coach at Whittier was a life experience. I have followed your example of teaching and coaching, and my husband teaches the way you do, too. The two short seasons of track in 1980–1981 helped define my entire life. Your dedication to

the young people of Albuquerque is amazing. Your ability to get the most out of athletes, so they can achieve the most success is a wonderful gift and great talent that you have. I wish my children could have the experience of having a coach that was half as good as you. I am going to come back to Albuquerque some time in the future. I would hope to become reacquainted with you and introduce you to my family.

Proud to have been coached by Jim Ciccarello,

Allison Clower Adams

When I receive letters like this I feel that I have made an impact. My athletes are all important to me. As the years go by, I can remember each and every one of them, and as I write this story, it comes back to me as if it were yesterday. I never did marry and have my own family. (I was probably too busy to commit.) The kids I have taught and coached are my extended family.

Now, you may not believe this, but Shannon Ryan made another big mistake. It was her sophomore year, 1981. She was by far the best hurdler in the state, and also ran relays and a great open 400m. Shannon was as tough a competitor as you would ever want. Dolores Archuleta, (Cibola) was another in that category.

Toward the end of the season we had a big meet called The Albuquerque Invitational. There were about 25 teams and it was billed as a preview of the State Meet coming the next month. That year all the good teams showed, including Alamogordo. We had a very good 400m relay and Alamogordo had beaten our time in the preliminaries by about 1/100 of a second. This did not sit well with Shannon. Running last for Sandia's 400m relay, she was racing the fourth girl from Alamogordo to the finish line and in a desperate attempt to win, she became airborne. She crossed the line first, but hit the track, and broke her collar bone.

We won the race but lost the war! This meet was over for Shannon Ryan, as well as Sandia, with the rest of the season still in front of our team. She recovered in time. As I counted the days to the State Meet I knew we were running out of time.

I was in a panic. I knew we had a good team, and could win the State Championship, but we needed Shannon to lead the way. I started looking around for any sprinters that I may have missed. One of the kids suggested, "Coach, how about Melina." On the JV softball team there was a young lady named Melina Walker with a reputation for speed. I approached the softball coach, Weggy Poston, and asked if we could borrow Melina. Since softball coaches do not like to share athletes, and being in the same season, I did not have much hope. I was surprised when Coach Poston agreed to let me test her.

The following Monday we went to Montgomery Park and took a look at Melina Walker. Coach Henry and I have seen many athletes over the years and when we took our first glance at Walker, we knew that she was gifted. At 5'10", she had shoulders like a Dallas Cowboy tight end! She was a specimen of an athlete and should have been out for track many years before this. All the girls were anxious to see her run. After a warm-up, we put her beside Allison Clower, our second-fastest, to run a 100m dash, hard. This was a Monday practice and you would have thought it was the NM State Meet, the way our girls were focused.

Allison had a 12.20 100m dash. At the previous meet this had put her in the top 10 for the State Meet. Allison asked how hard I wanted her to go. I looked at her and said, "You run your very best." The gun went off, Melina took the lead, and won by almost 10 yards. Coach Henry and I were speechless. The girls were all hooting and hollering. Even Allison was happy. All Melina asked was, "Coach, was that good?" I replied, "Yes Melina, Very good." I was in shock.

We had four days to get her ready for the City Championships. That meant she had to learn how to use starting blocks, how to stay in her lane, how to listen for the starter's pistol, and most of all how to take a handoff. Melina was very smart and focused. She soaked up everything we taught her and was ready in time. She qualified in the preliminaries of the 100, coming out of the slow heat with a 12.80 time—not a *great* time, but respectable. Other coaches of course were asking who this new kid was. I replied, ".... Just someone to take Ryan's place." Meanwhile, Shannon was in the stands, watching this unfold with more than a little interest.

In the finals we won the 400m Meter Relay with the best time of the year (48.90) and Walker ran pretty well, despite a less-than-perfect handoff. As the finals of the 100m dash came up, all eyes were on Reator Golston, the number-one ranked sprinter from Manzano. Two lanes over was Melina Walker, in her first 100m finals race ever.

When the gun went off Melina Walker bolted from the blocks. It was surreal. She utterly dominated the race. She won with a time of 11.80 and set a new City Championship record. Melina Walker is the most gifted athlete I have ever had the pleasure to coach! When I'm done with this story, you will be shocked.

We had two weeks to prepare for the State Meet. We were going to try to bring Shannon back to run on a relay. She had her arm in a sling and the hurdles were out, but after seeing Melina compete, Shannon wanted to be part of the big show. At practice we now had time to try Melina in other events. We soon found out that she was blessed with fast twitch fibers and power in her whole body. (She once picked me up in a bear hug and carried me the full length of the football field. I was truly humbled at that moment, as I had never seen that kind of "girl power." How many girls do you know that can pick up a grown man and carry him for 100 yards?) We tried her in other events and found that she could throw the shot put 35 feet and the discus over 100' on her first day. This was with no technique—just sheer strength. She could also long jump over 17' quite easily. This was her senior year, and we had only two weeks. Could we make something great happen?

The day before District, the girls JV softball team were in the championships. Our agreement with Coach Poston was that she would finish the JV season. We were just happy to have her run, so that was not an issue. We felt that at this point, even with Shannon out of the hurdles, we now had a chance at that elusive state title. Melina would fill in the extra points.

The night before the meet, I got word Melina had been hurt sliding into second base, and was out for the season. It was almost as devastating as the year before, when Shannon had hit the hurdles. It turned out Melina pulled her quad muscle and could hardly walk. The next day we got our trainer to treat and help her to get some motion back in that thigh. We still held hope that we could get her ready to help at the State Meet—the District Meet was completely out, but maybe we could salvage something for State.

We kept trying and never gave up. The State Meet was held in Hobbs, NM. It turned out to be our best ever; the times and performances of the boys and girls were outstanding. On the girls' side, Hobbs, Alamogordo, Manzano, and Sandia were hooked up in a fantastic meet. The team from Alamogordo, under Marilynn Sepulveda's direction, was outstanding. Alamo had the great Lisa Valle, who would win two gold medals herself in the distance events. Hobbs had some of the fastest girls I had ever seen. We had Shannon and Melina taped up and tried to pick our spots. It was a rain-delayed finals—lighting filled the air and sparked the track. At first it did not look like this State Meet would finish, but eventually it cleared.

We had both Shannon and Melina on relays as it would be too hard for them to compete while injured in the individual events. All of our relays finished high and we scored well. But there were State Records being set in many events. In the 800m relay we ran a 1:42.20, taking third. Any other year that would have been a new State Record for our team. In the mile relay we ran a 3:56.89 and scored in second place, Hobbs taking the State Record. Both races were close but we were on the wrong side of the photo at the finish. All the other points were spread out and we finished third at the meet behind Hobbs and Alamogordo. We had our best team ever at Sandia in 1981, but because of two freak injuries, we could not finish and show everyone what we had.

In 1982, we came back with a great team again. We graduated some good athletes, but still had Shannon. We won all our meets going into state.

We didn't have the dominating team we'd had in the past, but we had points in many different events. As the meet went on, all we had to do was win the Medley Relay and the title was ours. Back then, the sprint Medley Relay makeup was 100m-100m-200m-400m. Ryan, a great quarter-miler, was running the last leg. We had our best team lined up. If we won the Medley Relay, we would win State!

When Shannon, who was running last, received the baton, we were in first, with a huge lead. As she ran the first curve of the 400, I noticed she did not have the baton in her hand correctly. Her hand was on the top of the baton which meant she was in danger of dropping it. I was sitting on the East side of the track and she was about to run right by me. Shannon tried to correct her baton position and hit the bottom of the baton on her uplifting thigh while running. To this day, I remember that stick flying over my head into the stands two rows behind me. I could barely turn my head as I heard the clang of the metal rolling under the bleachers. When I later looked up, Shannon was in shock and could hardly talk. Our hope for a team championship was rolling down the bleachers with that baton. Shannon Ryan was always a team player and wanted the team title for her teammates, but fate kept denying her one final step.

In 1983, we had our last chance with Ryan at the lead. In an early season meet, she developed knee problems and could hardly finish the season. Lisa Longerot had become a State Champion in the shot and discus, but it was not enough. Our team took third and the elusive Blue Trophy was awarded elsewhere again.

Those four years at Sandia produced some of my best teams ever. The kids always responded to coaching and demonstrated good values. We gave them our time, and they responded with effort. They were good athletes and students, and true community role models, volunteering at the neighborhood elementary schools.

Richard Romero had been the principal the previous two years and he was completely supportive. He was one of the most upbeat administrators I have ever met. I had first met Richard when I was a first year teacher at Riverview. Between Richard and Jim Ottman (the athletic director), I felt like I had the best administrative support in my high school coaching to that point. The parents were great, too. We had the most respected track program in the state. The only thing we did not have was that blue trophy!

Even in a rebuilding year, in 1984 we took fourth at state. The athletes had a great attitude and worked hard. Lisa Longerot continued to dominate the shot put and the discus.

WHITTIER-HIGHLAND HIGH SCHOOL, 1985

I had so many good athletes and students at Whittier who went on to Wilson Middle School and Highland High School it was hard for me to keep track of them. Education was still evolving and the Southeast Heights was in flux. Boundary lines changed and kids started to move into different districts.

Those who lived in the Whittier district now transferred to Bandelier. Even those who lived right across the street from Whittier now went somewhere else. It was crazy, but it was clockwork: the local news kept publishing tests scores and parents would move their kids to the higher-performing schools. I would be teaching on the playground and watch a student directly across from our school get in his mom's car and drive several miles away. Some of these students would have been good role models, the kind of academic leaders we needed at Whittier.

While Dr. Nell New was still our principal, I saw TV cameras in front of our school, presenting test scores to the public. Sure, our scores were lower than those in the Northeast Heights, but this was a slap in the face to all the good teachers and students who worked and studied here. We had great students at Whittier with good test results being compared to a higher-achieving school. If the media said we were a "bad school," we became one. As each achiever left, we lost another shot at respectable scores.

The kids in my PE classes still had fun and responded. Students don't understand test scores. All kids love to be recognized. They will try harder for you when you look at them. They do not realize they are being compared to kids on the other side of town or in another state. Teachers told them to try their hardest on the test as it reflected on Whittier. That was unreasonable pressure, and the emphasis on scores detracts from student progress. Students are taught to the test, and not encouraged to develop their individual creativity. There is simply not enough time to do both.

Many of our kids came to school at Whittier with a different home environment than other kids. Parents may not have read to them or perhaps there were no reading materials. Maybe the TV was their babysitter. Diet plays a big role, too, and they may not have had enough nourishment before and after school.

In the late '80s these changes were happening at Whittier as they were happening all over the country. My friends in Connecticut, Florida, and California were telling me the same thing: classroom discipline was breaking down. Corporal punishment was being replaced with gentler, friendlier, positive reinforcement.

Done right, this works wonders! Remember this though: if you have even one discipline problem in your class, learning is disrupted for the entire class. Imagine a classroom where a teacher is dealing with *five or six* problem children. This is what we were now seeing. What happened in the classroom was also taking place on the field. As kids started to come to the public schools with lack of self-discipline, teachers had to reimagine how to control them.

I particularly noticed parents enrolling kids in private and parochial schools. These schools did not have to answer to the same guidelines as the public schools because they did not receive federal money, which was tied to test performance. Additionally, private schools could deny entrance to children who did not meet their standards. In APS we cannot reject any kid with a behavior problem, leaving us to try to change his attitude. We work with any child, regardless of past behavior or test scores. More parents are choosing the school their children attend. Public schools are expected to achieve despite the growing adverse conditions. This is how standards disparity is fostered. Eventually all the good students only want to go to certain schools, which become *elitist schools*.

One child's behavior problem interrupts another child's schoolwork, which develops behavior problems for the second child. Whittier was a prime example of this pattern, but it was happening across APS. Educators in every part of the system were dealing with this.

In my classes we were spared academic test scores. Our kids were asked to work to the NM state standards, that are aligned with national standards: fitness and motor skills that all PE students were being asked to improve.

I had always designed my program for fitness activities that developed the following areas: endurance, power, speed, motor skills, spatial awareness, large muscle movement and fine motor movement, all of which are included in the state standards. Most importantly, *we tied this all to having daily fun*. Children carry fun associations into adulthood. Daily exercise and fitness are lifetime commitments and all students must appreciate them, staring at an early age. At Whittier we start the students in fitness activities in kindergarten.

I had kids playing Blast Ball, T-Ball, basketball, soccer, and running track and field. Blast Ball consisted of blasting volleyball with a baseball bat! Kids never forgot that one. Imagine if you will, the sound of a volleyball filled over capacity, (one of my tricks) and hitting the over inflated ball with a medal bat. It not only blasted off, it sounded like a rocket! I always organized that game with the fifth-graders against the staff. The game was not over until a teacher hit the ball on top of the roof. Over the years I always knew which teachers could do that and I counseled them to wait a while before hitting the big Blast Ball on the roof. That meant the game was over and the students had to return to class. If you hit the volley ball on the roof even once, you were a legend! Jim Rayborn, a special education teacher, became a big-timer for that reason. Kids like Jim Roach came to me years later and said, "Coach, that Blast Ball game with the teachers was so much fun."

In the early '80s Karen Ogas and Kelly Taylor were two of my top PE students. They were on my gymnastic teams and ran track. Later on they would run for me at Highland. Kelly O'Brien was one of my top gymnasts and remembers PE as if it were yesterday. My nickname for her was "KOB FM," a local radio station I listened to on the drive to work in the morning. She saw me at Smith's grocery store 30 years later and said, "Coach Ciccarello thanks for telling us kids we could do anything we imagined we wanted to." I did believe that and tried to pass it on to the Whittier students. Later, during my career at La Cueva, someone designed a T-shirt for our track team that said, "If you can dream it you can do it." Considering our history at Whittier, I found that to be very appropriate.

I had twins, Cordy and Claudia Gonzales, who were friends of Kelly's. Both of these sisters had great attitudes. They also loved PE and gymnastics. Claudia had a rare form of cancer. I always included them in our activities and asked the other kids to respect them. One day when, due to chemo, she had to wear a wig, we were doing forward rolls in a PE gymnastic class, and her wig fell off. An unusual silence pierced this fourth grade class.

Elementary kids can be cruel, but not this time. I immediately sat the class down and talked about cancer and the things that can happen to children, like losing your hair, and the kids were good after that. Claudia still remembers that moment to this day. It helped her to get through some hard times. At the time I was just trying to soften a hard blow; I now realize it was the right thing to do at a critical moment in a child's life.

Teachers on a daily basis are dealing with special moments like these. Rest assured, all teachers are in this business to help, and while we may not get an immediate response, many years later they often realize the difference someone made in their lives. As you read this, think back in your own past—who was that teacher you always wanted to contact or share a story with, to thank, or just visit? Call or email that teacher and let them know! I myself have done this many times!

In 1984 an opening for a head girls' track coach appeared in APS's newsletter. Whittier is five blocks from Highland and is their number-one feeder school. Even though I loved Sandia, I was ready to try a new beginning with some of my old Whittier kids, now at Highland. I agonized.

The school bells at Whittier had changed and I now finished my last class at Whittier an hour later, leaving me less travel-time to get to the high school. Highland's closeness made it appealing. Though I was not on Highland staff, I was close, and knew most of the kids from their Whittier days. Keith Whethersby was the new principal at Highland, coming from Sandia.

I asked for a PE job at Sandia, but they gave all the PE jobs only to football and basketball coaches. I had never held a PE position at the high school where I coached; having one would give me a recruiting advantage, as I knew the kids and figured I could get a larger turnout. All in all, it sounded like a better position, and I went for it. I was interviewed and hired, and started all over again.

Henry Sanchez was the head boys' coach, and his son Gary was his assistant. I really liked Henry, and had always respected his coaching. The boys' program at Highland was maybe the top in the state, and I knew I'd have to work hard just to keep up with them. But I went in with a productive attitude.

That first year I was reunited with some of my former students. Karen Ogas and Kelly Taylor were the first to sign up. Susan Kreis was new to me, but she turned out to be a great hurdler. Shanta Mcgloclin was a sprinter and a high jumper. Tammy Meade was a former elementary student of mine who had turned into one of the best sprinters in town. Many years later her son and daughter also went to Whittier. Sonya Esaw turned out to be the best freshman sprinter in Albuquerque. Susan Kreis finished third at state in the 100m and 300m hurdles. Our team won district and placed third at state. This was a very exciting and successful year for the Highland Girls Track Team. We had a very competitive team and won most of our meets.

The following year we received a couple of new athletes. Jessica Sanchez and Kelly Delaway were solid runners and great team members. Jessica became an assistant coach at La Cueva many years later. Heather Case was a distance runner who improved each week. Many years later I developed a good relationship with her parents, as we ate at the same Italian restaurant. Ed and Shirley Case always knew where the best pizza places were. On Wednesdays I would eat at Giovanni's, and the Cases were always there and sharing stories about Heather. After she graduated, I always knew where she was and what she was doing. Heather was extremely bright and eventually went to West Point, becoming a great role model for all young female students.

Natanya Jones was a freshman talent with great speed. Susan Kreis was our determined free spirit. It was said of Susan that she was a throwback to the "hippy years." I think this was because of her adornments and earrings. She at one time had seven earrings and was quite the attraction at the State Meet. She won the City and District Meets in both hurdle events and finished third at state, behind Sandra Crowe from Alamogordo and Anne Frost from Farmington. With Susan Kreis, Karen Ogas, Natanya Jones, and Tammy Meade running the relays, we took second at state. Our biggest win that year was in the upset of Eldorado High School in the City Meet coached by Jimmy Knop, a friend. In some ways the City Meet is bigger than the State Meet; to take it, you had to show some depth, placing in many different events.

The next two years we had one of the top four teams in New Mexico. Our biggest accomplishment on the track was turned in by Natanya Jones. She became a New Mexico State Champion and State Record-holder in the 300m hurdles. She followed her high school track career with a four-year scholarship to UNM.

Natanya was another quiet athlete who proved herself on the track. It was a pleasure to watch her receive her gold medal in the 300m hurdles. It takes courage to clear the hurdles at a top speed, and some seem to accomplish this better than others. Natanya Jones mastered it. She would work hard and compete harder. It was as pleasure to come to practice and spend time with her. Natanya was another athlete I kept in contact with over the years. She got a job with Nike and moved to New York. When Val Boyer was inducted into the Albuquerque Sports Hall of Fame, Natanya attended the ceremony. My athletes still make me proud.

Eldorado and Clovis won a couple of state titles in the late 1980s. Both of those schools had quality athletes and had established the standard in New Mexico. Highland also won a couple of district titles and finished in the top four at state several times.

In New Mexico, you have a one year contract *only*. Highland received a new principal in 1990. The new administrator hired a former friend to take over, and despite my program having made big strides and remaining very competitive, I was relieved of my duties. I felt that I worked harder than any track coach in APS at the time. Politics in education and cronyism did not sit well with me. I took a break from coaching until the new decade.

While I left coaching I kept right on teaching elementary physical education. In 1990 I had been teaching and coaching over 21 years. Who would have guessed I had not yet reached my half-way point?

NEW GYM AND JUMP-ROPE

In some ways the 1990s were the biggest change of all. First, Whittier built us a gymnasium. Across APS gyms began to appear next to playgrounds. We were not the first school to get one, but with it our program took a giant step forward. The politicians decided that, if you had a better PE program, you might have healthier kids, which would find its way to academics. Finally!

One of my friends, John Gonzales, from Arroyo del Olso Elementary, spearheaded this project. He had one of the first gyms built at his school.

An indoor facility is a must for a good PE program. In 1948, PS Number 35 in Jersey City had an indoor gym, which made good sense, because New Jersey is cold in the winter. A cold, damp wind outside will make you miserable and tired. I was lucky as a young student to have a warm building for PE classes.

For almost 25 years in Albuquerque, I was teaching PE outside, year-round, whatever the weather. This may not have been coastal New Jersey, but at nearly a mile high, the cold catches up with you. Sure, there's lots of sun, but the wind makes a huge difference. In the early fall and late spring it is often so hot on the playground teachers would carry umbrellas. All this time my elementary students and I would carry on PE classes outside. We looked for shelter in the form of trees or a roof overhang for protection. All high schools and middle schools had an indoor gym, but most elementary schools did not. We had occasional use of the cafeteria or a portable building.

I planned my activities around the weather. On those days the wind blew at 30+ MPH, there were no gymnastics, not much individual motor skill development, no balance activities, and not much partnered cooperation games. We could not even play T-ball, as the wind always blew the ball off the T. If we were doing high jump in track and field, the wind would blow the bar into the street. Kids were always distracted by the wind. They would face the opposite way and huddle up while I talked. On those days we got in plenty of pure running and soccer.

A fellow PE teacher and friend, Stan Chavez, from Osuna Elementary, received one of the new gyms and said, "Jim, your professional life will change the day you get a gym over at Whittier." At the time I was thinking about early retirement—the weather was making an old man of me. I earned my money in those days.

That kind of weather makes skin crack, hair thin, joints hurt, feet swell, eyes hurt, and legs cramp! Many PE teachers look for early retirement, and have to guard against skin cancer. Ask Mike Sheridan (Pajarito Elementary) and Ken Medley (Cibola/Albuquerque High) about the skin problems they encountered over the years being outside working with students. Twenty five years in the elements is a long time to go for a retirement benefit if you are all beat up by the time you receive it. If classroom teachers were on the playground for 15 minutes of recess duty on a cold windy day, they would show up late and leave early. Administrators sent an educational aide to the playground. That was just the way it was.

So the Whittier gym was a godsend. I wanted to recharge and start something new. I knew that the Whittier kids needed some kind of activity to get excited about. Coach Stan Chavez told me, "Why don't you start teaching individual jump-rope skills?" I had always taught long rope chants in rope-jumping. Games with chants like "Cinderella Dressed in Yeller" or "School, School I like School," were always the order of the day. They were fun but they were not that athletic, and they came with a long line of kids standing around. I have always believed in participation by all; kids need to move and become physically involved to use their stores of energy. Coach Chavez invited me to come to Osuna and bring some kids to observe. He had already had his gym for 10 years, so I was eager to see how he used it.

The Osuna kids were in an upscale neighborhood. I set a date, and I asked some of my most athletic Whittier kids to get ready for a "road trip." Bridget Ruiz, Shelly McNeil, Devon Marquez, Cerone, and a couple of others were invited and I told each to learn five new tricks to bring back to Whittier. Needless to say, it was a complete success. They were excellent rope-skippers and put on quite the show. That day sparked a new era at Whittier. Who would have thought that we would become the premier jump-rope school in New Mexico, just because of that trip up the road?

What I liked right away about rope-skipping was that it was an individual event, and cheap. Without much space or equipment, it provided fun, and maximum cardio. For a school like Whittier, which now had primarily disadvantaged kids without home athletic equipment, this was a great chance to get involved in something big with little investment. Thank you, Stan, for the idea.

Years later we returned to Osuna and put on a jump-rope show. The kids were impressed! The Whittier Jump-Rope Team had begun.

Whittier needed a low-cost after-school and down-time activity. This was especially true for recess. I always remember the kids from Harlem, NYC jumping Double Dutch on television. Those kids were ahead of their time! They looked very athletic and were having fun. Why not the kids at Whittier? I just wanted to stress individual skills.

A friend of mine, Jeff Turcotte, who coaches track and field at St. Pius High School, told me, "If you raise the bar, they will excel! But if you lower it, they will do the limbo." What a profound statement that was! When I am at jump-rope practice, my eyes are on everyone and I point at them as they jump. This is a visual improvement signal. When I compliment them they beam, and try harder.

We had a young jump-rope kid named Shelly McNeil who invented tricks I had never seen before. I often made an example of her, and the kids looked to her for leadership. One day she moved the rope behind her back and over her head, then back to a basic jump. We named that trick the "Shelly," and her parents were very proud. Twenty years later we still call it the "Shelly," and kids always ask me about who Shelly was. When the family moved to Connecticut, I went back to visit on a Thanksgiving vacation. They welcomed me like a king. One day, years later, Shelly came to visit and she mesmerized the young kids. They had not even been born when Shelly attended Whittier. She had become a legend. Her legacy as a great jump-rope athlete lives on. And she could still do the "Shelly."

I have seen teachers and coaches who socialize instead of acknowledging the athletes working in front of them. When approval comes from their mom or dad, it is very special, but not all children are nurtured equally. Some grow up without much attention. Today, TV has become the babysitter and substitute caregiver. When kids are in another room on a PlayStation, or Wii, or X-Box, un-monitored and without validation, who is nurturing them?

How can our kids have great futures if we adults do not foster it with our guidance and presence? A very good friend of mine, Spencer Sielschott, who teaches math at Sandia, is a longtime track and field coach. He wrote a poem that addresses this very issue. Spencer and his wife Sandy have raised several kids and now have many grandchildren. They have flourished, as they have always been there to support their own children. Spencer does the same for his students at Sandia. He supports other people's kids. His words are profound.

Knowing I was working on a book called *Coach, Coach, Look at Me*, Spencer played with my theme. While we agree that the parent should be the main caregiver and nurturing force in a child's life, a teacher, coach, or another educator must step in to fill the void. This poem represents the importance of a parent's/coach's impact on a child's life.

COACH, COACH! LOOK AT ME!

An open verse to acknowledge…

A show to excite more as confidence builds mastery.

Plant a seed, nurture it… it grows;

Recognize a child's zeal… respond with eyes of a smile… it grows

This cycle takes on a life of its own.

Daddy, Daddy, look at me;

This sensational experience compels one to notice a willingness to please.

The eyes tell the soul to sustain giving more than to receive.

What grows from this Opens the Future

To enhance

Coach, Coach, look at me!

Who What spurs action of excitement?

A child's determination to give;

'I want you to see me do what you want me to do.'

'I want to show you I can do what you want.'

Can it transfer the future and complete life's circle to: Look, Look at me?

Your eyes will tell.

Spencer Sielschott
Sandia High School math teacher, girls' track and field coach

Though Spencer came to Sandia High School 20 years after I left, he shares my philosophy. In my career I have met many unsung heroes, visionary educators and coaches who do the job correctly and with passion for students. They are the quiet ones. Spencer, in some respects, is a quiet coach. He is very effective and he helps all students as if they were part of his family.

Jeana Beach, mother of Curtis Beach, sent me a John Wooden quote: "You have not lived a perfect day unless you have done something for someone that they cannot ever repay you." She then added, "You, Coach Ciccarello, you have lived many perfect days." This was a very special moment for me, as Jeana has always been one of those nurturing moms!

Having a gym meant I could get double the work from these students. I played music with a fast beat and discovered you need a minimum of 120 beats per minute (BPM) to improve a cardio workout. (180 BPM, with an average of three jumps per second, was my target). I also believed that if you played catchy tunes from the radio, you could put on a better show; athletes perform better with an audience that knows the tunes. We always updated our music.

I like all music, but soon realized we needed something faster. I grew up in the 1950s, and Rock 'n' Roll was fast and fun. I started playing "Johnny Be Good" (Chuck Berry) and "At the Hop" (Danny and the Juniors), knowing I was onto something. If you never said a word, but just played music, kids will jump to the beat. All I had to do was choreograph the routine. I have a little Hollywood in me, and I passed this attitude on to the kids. We had this dance tune from the 1940s, "In the Mood" (Glenn Miller). I would have the kids shake their hair to it and smile widely. It was kid-tested, audience-approved!

The kids practiced their routines at recess. When we got proficient, we would invite the kindergarten classes to watch us perform. Gradually, we expanded, and all grade levels loved it. I went to the principal and asked for a school-wide assembly. We were a hit. I then asked the PTA for a night-time show. I bought T-shirts for the kids with a nice logo. When I passed them out, you would have thought they were already in Hollywood! They wore their shirts on the playground, and soon other kids wanted one; even some of the teachers wanted one! This was an *event* at Whittier. I started planning how to make it even better.

In the past I had taken my gymnastics teams to the UNM Pit to perform at Lobo games. This was always huge and we received such a great welcome from the crowd. I was wondering if we were good enough to do a halftime show in jump-rope; it would be humiliating to have kids make mistakes in front of 17,000 people. We scheduled the UNM show and started a string of small performances at other schools to prepare. I had Bridget Ruiz, Devon Marquez, Cassie Wilson, Amanda Staeline, Dominique Hagins, and several others ready.

The big night arrived. As we came down the ramp and looked up at the crowd, it was scary. We all pumped the same adrenaline. Athletes and coaches alike stood on the ramp watching the seconds tick toward halftime. People were yelling, "What've you got now—who're those kids?"

We had exactly six minutes to perform. As the Lobos left the court, my kids were giving them high-fives, and all I could think was, "Don't trip them or we'll never get invited back."

I had already given them a CD with our music to play. The first song was "Who Let the Dogs Out" (Baha Men). When we went out there, the student body went nuts, even barking. I guess I picked the right song! Our kids heard that yell and performed better than I could have imagined. When we got to "At the Hop," where our kids jumped on their bottoms, we had the crowd in our hands. They loved the old-time music and the little kids. We left the floor to a standing ovation! I knew that not only was the coach looking at them—but 17,000 others! It was a jump-rope love-fest. Again, I set about thinking how to make it better.

The next day the school was getting calls. Parents, teachers and administrators would start supporting our team. More kids started showing up to practice in the gym and I had to reorganize my time. Remember, this was not an after-school program; kids learned all their jumping skills in PE class and recess.

After 25 years, I had reinvented my approach and recharged my batteries. I still acted from my belief that physical fitness is for everyone, not just the gifted. The whole school was jumping and getting healthy. Kids with marginal natural talent could still could jump-rope and feel good about themselves.

I now had an indoor facility and was motivated to reach more kids and try new activities. My basketball program improved; gymnastics, though fading, was still in the program. Jump-rope was now the number-one activity choice, and I had the beginnings of an aerobics team. Agnes Redmond, our new principal, supported us immensely. We had a night when our team dressed up like *Men in Black* with sunglasses, dark suits, and the parents in the audience went bonkers. We were a hit once again.

Meanwhile, as I was not coaching after school anymore, I looked for something to keep myself busy. A couple of years earlier, I had helped Lee Hays run a movie theater in Rio Rancho. One day I read the Lobo Theater was going out of business.

I made a phone call and learned with an investment of about $35,000 I could keep it going. Somehow I came up with the money and I enlisted my brother Richard to run it with me. We remodeled, cleaned the lobby up and put nice Hollywood pictures on the wall. Old-time movie stars were out choice, which appealed to our audience's nostalgia.

We offered an unbelievable deal: a movie, soda, and popcorn for $3. We called that the "Lone Lobo." For $6 you got two tickets, two sodas, and super-large popcorn: the "Budget Buddy Special." It was the cheapest date in town! We started to get crowds of 500–600. We showed art films, independent film, foreign films, and midnight movies such as *The Rocky Horror Picture Show* and all the Quentin Tarantino noir; *Reservoir Dogs* was always a big hit. The new Lobo Theater made quite an impact on Nob Hill.

We also became involved with the local schools. We would have special Saturday cartoons for the elementary schools and donate the drinks and popcorn. Whittier, Bandelier, and Monte Vista received most of it.

The Oscars were a big night on TV. We thought, why not hold a giant fundraiser and show the Academy Awards on the big screen? We would do it up right! We would have dinner, tuxedos, drinks, an MC, door prizes, and of course, a good time. Profits would go to schools. This turned out to be the most successful event of all time at the Lobo. We sold out every year and received generous local media coverage. We were able to donate over $3,000 to each participating school. We helped fund the PTAs and had a blast.

At Whittier we always had a talent show for the parents. We would go into the cafeteria or gym and have the kids, dance, sing, or play act. It was always a big event. Now that I had the Lobo Theater, I thought why not take it to another level. I went to Agnes Redmond and asked if we could host the talent show there. Agnes, always an inspired and supportive leader, thought it was a great idea. So we had the Whittier kids perform for their parents on the big stage, with balcony spotlights (manned by Freddie, our custodian) and "Hollywood Curtains." Jennifer Carter, Becky Peters and Nancy Huerta helped organize the student body. It was a packed house. You would have thought the kids were in LA; Whittier pride was everywhere. It was a night of, "Mom, Dad, Look at Me." Ladies and gentle-man, just look at your own children!

While the Lobo Theater became a community resource, we were still putting on jump-rope shows. We even hosted a couple of shows at the Lobo. As we developed as a performing arts jump-rope team, we started to travel, teach workshops, and establish a reputation for passing on the "love of jumping." The beauty of jump-rope is its low cost and space needs, and ease of learning. We improved and increased our skills, which gave the kids greatly increased self-confidence.

Self-confidence is as important in the development of an individual as are reading and writing skills. You must be able to express yourself, relate to others, and take charge when necessary. I have seen firsthand students who excel in athletics become role models in the classroom, and I have seen kids fall between the cracks, because they were denied opportunity or recognition. Role models are critical to an infrastructure of support and growth.

KIVA: THE "EVERYTHING GIRL"

In the early '90s I was teaching on the Whittier playground when we still had a lot of dirt and a 3' perimeter wall. One of my former parents had her baby girl in a carriage, wheeling her around the block. I asked who she had there. "Coach," Misty said, "this is Kiva, Kyle's little sister." I looked in the carriage and saw the *cutest* little girl, about a year old. As she looked up at me I told her, "Someday I am going to teach you PE and put you on my gymnastics team." Misty said, "Coach, are you still going to be here?" "For that little kid, I will stay here forever." Who could have known how true that statement was?

Not only did Kiva grow up and attend Whittier, she became our top PE student of all time. Kiva could do any physical activity she wanted. Her favorite at first was gymnastics; later it became soccer. As a first-grader Kiva was always doing handstands and cartwheels across the playground. The little kids would follow her everywhere. Her great attitude was infectious.

Lloyd McPeters, the Hall of Fame all-state quarterback for Highland, who also spent 20 years refereeing in the NFL, told me, "Ciccarello, always remember there are two kinds of role models: positive and negative. At some point individuals come to a fork in the road. If you have a great role model, your chance for success is multiplied. If no role model is present, you are leaving it all to chance!"

Sometimes our superstars in athletics and the entertainment industry say, "I'm not a role model." They are wrong! It does matter if you are a super star in the NFL or jump-rope leader in an elementary PE class, those kids behind you look to you for guidance. Kiva was that kind of person who then, and now as a college graduate, still returns to Whittier and models for our kids. At no time did Kiva ever deny her responsibilities. After Kiva would jump, so many kids started to rope-skip in the gym you could hardly see for the dust in the air. She would get a soccer game going with 50+ kids. How are you going to tell the kids that there are only 11 players on the field at a time? They all wanted to match skills against Kiva. A perfect day in PE involves warm weather, motivated kids, and teamwork. Having a Kiva Gresham on-hand makes a great ace in the hole!

When Kiva graduated from Louisiana Tech University and was working with children in the country of Trinidad &Tobago, she sent me the following letter:

> My first memory of Coach Ciccarello is from when I was six years old, and he took me to my very first jump rope show at Highland High School. I remember climbing up on that big stage in my light blue jump rope shirt, my long blond ponytail bouncing up and down behind me. I felt so special not only because I got to perform in my first show, but also because I finally got the chance to "jump with the big girls," who I idolized. Back then I wanted to be just like Bridgette Ruiz. I would watch her and try to copy the tricks that she had mastered. Tripping over the rope, I would keep Coach's words of wisdom, "Practice makes perfect," in my mind until I got it just right. Pretty soon Bridgette was gone, all her moves were mastered, and we had to start making up our own.

> Traci Book and I would practice every day before the bell rang for school, at recess, and after school until the streetlights came on and I had to be back

home for curfew. Then I would stand in front of the TV and make my parents count how many "Shelleys" I could do without stepping on the rope. Jumping rope was a part of everyday life back then. I would jump to be with my friends, perfect my tricks to show Coach, so that hopefully I could do them at our next show, so that I could win either the Double Under or Shelley contests. Whether it was to build friendships, to get a high five from Coach for showcasing our moves, or for competition, Coach always gave us motivation to practice and improve our skills. Coach did not just get your feet and heart moving, but he got your mind moving as well. If you made up a trick, Coach would name it for you. Coach's motivational techniques taught us that in order to master a skill and be rewarded, you have to practice, practice, practice, and any successes in life come from learning this at such a young age.

Pretty soon Traci Book, Aly Hill, Lillian Cutter, and I were the new Bridgettes, and the first-graders were copying all of our moves. When we learned new tricks, we would teach the younger kids how to master the new tricks. This is one of my first memories of reaching out to children. Since then, I have always had a passion for "reaching back and working for the ones behind me." I continued to help the jump-rope team through middle school and would visit the Whittier gym while I attended high school to teach a new generation of jumpers. It just didn't stop with jump-rope though; I began teaching soccer to children about six years ago, and spent many evenings in college passing the love of the game onto the kids of the Ruston Soccer Club, with the help of my teammates. Currently, I am in Trinidad & Tobago coaching soccer for underprivileged children. Looking back, I now realize that Coach Ciccarello does not just have the gift of giving back to children, but he also has the gift of teaching children how to give back to other children. Once you experience the joys of helping a child, you never want to stop.

I consider Kiva the ultimate PE student and athlete. She became one of the greatest female soccer players in Albuquerque, playing for Highland High. She was a team-player and respectful of everyone. Included in her love for all skills were soccer, gymnastics, jump rope, dance, fitness, basketball, movement activities, and all games that involved a competitive challenge; it's why I named her "the everything girl." Eventually she played soccer for Louisiana Tech University. She is also a superior student. What separates Kiva from others is her commitment to giving back, wherever she is. Kiva Gresham is just starting out as an adult. Our world will be better because of her.

Lloyd McPeters said, "The perfect role model, of course, is the parent, but as we know in today's society, that does not always happen. So the parent's position is often filled by others who have an influence on our children, such as teachers, coaches, and other students or athletes." In his own family Lloyd says he is always talking to his children, even when it appears they are not listening—they are—and their age does not matter. His kids are in their 30s now, and it is an ongoing process for him. He knows they are watching. I personally return to my elementary and high school and think about how student role models like Kiva contribute to both our program and individuals' lives.

Hannah and Ari Macpherson were two sisters who attended Whittier in the late-'80s/early-'90s. They were perfect academic students and very good athletes. Ari was particularly adept in track and soccer. She ran on our little Whittier track team and we took her to UNM several times for meets. Their parents supported their interest in both athletics and in the arts. Hannah went on to become a film director and has received many awards; Ari turned into an outstanding high school soccer player at Highland. Angus and Melissa, their parents, became involved and served on the Whittier PTA. The entire family served as fine community role models . We were blessed to have the Macphersons on-hand.

Gymnastics continued. Kiva hooked up with Traci Brook to lead our team into several outstanding performances. I should point out that we were only a performing arts team: we went to the Pit, did gymnastic shows and jumped rope at halftime, but never competed. One year Kiva could not make the Pit show and Traci took leadership, wowing the audience in an all-jump-rope show. Traci ran to the middle of the floor and did a forward summersault flip with her jump-rope—the crowd went wild. She finished it off with a combination gymnastics-jump-rope routine. The Whittier students had an outstanding reputation and a far reach in APS because of these halftime shows. We were not only role models for our own community, but we touched all elementary students in the city. The day after a halftime show, I would field numerous phone calls from other PE teachers and students.

Jump-rope at Whittier was getting bigger and bigger! I received a phone call from the American Heart Association asking if we would like to be the official New Mexico Demonstration Team. Patty Ross in charge of this region, and immediately scheduled shows all across the state. We traveled to a school, demonstrated our skills and talked about the value of fitness, endurance, and developing a healthy heart by jumping rope. The school would then host a fundraiser for the American Heart Association.

We were provided brand-new T-shirts and black shorts, and transportation. All this for a low-income school on the southeast side of Albuquerque. We were very proud of this team and the students involved. And as they performed on the court, they were performing in the classroom.

In 1998 we were asked to perform in Clovis, NM. It would be a road trip with a six-show format. We would be staying in a hotel and would have two vans provided. Barbara Murchinson, a teaching aide, went along to help supervise. Can you imagine the group's excitement? Some of these kids had never been more than 30 miles outside of Albuquerque, and here we were with our new spiffy T-shirts, representing the American Heart Association.

We did multiple shows in Clovis, each about two hours, including set up and travel. You would have thought we were a rock band. Audiences greeted us with hoots and hollers! Our kids were full of self-worth as they passed on the love of jump-rope.

We had great Rock 'n' Roll music, skipping and jumping to tunes they knew and loved. The Clovis kids had never seen a show like this. We were jumping on our rear ends to "At the Hop." The theme from *Rocky* was our lead-in and we came charging on to the stage like heavy-weight boxers ready for a big fight! In two days we did six shows at the elementary, middle and high schools. Each was a blast, and our kids were very well-behaved.

At each show Patty Ross spoke about fitness and how jump-rope helped the heart and contributed to overall health. We held a Q&A at the end: *How old are you? How did you learn those tricks? When do you practice? How much do the ropes cost?*

What grade is that little kid in [a first-grader]? Where is your school in Albuquerque? Can you come back? This trip was an experience that the Whittier kids would never forget. Clovis looked right at us and saw success.

We continued to do shows at elementary schools and special community organizations in our area. We were invited to perform for a big nursing convention at the Albuquerque Convention Center. A few years later, we went to six different Pueblos. This was very important, as there are serious obesity and diabetes problems on the reservations. We did our part by demonstrating a jump-rope exercise in daily life. The tribal leaders always welcomed us with open arms and treated us with much respect, feeding us and giving us treats. Some of our students were Native Americans themselves, and the audience could relate more easily to them. They were perfect role models to show other communities the value of being fit.

When we do a show or clinic, I encourage both kids and older folk to become involved. We have done clinics where elders jump right along with the children. This can be a family exercise and a health benefit to all. Some of the skills are very easy to learn; a simple hand swing of the rope from side to side to a rhythm is a lot of fun. We even have kids in wheelchairs that just swing the rope with their arms; even they get some valuable exercise while having fun.

Kiva Gresham could amaze with the rope. I think she was blessed with an understanding and feel for space around her others could not mimic. We would come to practice and have Kiva demonstrate her tricks. Practice was only during recess, and it lasted only 15 minutes, so we had to focus!

We had a kid by the name of Jessica Soto who could do amazing combinations. One day she challenged Jeff Simbeida, a local sportscaster who always had kids on TV doing impressive things. They would do a trick which Jeff would try to duplicate. A kid might dribble a basketball through his legs or spin a ball on his finger. Jessica chose jump-rope. She did a combination and added a Butt-Bumper. Jeff froze up; this nine-year-old was out of his class. The Whittier phone rang off the hook the next day.

Around this time we got two new jumpers: Briana and Erica Brown. They were the daughters of Mary Lynn Griffin, a former Whittier student and ATC athlete. These two girls complemented Kiva and became jump-rope leaders, helping the young jumpers develop. A few years later, they moved to Colorado. Mary Lynn told me that at their high school they did a jump-rope routine at school assemblies, always to standing ovations. The audience was particularly appreciative of the "Butt Bumper," which of course was a Whittier trademark. It is remarkable to teach a kid, and years later, their own kid.

Our gym is designed so that my office looks out at the half-court line. I would position myself so that I could see all the kids, if peripherally. Their eyes were always on the Coach's office while they worked. We would practice nonstop and dust would fill the air; the untrained eye might think it was chaos, but they were always in control, learning in a small space. One day Kiva was doing a trick I had never seen before and I liked it so much, I named it for her. It is still called a "Kiva," to this day. When asked, "Coach, what is this?" I would just name it after the person who came up with it. It is a very effective motivational tool.

If you like kids and want them to excel, talk to them, and compliment their efforts. Students will surprise you. One day Kiva took a short rope, entered Double Dutch and did a series of tricks inside the two ropes. I had never seen that before, but it looked intriguing. We incorporated it into our show, and named it for her. We encouraged their creativity, and they rewarded us with new tricks.

COMEBACK

In 1999 I was sitting in my gym office when a strange man walked in. He asked, "Are you Jim Ciccarello?"

"Yes," I said, wondering what this guy wanted.

He said, "My name is John Dufay. I'm the girls' track coach at Sandia High and I've been looking for a hurdle assistant coach. Buddy Robertson, APS Athletic Director, told me to come see you."

"Is that so?" I replied. "I'm done coaching track and field. I did my time with APS and at Sandia High School. I like my free time at the moment."

"Coach you only have to come twice a week and on the weekend. If you need free time, don't worry, we'll cover for you."

He was very persistent and I did agree to look at the girls that Monday. I figured it would not hurt to look. Little did I realize he was setting me up! When I went to practice that Monday, he had seven *very* athletic kids, all very polite. They listened and asked excellent questions. I had them do hurdle drills and they followed my directions with no argument. They even said, "yes, sir" and thanked me at the end of the session.

So, next thing I know, I am out at the Sandia track two days a week. Emily Goodwin was a sprinter-turned-hurdler and was so nice that I could not wait to get to practice to work with her. Her sister Sada, also polite and nice, was an up-and coming-track star, and their parents, John and Donna, were very supportive. Abby Dufay was the daughter of John, the head coach, and was eager to please. Jessica Hartinberger was a tall girl with some speed who performed every drill perfectly. Sara Belcher was the daughter of a girl I helped coached years before with the DCD. She would do anything I asked of her. These nice kids encouraged me to a new beginning. In a way, they had "looked at me."

My specialty was hurdles, and I started to develop the Sandia team. I wanted to score high at the District meet and then qualify some athletes for the State Meet. This was not a hard job—*assistant* coaching is easy.

I had a lot of free time, only attending practice on Tuesdays and Thursdays, and not burdened with negotiating discipline. My energy picked up. The girls were very respectful and appreciative of my work. At the tender age of 57, I was starting over again, coaching track athletes. Not realizing it at the time, this was the start of a new and exciting era of coaching for me.

That year, 1999, was one of my most fun ever. Sandia did not have a State Championship-level team, but they had some nice speed and could contend with Eldorado for the district title. I told John I would bring in points from the hurdles. Each week the girls kept improving, and I knew we would do well. Emily Goodwin was developing into one of the top hurdlers in the state and qualified early in the season. And then we had a problem.

Emily was ranked first in the 300m hurdles in the city, but she hurt her foot on a relay. We had to give her time to heal. Jessica Hartinberger, meanwhile, was ranked first in the 100m hurdles. We had four others who could run a good 300m hurdle race: Sara Belger, Sada Goodwin, Leann Komorowski, and Beth Deham.

At the District meet, we placed all five girls in the 300m finals. Emily won the 300m and the others finished second–fifth. Jessica won the 100m and Beth and Abby placed in the top five. It was a great season and we scored more points in the hurdles than all of the other district teams combined! In the end, though, Eldorado took the District Team Championship in a close finish.

It was a good comeback and I thought maybe I would return the next year to try it again. Those Sandia girls worked hard and appreciated my attention, and I enjoyed teaching a new generation of hurdlers. Years later, Jessica and Emily told me, "Coach we would always wait until you were watching the hurdle drills before we would do them… We wanted your approval!"

LA CUEVA HIGH SCHOOL, 2000

In 2000 I was planning to return to Sandia part-time to work with the hurdlers. Just before school started, I was reading *The Albuquerque Journal* sports page. I saw an ad for a girls' head track coach at La Cueva. Mike Soloman, a former Lobo runner, had resigned the day before, and La Cueva was looking for an experienced coach. I soul-searched and began the application process.

The head boys' coach there was Matt Henry. Matt had student-taught under me at Whittier, and his wife Lisa was a former assistant of mine at Sandia in the '80s. It started to look like a natural fit. I knew a head coach worked ten times harder than an assistant and that I was getting up in age. Did I want to start all over again? Starting a new program at a high school is hard; you must learn the system, manage athletes, address new parents and new administrators, hire assistant coaches, start a booster club, work alongside other programs, order uniforms, inventory equipment, and do whatever is left to assure a quality program. I'd have to do all that on top of eight daily PE classes a day, and working my jump-rope team. Well, you know what I did. I turned it down.

Gotcha! I scheduled my interview with Larry Waters, the Athletic Director, in the principal's office. Also present were Joann Coffee, the principal; Sam Soto, the assistant principal; Buddy Robertson, APS Athletic Director; the La Cueva school secretary; and a parent I did not know. They were all very cordial.

I could tell La Cueva took their interviews seriously. It was exhaustive. What were my qualifications? How would I handle the parents and the booster club? How hard were the workouts? Do you believe in kids being in other activities? Did I have assistant coaches ready to help? How would I check on kids, as I was an off-campus coach teaching elsewhere? How often would I check my box and my e-mail? Would I be accessible during the day? Finally, I asked what they would do to support developing a good program. Their answer was simple: whatever it took to support the girls' track and field team. All questions asked and answered were right on. It was decision-making time!

It took over a month. I was expecting to pick up the *Journal* and read about their new hire. (Sometimes you hear about a coach being hired in the newspaper before the coaches are notified. In 1980, I had applied for the head coaching job in track and field at UNM. Several months later, I read about someone else being hired in the sports page.) This time, on a warm October day, I was teaching a PE class at Whittier when my cell phone rang.

Larry Waters said, "Jim, how would you like to be a La Cueva Bear?"

"Da…" I said. "Larry, I will try my best to do you a good job. And thank you."

Matt Henry called me the next day and said, "Jim, you've been around the block and kicked a little bit. But this is going to be your real home." And it is, still. La Cueva girls' track and field became my future!

La Cueva is located in the far Northeast part of town—the upscale part. Kids here have been exposed to athletics their entire lives. Their parents are well edu-cated and many of them have been athletes themselves. The students perform well academically and score high on APS's educational tests. All in all, I would be working with students who were motivated, smart, naturally athletic, and had high expectations of themselves. Their parents would be supportive and challenging. I was eager to prove to them that the La Cueva girls' track and field program would be professionally managed.

A potential scheduling conflict I needed to resolve was how to share athletes with a private soccer league, which meant kids missing certain days and some of the meets. It was made clear to me that La Cueva liked to share athletes and it was my call as to handling athletes competing simultaneously. This has been one of the hardest coaching skills I needed to learn. The athletes wanted to excel in all their sports, and expected the coaches to support that effort. Some schools' parents don't even know your name, but at La Cueva they know your *history*. I was proud of my accomplishments and had a plan to make it better still. The "soccer kids" could do both, as long as they checked in with me and made up for missed practice. It was not perfect, but it would work.

My first order of business was to find a couple of good assistants. Most successful programs not only have a motivated head coach, but also a motivated support staff. I called one of my former athletes, Dolores Archuleta Black, who had coached at Cibola High School. She agreed. Dolores is one of the most knowledgeable athlete/coaches you will ever meet. She was a multi-event athlete, articulate and aggressive. She would be an assistant to fill many roles. Coach Black and I shared the same philosophies and developed a close relationship. She also believed in hard work and taking the athletes to the top of the mountain!

Though Dolores was a perfectionist, she understood that the 2000 athletes could not all live up to her legacy as an age-grouper. Dolores was another in a long line of former athletes who were very loyal to my program. As well as being a dynamic coach, she was a good bridge between the coaching staff and the parents. She looked out for the girls' best interests and communicated with the team moms. This being a first-year program for me at La Cueva, it would be a trying one. We had to prove ourselves! Coach Black certainly helped me accomplish that mission.

Next I asked Mike Soloman, whose position I now occupied, to work part-time. He was now driving a route for FedEx full-time, so he was limited on the field, but he understood the La Cueva program and helped me with adjustments.

Ken Medley, a friend from the old Albuquerque High and the Cibola High boys' programs, also joined us. Ken, like Coach Black, was a multi-event athlete and coach. He was a former long-jumper at Valley High and UNM. He could also triple jump, pole vault, and sprint. He learned how to coach the javelin; Ken had 30+ years in coaching and could learn any event well enough to pass it on. Dan Ashcraft, the boys' pole vault coach, and former vaulter himself, agreed to coach the girls also! He had two boys vaulting for La Cueva. With all events covered, we were good to go.

When I checked on the uniforms, I found that our warm-ups had disappeared over the summer. This happens more often than you can believe. Buddy Robertson, gave me a rush on 40 new warm-up uniforms. This is what I call great administrative support!

The Booster Club bought me some new jump-ropes and throwing implements. Equipment and proper uniforms were now in order. The La Cueva track was in decent shape. Later I found it a bit too hard, which caused shin splints. I met with Matt and Mark Henry, the boys' coaches, and we worked out the sharing schedule. My Whittier schedule meant I could be at La Cueva by 2:45 p.m. each day. Now, to meet the athletes!

I called a meeting of all interested track athletes and their parents in December of 2000. We met in the lecture hall and, to my surprise, about 100 people came. This was exciting, as I knew the more kids you have the better the program's chance of success. I did not recognize any names except for senior Amy Warner, the fastest kid on the team, who had scored in most of the meets in years past. La Cueva had always placed high at the State Meet, but had trouble getting to the top of the podium. My coaches and I wanted to change that.

We knew that to get to the top, kids needed to buy in, to sacrifice for the team. Our goals had to be both high and reachable. We also needed to diversify across events. We told those girls that we expected their best; if they gave it to us, we would reach the top. We were going to push them with workouts they had never heard of and urge them to push harder than they thought they could.

Coach Black and I knew that the State Meet would come down to the 4 x 4 relay, the final event. Amy Warner had never run the 400m and she was used to short sprints and relays. Our first order of business was to convince her to run the 400m. At first she balked, but she warmed to it after running a couple of 600m's in practice with some fast times. We knew that Lauren Lemanski could run a good 400m, as could Haley Bennett. We developed a new athlete, Rebecca Foutz, into a good quarter-miler. Tristan Ryan was a mainstay on the short relays.

We won our first meet in Las Cruces. Our 4 x 4 relay ran a 4:03. That was unheard-of early in the season! And when the girls saw their time and potential, they felt more empowered, and were easier to push. Meanwhile, we were working high-jumpers, long-jumpers, pole-vaulters, and the sprint relays. I knew this team had a chance. I also knew Manzano and Eldorado were good.

It does not matter how much money or prestige you have, but how much you want the coach to recognize your efforts that counts. I learned early in my track coaching career of the breakdown and build-up philosophy of training: push athletes in practice and they come back stronger the next time. The La Cueva girls were about to experience a change in routine. They had never done whistle fartlek or 600m's before, but they did it for us. They were on a roll, and the coaches encouraged them. As long as we watched them, they went hard.

We were undefeated going in to the 2000 State Meet. This does not happen often. During the season you try different kids in off-events and you do not run kids in their favorite events all the time. You give up points to develop new skills in an athlete, and because of that the team may not take top honors. But this La Cueva team had a lot of depth, and could compete in every meet ,regardless of strategy. We were the favorite going into state, with Manzano a close second. This meant we could not afford to make a mistake.

In track and field, mistakes are made in the relays, in the blocks, and in disqualifications. Coach Black and I had read the athletes the riot act. We insisted on complete focus. This was our first year at La Cueva and this team and their parents were still not 100% behind us; we had made changes in workouts and events that not everyone understood, or was comfortable with. Coach Black and I stood steadfast in our approach. We knew we were doing the right thing.

When we win, all is forgiven, and we look like geniuses. We are the same coaches working hard with kids *whether we win or lose*. In the final analysis, the drive to win is just a means to participation and discipline, to experiencing fitness as a way of life. As Vince Lombardi once said, "Winning is not everything—but making the effort to win is." If you don't win, move on to the next competition. "You win today; I win tomorrow" has always been part of my philosophy.

I love the thrill of competition and, as a coach, I anticipate going to the first meet of the year and waiting for that first starter's gunshot on the 4 x 1 relay. Every year, I think, "Here we go again!" and maybe that is why I have lasted 40+ years in this role. How about that new kid on the block; I wonder what she can do on the track? It's a new season and I wonder how we stack up? The excitement of that first meet each year is shared by athletes and coaches alike.

The 2000 state preliminaries did not go as we hoped. We qualified almost every event we needed to advance and score in the finals, but in the 4 x 2 relay, we made a costly mistake. One of our runners received the baton out of the zone on the second exchange and we were disqualified. She later had a great 400m leg of the 4 x 4 relay. We won the 4 x 2 preliminary heats, and had the fastest time of the meet, but did not advance the relay. We had given up 10 points in our final team score, which opened the door for Manzano. Henry Ford once said, "Even a mistake may turn out to be the one thing necessary to a worthwhile achievement." This was very true for this La Cueva Girls' Track Team.

The coaching staff told the athletes the next day to start over and run for each other. The finals the next day started with a great race for us. We won the 4 x 1 relay and set a new school record. Amy Warner won the 100m dash. We placed in the sprints, the 800m, Jade Mallory in the long jump, Amanda Grover in the javelin and Heather Kaiser in the pole vault, tying for the gold. The pole vault had just been added in New Mexico.

Allison Haar, who tied for sixth place in the pole vault, scored what turned out to be a very important quarter point. Sixth place was worth one point and four girls tied for that competition. Each athlete should have received one quarter of a point, and Coach Black insisted that we receive it. She went over to the scorer and fought to get it added to our score. We were making a comeback. Amy Warner placed in the 400m. She and Lauren Lemanski went 2–3 in the 200m. With one event to go, we needed to win the 4 x 4 relay and hope Manzano finished fifth, or lower. If that happened, the tie by Allison Haar in the pole vault would give us the quarter-point for the championship. This made for an exciting finish!

With the gun, the first runner on the 4 x 4 took off and we were in the lead, Manzano close behind. By our last runner we had an easy 50m lead, on our way to a gold finish, five teams battling for the rest. Manzano and Clovis were separated only by inches down the final stretch, fighting for fifth.

Everyone knew that this 4 x 4 would determine the team championship. All eyes were on the battle for fifth place. Coach Black and I almost fell off the bleachers as the race came down to the last 10m. With one meter to go, the Clovis girl outleaned the Manzano girl for fifth place. The final score for the 2000 State Meet: La Cueva 50.25 points; Manzano 50 points. As Lauren Lemanski said, "It is the best feeling in the world." The La Cueva team busted the school's former 4 x 4 record with a time of 3:58.54. This time we did prevail.

The La Cueva girls won the 2000 New Mexico State Championship by a quarter of a point. If Coach Black had not insisted on that quarter-point in the pole vault, we would not have won. The officials at the scoring table did not want to listen to us, but Dolores stood her ground: "I'm not leaving until you get this right." Eventually, we received our earned quarter-point. The Clovis coach, Darrell Ray, aware of the score going into the 4 x 4 relay, told me, "Ciccarello you owe me a breakfast at the Frontier for helping your team." Some day, I still intend to buy Coach Ray a hearty Frontier breakfast.

The seniors on that team, Amy Warner, Lauren Lemanski and Haley Bennett had finally won the blue trophy. There were tears of joy, hugs, and high fives everywhere. The coaching staff was ecstatic. Most people do not know how hard it is to take first place at the NM State Meet. Athletics is about dedication, attention to detail, self-motivation, teamwork, commitment, hard work, persistence and luck. We celebrated the moment.

We lost some very good athletes to graduation and went into 2001 thinking about a rebuilding year. In coaching you are always starting over, as new faces and names appear in your program. We had a few freshmen who showed promise. Michelle Romero, Allie Snell and Michelle Falzone could help this team. We wanted to again develop athletes in all events. Megan Rice, Anna Bellum, and Hannah Kunkle would all contribute to this team. Tristan Ryan, Heather Kaiser, Amanda Grover, Allison Haar, and Rebecca Foutz were ready to go again. We had some raw talent, and if we could motivate these kids at practice, we could get them to run hard and score at meets.

Coaches must spend time each day with athletes in order for them to develop. The coaching staff added Jessica Sanchez Field, a former athlete of mine at Highland. This team exceeded expectations, winning most of their meets and finishing third at State. Any finish in the top three in New Mexico is a good year.

Jimmy Valvano, North Carolina State basketball coach, while dying of cancer, said, "Don't ever, ever give up!" Athletes, coaches, teachers, and everyone else alike should heed those words. That year, 2001, we set the foundation for great success.

CANCER

The next year, 2002, was not stellar for me personally. I was diagnosed with prostate cancer. It was a nightmare to hear I had cancer of any kind. I don't smoke, drink, and I have a healthy diet. I exercise, sleep well, and keep a healthy weight. How could I have cancer? Sitting in the doctor's office in November, 2001, I was in shock and could not begin to ask questions when I heard the words.

I remembered Jimmy Valvano's words. I wondered if my coaching and teaching career was over. I researched and assembled my options. But if I taught my athletes not to give up, how could I? I made many phone calls and received much advice. A 50-year-old man in Denver, CO, had attempted radiation therapy for his prostate cancer, and it had come back on him. This scared me. I talked to doctors, cancer patients, relatives, and many people I did not know. I read books and articles. Johns Hopkins Hospital was the main treatment center for this cancer in the United States. There were many treatments, and because I had caught it early, I had some viable choices. My best chance for a full recovery was to undergo a surgery. Dr. Phil Vitale, an urologist, and former golfing buddy, told me to do it.

We scheduled the surgery for February, right after our preseason workouts. I was eager to get back to school. At the time I was eligible to retire, and could have stayed home forever, watching daytime TV. But my role models never gave up.

They included Jimmy Valvano (North Carolina State), Jim Boeheim (Syracuse), Jim Calhoun (Connecticut), Pat Summit (Tennessee) and numerous others. They all returned after a major sickness or surgery.

I called Sandy Beach Warfield and Jimmy Knop (a former coach from Eldorado). I asked them to cover me at the beginning of the track season. Out of respect for our prior relationship, and their kind hearts, they agreed. When I coached at Highland, Jimmy Knop and his team was our biggest rival. We always respected each other. Sandy was now a middle school PE teacher.

Most surgeries are serious, and anesthesia only makes them seem moreso. This was my sixth, and the one that scared me the most. When I was wheeled into the operating room, I noticed how cold it was; it reminded me of my visits to Alaska. I was so sedated I thought I was dreaming. Hours later, I woke up in the recovery room thinking I was watching a movie of nurses and doctors pushing patients around. The head surgeon, Richard Conn, told me, "Jim we got it all out and you're going to be okay." I was so relieved I took a ten-hour nap.

Jimmy and Sandy kept me updated on the team. I knew their times and events; all I had was downtime! I coordinated workouts and events for the first meet. The second was at Wilson Stadium; I was there, ready to go, in a folding chair on the track. I was not 100%, but I was motivated. Many coaches came over to wish me well. One thing they did *not* do—cut the La Cueva girls any slack on the track. That was okay with me. They were ready to compete. I was ready to help them.

SANDY BEACH WARFIELD

Sandy stayed on as an assistant coach. My former athletes make great assistant coaches because they know the workouts and have great loyalty to me and my program. Sandy was a great mediator in the coaching process. She was not only a great age-group champion, but went on to become a great teacher and track coach, and a most important asset to my coaching career.

Sandy would handle disputes between individual athletes, parents who thought the workouts were too hard, uniforms problems, long practices, and athletes who wanted to be in certain events or run in certain relay positions. The list goes on. Sandy was the unofficial mom of the La Cueva Girls' Track Team. Of course, what the girls did *not* know was that Sandy and I addressed each problem daily. They hoped that Sandy would immediately change things on their behalf; this wasn't often the case, but Sandy did bring their issues to light.

We had a plan. I was the "bad cop" and she was the "good cop." Ciccarello would give the hard workouts; Warfield would help the athletes negotiate them down. They did not realize that Sandy had done these same workouts for me 40 years before and believed in them, also. Sometimes before practice, I would have the workout schedule on a clipboard and Sandy would say, "Coach, those four 600s are too much. When they come to me I'll negotiate for them, and you drop two 600s and add two 200s instead." We knew even before they started those girls would question a workout.

They always felt that Sandy was looking after their interests and developed an open relationship with her. So they always went hard, knowing that Sandy was watching. We gave the appearance of overshooting, so that the workout we knew they needed did not seem out of reach. Sandy would look out for the girls and question my workout plan if it was too hard.

My relationship with Sandy was very near perfect. My coaching style changed as kids changed. Our team always listened and looked. I never cussed or screamed. One day, I heard a tirade of cuss words from the football coach toward his athletes. The girls' track athletes were shocked. They told me they were so glad for my personal approach. Of course, if I had used the language I heard other coaches use, my career at La Cueva would have been over. Our society is full of gendered double-standards. Some coaches yell and cuss at boys; at times, I've seen boys physically pushed around, coaches striking them to get their attention. If I was coaching strictly boys, I would never use that approach. I have coached both boys and girls and my philosophy is invariably one of respect toward young people.

In some form or another that double-standard will never go away; it is too in-grained in our culture. "Boys need to toughen up" has always been the approach, particularly in football and wrestling. My approach was to ask kids to do something for their own good, and incentivize it. I put the decision on the athlete—does he want to work or not?

I always had respect for the athletes and their concerns. If they *needed* a break, I gave it to them. All my athletes and my assistant coaches know my approach by heart: "If you are healthy, go hard—and if sick or hurt, back off." We encourage athletes to always be honest with us. Have you had a day when you don't feel good? Have you ever gone to a practice or to work and needed some quiet time or rest? Every human being on this planet needs a break now and then! I have seen coaches that push kids hard when they don't feel good, and it does not work. Give a kid a break today and he will do better for you tomorrow. Sandy and I not only believed this, we demanded it. Over the long run it paid off, as athletes *did* run hard and *did* compete hard for the team. Coach Warfield and I always communicated to each other about the health of our athletes. Sandy stayed with me for ten years and I give her much credit for our accomplishments on the track.

In the years 2002 and 2003, we again had good teams at La Cueva. We placed first in our district both years. At the State Meet in 2002, we finished in fourth place. In 2003, we finished second. The team now counted on Katie Candelaria, Brianna Paxton, Rebecca Warin, Marian Andersen Abby Schubert, Allie Snell, Sara Guylinger, Napolonia Harper, Laura Hughes, Whitney Hughes, and Tori Graffman. Our team was young and we were seeing success as we developed.

In the 2002 New Mexico State Meet our little freshman Katie Candelaria won the open 400m in a huge upset. Katie was ranked fifth going in, but she was always unpredictable. As Katie came off the far turn, she had a five-yard lead and held it all the way to the end. When she ran on relays it was, "Katie, bar the door," because if she decided she wanted to run hard, no one could catch her.

The next season was very interesting, as our chief rival now was Cibola High. We won most of our meets and took first in City and District. They had the great Tressi Richardson, who was, inarguably, the best sprinter in the state. We stayed overnight in Alamogordo for the State Meet.

We thought we had a great plan. It would hinge on the 4 x 2 relay. Tori Graffman won the high jump and Jade Mallory the triple jump. The preliminaries went as predicted. That night, unknown to the coaching staff, two of our 4 x 2 relay members were wrestling in their room and our best 200m runner dislocated her knee. In the finals, we had to run an athlete who was two seconds slower. Needless to say, we did not get the points we needed. We were tied going into the last event, the 4 x 4 relay, and Cibola took the relay and the meet, La Cueva finishing second. Over the years I have always known it is tougher to control athletes on a road trip. They are still kids.

Certain competitions get away from you: the New Mexico State Championship in 2003; the 1980 State Championship, when the Sandia team finished second. Someone once said finishing second is like kissing your sister. Almost. General Douglas MacArthur said, "In war, you win or lose, live or die—and the difference is just an eyelash." It is more fun to win, but if we fail, at least, in athletic competition, we (probably) have another opportunity waiting. In the final analysis, finishing second is not really that bad. Just ask the teams that finished behind you.

In the summer of 2003, I received a phone call from a former athlete of mine, Ann Bernitsky. She asked me to look at her nephew, Will. He wanted to work on hurdles and she knew I had worked with Curtis Beach. It was quickly clear Will could be a great hurdler. He was smart, fast, agile and *motivated*. That summer we practiced and competed in local meets, and Will qualified for a Junior Olympic National meet in Miami. Curtis and Will would do drills together, and pushed each other, Will was older and the better athlete. Both Will and Curtis made the podium in Miami. Will returned for two years, and at Albuquerque Academy dominated the hurdles, setting a State Record. The young Curtis then proclaimed, "Someday, I will break your record in the hurdles."

It was a busy summer. I also taught the hurdles to Will's younger siblings, Laura and Alex, in age-group competition, and a young Alex Darling, daughter of former ATC athlete Christine Roybal. Alex was running the 800m and 1600m. I take a great deal of pride in coaching second- and third- generation athletes.

In the fall of 2003 Sally Marquez, a key member of our 1977 Manzano Track and Field Team, was voted into the Albuquerque/NM Hall of Fame. Sally had run the anchor position on the record-setting mile relay, and went on to play college basketball. She followed that with a few years coaching basketball, and then administration. Today she is in a high-profile position with the NM Activities Association, helping to improve state athletics for females. Now I had two former athletes in the Hall of Fame. I thought, why not see what else the future will bring?

WHITTIER/BANDELIER

School climates really began to change in the early 2000s. Discipline waned across APS. Whittier, with a population of mostly Hispanic, Native American, and African-American students, lost still more socioeconomic ground. We added many bilingual programs. With No Child Left Behind, and our test scores still public, we lost more students. If Whittier did not meet certain standards, the state had threatened to take over the school administratively. Our principal, Agnes Redmond, was instructed to raise test scores. She worked diligently with teachers to restructure the curriculum. Meanwhile, people were retiring and moving on. We were starting with a staff mostly comprised of new educators.

For my part, I stayed and helped. Agnes told me, "Coach, keep the kids engaged, and I will support you." And she did, in the form of equipment and supplies.

I started an aerobics team in which kids dressed up and danced as *Men in Black*. The music was from the movie's soundtrack. The students would create their own routines in groups and do step-up aerobics. We practiced at recess, put on several assemblies for the school, and finally held a PTA show, with a "Hollywood Look." I was trying anything to keep them engaged.

On January 7th, 2002, we did a Lobo basketball halftime show. Harold Smith, a sports reporter for *The Albuquerque Journal*, happened to be covering the game that night. He was so impressed he did a special story the next day. This was the most exposure we have ever received, and the headline was clear: "Go Ahead and Jump-Rope: Whittier Puts on a Show." The article featured two half-page photos of Brandy Shock doing a "Butt Bumper" and Kiva Gresham and Robin Ledesma doing a "Sneak and Peek." This article did more for our team than any other show or press release. Now all of Albuquerque could read about them. The Whittier jump-rope students who performed that night were: Pilar Garcia, Dominique Hagins, Nichelle Hall, Jacob Jaramillo, Meena Lee, Gabrielle Lopez, and Brenda Rios. Chelsy Leeper, Brandy Shock, and Kiva Gresham were students at Wilson Middle School, and still members of our jump-rope team.

Several teachers and the principal had attended. Maria Cassanova, a fifth grade teacher, was one of them. Maria would always visit a practice in the Whittier gym to see how her students were doing. She knew if her students focused here, they would focus in the classroom.

Maria saw the value of jump-rope. Whenever we needed to release a kid from her class for a show, she let him go—and attended the performance. We shared the students; not all teachers did this. Some actually said, "If you don't perform here, you can't perform in the gym." It was heartwarming to meet a teacher who shared my philosophy. When I look back on all my years of teaching, I can distinguish those who care from those who go through the motions. Some teachers show their authority by denying kids a special activity. The great majority, however, see an opportunity for motivation. I find it interesting that after a few years of teaching Elementary Ed., Maria moved to the high school, at La Cueva. Some of her students are running track for me, and it is delightful to have her support, still.

We have to put a "spark" into a child's day. It is a chance for students to release some of their huge stockpiles of energy. Young kids do not understand the consequences of being taken out of an activity because their "attitude" is not right. I have seen thousands of students behave *worse* for being denied. They start being disruptive in other areas because they do not connect their behavior with its consequences.

This is particularly true of low-income children. Schools must provide disadvantaged children with activity-focused after-school programs. Middle- and upper-class neighborhoods offer these programs starting as early as two years of age. I have seen gymnastics and Tumbling for Tots programs in the well-off neighborhoods, and they are fee-based. These kids get a jump-start on less-advantaged kids, and it affects them their whole lives.

Of course, the same happens in academics. The highly-educated always supplement their kids' education. They read to their own children, hire personal tutors, and sometimes even personal trainers. We need to equalize the opportunities. And it does cost money, which the schools, committed to teacher salaries, supplies, equipment, and insurance, among other expenses, do not have.

Liz and Marisol Baraza were two sisters whose parents emigrated here from Mexico. Both were athletic, but had never been exposed to an athletic program of any kind. In the classroom Marisol was sharp, while Liz struggled a bit; English was their second language.

The fastest hands with a rope I had ever seen belonged to Marisol. She was short and quick, with great potential. They never missed a recess practice. When we had a show, they were on the bus. Their dad was in jail, and mom was raising them alone; they were survivors. I had seen this in my own neighborhood in New Jersey, and I hoped to help them.

Jump-rope was the best time of the day for these girls. If they needed a ride to a show, they rode with me. I had been doing this my whole career and I knew if I did not, the kids would fall between the cracks; the liability seemed worth the risk. Others did it, too: Marsha Conglin, an occupational therapist, helped them for a while when they moved to the West Side; she picked them up and I would return them home when the show was over. This was never easy and eventually the logistics became too great.

The sisters went to a new school, where activities were not offered. No adults helped them, and soon they dropped out of the jump-rope scene. If the schools don't help low-income kids, they disappear.

For about seven years we lost contact with the Baraza sisters. As this book was headed to print, I received a call from Marisol, now 19. She had just had a baby girl, Paris. Even as a new mom, she asked if she could perform in our next show. We will find a way to honor her request.

Teachers like Mr. Earl Lyon, Meredith Vargas, Steve Clapper, Lee Hayes, Mr. Monceballez and Maria Cassanova share my views, and have become involved. I personally want to thank these teachers for their extra commitment to children at

Whittier. My brother Richard reminded me of a Winston Churchill quote, which recalls me their sacrifice: "You make a living out of what you get, and you make a life out of what you give." The real heroes in our society are not our Hollywood stars, our recording artists, or our super-professional athletes, but our teachers, who do not receive fame or fortune for all the "extra" they do to help our children.

I am very proud of my students and all they have accomplished over the years. These kids always remember the extra effort that adults give to help them improve. At Whittier I had been taking kids to perform in the Pit for many years. I occasionally receive a letter from one of them. Following is a letter that was sent to me by a former Whittier gymnastic student:

Dear Coach Ciccarello,

The other day my husband and I were at a Lobo Football game and a zillion little girls got to come out and do cheerleading at halftime. That reminded me of when I was little and you had the Gymnastics Club at Whittier. You were such a good coach. You made that club fun for everyone regardless of ability. It must have taken quite a lot for you to arrange for us to go do our little routine at halftime at the basketball games and I don't know if any of us or our parents ever thanked you, but we should have, because it made each and every one of us feel special.

The fact that you did Play Day where we could all (the whole school!) win ribbons and have fun, is really amazing. I also remember you being with us kids at recess and always interacting, with us, whether it was hula hoop contests or any other kind of activity. When new kids came, you always found a way for them to feel good. You were a really great coach, and I just wanted to finally take the time to say, "Thanks!"

Sincerely,

Lesha (Rupert) Harenberg

PS: I still have your school picture! I am a teacher at Eldorado now myself, and it's funny to be an adult & still get school pictures, but it's neat that you gave them to us kids!

Another letter, from Cody Langdon:

I learned a lot from you, Coach Ciccarello. You made me work and taught me multiple things like teamwork, respect, and "practice makes perfect." That has been with me for all of my growing years. My sister, Cheryl Luna, helped kids become active, by doing what she did when she was a kid. Gymnastics was very exciting for her. She learned it from you, one of the most respected coaches of her childhood.

Sincerely,

Cody Langdon

We do not always hear from former students, but when we do it is always special. I, myself, have always communicated with former teachers and coaches to let them know how important they were in my development.

As if I did not have enough on my plate, Agnes Redmond, principal at Whittier, called me into the office in 2002 and said, "Coach Ciccarello, you are going to spend part of your teaching day at Bandelier Elementary."

How could that be? I was just developing the track and field program at La Cueva, and the jump-rope team was getting better at Whittier! But, Agnes said, Bandelier has 300 more students than we do, and you need to go and help the PE teacher there so he can have a break. You will teach eight classes here and then drive over to Bandelier and teach two more." All I could think was that APS was adding more work, and I would have a hard time fitting it all in. I knew the budget was tight, but couldn't they find someone else to do this?

The next week Bandelier's principal, Mrs. Dennis, gave me a tour of the campus. Like Whittier, it was located in the Southeast Heights, and an older school, built in the 1940s. The two were a mile apart, and many more in demographics. People were very friendly and they welcomed me with a great attitude.

We went into the new gym, built just a few years earlier, where I met Chris Jarvis. Chris was the current PE teacher and in his second year at Bandelier. He had formerly been a classroom teacher and was trying his hand at physical education. He had nonstop classes from 9:00 a.m.–3:00 p.m., and he needed a break to eat lunch, which I would provide, and team-teach a few classes with him. I had a 15-minute window to get from Whittier to Bandelier.

Chris struck me with his professionalism and easy-going attitude. I knew we would get along. Many times when teachers work closely, some friction can disrupt the educating. But Chris was in a learning mode. I would rely on his youth and classroom experience, and he would rely on my years of coaching experience. You can teach old dogs new tricks, but old dogs can teach the young pups, too!

Chris had heard of our jump-rope team and wanted to try something similar. I balked at first, but with further thought, I figured we could join our groups. I agreed to it explicitly as a team effort: the Whittier/Bandelier Jump-Rope Team. At times, each team would perform alone, but more often, together. We designed new shirts with each school's name on the front, and both names on the back. Now all we had to do was train the Bandelier kids to jump!

I wanted to bring experienced students from Whittier. Both Mrs. Redmond and Mrs. Dennis were in. I took Leandra and Ariel, two excellent jumpers, and then we roped Curtis Beach into teaching. The first day the Bandelier kids saw the jumpers, their eyes were popping out. But even better were 'kids helping kids.' I have always believed in multi-age-grouping. The little kids learn from the big ones; sometimes your best role models are the children themselves.

The Bandelier kids were sharp. The school is a magnet for the arts, and in a middle-class neighborhood. We thought, perhaps, if we could mix the groups together, we would come up with the perfect team. It was imperative Chris and I collaborate. Dissension would not be tolerated. This team would now be the most diverse jump-rope team ever concocted in Albuquerque. The kids and parents both needed to understand the joint aspect of this team. I knew if this worked this team would perform like nothing we had imagined. Was I ever right!

My first class at Bandelier reminded me of my first year at Whittier. The kids came in quiet and sat down in even rows, with perfect self-control. They had a clean look, were dressed appropriately, did the things I asked them.

Chris observed me while I taught, and when he would teach, I would study him back. He had a calm demeanor. His behavior management techniques were solid from five years in a self-contained classroom. As I gave him new ideas he slowed me down. There was no power struggle in that PE class. Sometimes we would observe each other; sometimes we would teach simultaneously. It became a game, and the students picked up on it. You might say it was tag-team teaching.

A few years passed and Chris and I got real good at this. We wondered if any other teachers in APS could or were doing it. This kind of teaching only works when both teachers respect each other and their philosophies. Chris had only just begun to teach PE and I thought he had already worked himself into the upper tier of Phys. Ed. teachers. Among his strengths were his use of music to motivate the children, his preparation and use of lesson plans, use of the whiteboard, and his use of technologies, such as the boom box, laptop, and projectors. So, what I thought would be another burden, courtesy of APS, had made my career even more interesting. I again had my batteries recharged!

Chris's son Sean attended Bandelier. He joined the jump-rope team with imme-diate success. With his dad there to motivate him and my help to learn new tricks, Sean rose to the top; within just a couple of months, he was ready for shows. Sean was a hockey player who used jump-rope to sharpen his feet, hand-eye and foot-eye coordination. As Sean became better in jump-rope, his speed on the ice and his quickness in his hands were very apparent. Coach Jarvis was very aware of this and encouraged his son to stick with it.

Over the years I have learned to use the audience's tastes to hold their attention. Sean was also young and cute, unassuming and pleasant to be around. We did not have many boys like him, and he stood out at shows. At one such show at La Cueva, eyes gravitated toward him: his skills were paramount, he was the only boy on the team, and the high school girls called him "handsome." He made many new friends that day.

Julia Foster came to us around the same time as Sean. Her father had gone to Whittier, and knew about our track club. Karen and Leonard Foster encouraged Julia to run track and field. Julia became involved with the ATC and started to jump rope. I insist that all track athletes learn this skill. Julia was a tall Native American girl, and people would follow her during a show. One time at a Pit show, all the kids were on their rears doing "Butt Bumpers," and she did straight-up "Double-Unders." The crowd hooted and hollered for Julia—who was actually doing the easier trick. Her height and straight-upward jumping made her appear to jump "super-high." She was a highly skilled athlete.

At Bandelier, two former gymnastics girls, Nicole Ortega and Destiny Burrell, had come up with a complex routine: a combination of jump-rope and cartwheels with back walkovers. They synchronized their moves, and it became an instant hit.

We also had a very motivated student in Chloe Lee. As an age-grouper tennis player, she became one of the top players in the Southwest. Chole, daughter of Becky Lee, was one of the most skilled jump-rope kids we ever had. Becky said to me, "Ciccarello, I believe that jump-rope practice has been the best thing to help Chole become a great tennis player." She would come to practice and stand in front of a whiteboard with the entire trick list. She would then go non-stop for 15 minutes every day, repeating the list of tricks, never stopping for rest. She became determined to do the entire 15 minutes without a mistake. The other kids would try to copycat her routine.

The Coleman Tennis Tournament is a big deal, held at the Tanoan Country Club. We were invited to the finals and did a jump-rope performance for the tennis audience. Of course, Chole was our headliner, and it was a smashing success. Chole continued on to Albuquerque High and became the NM State Champion in the singles event. She was the number-one ranked tennis player in New Mexico for several years.

One day, in the Bandelier gym, Mikala Sterling came to me and said, "How about this, Coach?" She was on a pogo stick and jumping rope—simultaneously. Everybody stopped to watch. She held the stick with her legs, leaving her hands free to turn the rope. It looked both dangerous and athletic; I thought I was looking at a circus act. She was keeping control on a pogo stick while jumping rope in a room with 100 small kids. After several weeks of practice, we took six kids on pogo sticks to La Cueva and the crowd went wild. We used a metal spring sound that resonated across the gym floor.

Kids are risk-takers. One day, Josh, a Whittier first-grader, brought me a Disney song called "Jump In" to play for the jump-rope team. It had a hip-hop sound and the kids loved it. We played it every day; if kids like a song or movie, they rarely become bored with it. Another kid brought me the soundtrack from Michael Jackson's *Thriller*. This became an instant hit. The kids pretended they were graveyard zombies. Later we incorporated the Zombie Dance into our performances.

On February 23, 2006, *The Albuquerque Tribune*'s Jan Jonas did a story on our team. It was titled "A Jump on Health." There was a half-page picture of Hannah Glasgow from Bandelier doing a grapevine trick, with a story about our show at Los Padillas Elementary. Here is a small part of the article:

> Bandelier and Whittier Elementary students' Tick Tocks and Mad Dogs are inspiring other kids to take up jump-roping. After all, says one little master, "It helps you get stronger." How many kids do you know who can double under to "In the Mood" by Glenn Miller or mad dog to "Do you believe in Magic" by the Loving Spoonful? Kindergarten students at Whittier Elementary and Bandelier Elementary watch the jump-rope team execute those tricks. They begin practicing in first grade and are accomplished jumpers by the fifth grade. Coach Jim Ciccarello and Coach Chris Jarvis, PE teachers, oversee the program. Jump-Rope is so successful other schools have started teams. Painted Sky Elementary and Lowell Elementary in Albuquerque and an elementary school in Los Lunas are among the newer teams in the past few years. Last fall, some members of Whittier's team went to Bandelier Elementary and took on the responsibility of giving pointers to Bandelier students. "It keeps you healthy. It helps you get stronger," said Nicole Ortega, 9, a fourth-grader at Bandelier. You don't want to get too fat." When Glenn Miller wrote "In the Mood" in 1940, he couldn't have known kids in the next century would jump rope to his music. And the kids can't fathom 1940. But put the two together, and it's pure fun.

Every day the phone rang with a new request to perform and teach throughout New Mexico. There was no way we could honor all of them; our kids were students first. But in the next two years we performed in many places:

NM State Fair

Sandia Pueblo

Griegos Elementary School

Highland HS

Santa Fe School for the Deaf

UNM PE Department

Nob Hill Cultural Fair

La Cueva HS

EG Ross Elementary School

Eisenhower Middle School

Wilson Middle School

LBJ. Middle School

Peralta Elementary School (Los Lunas)

Santa Ana Reservation

S. Y. Jackson Elementary School

Tomisita Elementary School

Sandia Base Officers' Club

Durantes Elementary School

Eldorado HS

St. Michaels' HS (Santa Fe)

Los Alamos HS

Los Padillas Elementary School

Lowell Elementary School

UNM Soccer Tournament

Monte Vista Elementary School

NM Health, PE, Recreation
   and Dance Convention

US American Nurses Convention

Albuquerque Academy School

ABQ City Parks and Recreation
   Summer Program

The PIT (UNM)

Rio Rancho Special Events Center

Ann Parrish Elementary School

Winrock Shopping Center

NM Special Olympics

Wild Oats

Whole Foods

Wal-Mart

Pojoaque NM Wellness Center

APS Headquarters (Main Office)

NM State Legislature (Santa Fe)

East Mountain HS

ABQ International Balloon Fiesta

ABQ BioPark (Duck Pluck fundraiser)

North Star Elementary School

Buffalo Exchange

Bernalillo Tamaya Resort

Algodones Elementary School

Hodgin Elementary School

Coach Jarvis and I were extremely busy. We tried to schedule night and weekend shows. When it became necessary to go during a school day, we ordered a bus and had kids excused from class, and they had to make up any schoolwork missed.

We found that the kids on our jump-rope team were excellent students and the travel time did not affect their studies, especially when we explained that doing the show depended on good academics.

Many parents and students told us that they enrolled in our schools just to be part of this program. As more schools added jump-rope to their curriculum, we received more requests for information. The benefits of speed, cardio endurance, fast feet, hand-eye-coordination, and plain fun were passed on.

The team had great ethnic and socioeconomic diversity. Bandelier attracted mostly Caucasian and African-American middle-class students. Whittier had many students from Mexico, Cuba, Native American reservations, and South American countries, as well as low-income African-American and Hispanic students from the neighborhood. Coach Jarvis and I knew that we needed to provide fair and supportive leadership to all students. We had become role models for the entire team—and not just us, but parents, teachers and administrators, too.

We mixed the kids up to ensure a team "feeling." Chris and I would take turns bonding with all students. We had tricks and routines including kids from both schools. Our T-shirts reinforced both schools' identities. When we jumped, it was important that all kids looked the same. This developed team and school pride.

We raised the money and gave each kid their shirt the day they performed in their first show. Imagine a young kid receiving her first T-shirt as a team member. They earned the shirt by developing the skills necessary for a show. No one could buy his way on this team. Students learned as they earned their way in.

LA CUEVA GIRLS AND LINDSEY BARR RAISE THE BAR!

2004 and 2005 were special for girls track at La Cueva. In '04 we had returning athletes and new kids to help the team. Our chief rival was Cibola, who had the great Tressi Richardson, the fastest sprinter in the state. We had Katie Candelaria, hurdler Alex Darling, thrower Brianna Paxton, Allie Snell in the pole vault, and two promising sprinters in Whitney Hughes and Napalonia Harper.

My family. Back to front:
Helen, Rosemarie, me,
Ignacio, Richard, and Frank

In the US Air Force, 1962

Trabzon, Turkey Basketball 1965, Coach Dave Tucker

Riverview Elementary, 1971

Lowell Elementary, 1969

Duke City Dasher Coaches, 1969

Lowell & Duke City Dashers, 1970

Whittier/ATC Boys, 1971

Whittier Grade 6, 1971–1972

Duke City Dashers 400m Relay, 1971:
Tana Meadows, Val Boyer, Barbara Hobbs, Donna Corley

Duke City Dashers, 1971

Alice Watson

Val Boyer & Alice Watson

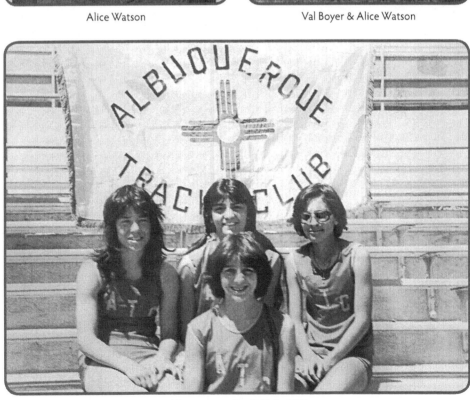

Albuquerque Track Club, 1974:
Mary Grace Lemaster, Glenda Padilla, Dolores Archuleta, Chrtistine Roybal

Whittier Gymnastics 1971

Whittier Gymnastics 1971

John Monceballez & Al Unser, Jr.

Phil Romero

Whittier Recess, 1971

Coach Ciccarello, National Champion Sandy Beach, Gloria Beach

Val Boyer (courtesy of cwpacksports.com)

Albuquerque Track Club, 1973

Manzano High School State Champions, 1977

Albuquerque Track Club, 1973:
Val Boyer, Denise Bailey, Christine Brockhoff, Alice Watson

Sandy Beach and Margaret Metcalf

Albuquerque Track Club, 1980: Sandy Beach, Val Boyer. Coach Ciccarello,
Cheryl Thompson, Dolores Archuleta (photo courtesy of Daniel Gibson)

Jewel Baty

Donna Corley

Sandía High School, 1983

Cal Guymon, Jim Ciccarello, Lee Hayes

Whittier Gymnastics, 1986: Coach Ciccarello, Coach Steve Clapper, Coach Earl Lyon

Natanya Jones, Highland High School State Champ, 300m hurdles, 1988

Whittier Jump Rope Team, NM State Fair, 1990s

Whittier Jump Rope Team at The Pit, 1990s

Alex Darling, Coach Ciccarello, and Curtis Beach at the Utah Junior Olympics

Trevor Perkins, Julia Foster, Curtis Beach, and Coach Ciccarello at National Competition, Baltimore

Curtis Beach, Daniel Gooris and "The Macho Boys"

Whittier/Bandelier Jump Rope Team at The Pit, early 2000s

Coach Jarvis, Sean Jarvis, Coach Ciccarello

Whittier/Bandelier Jump-Rope Team

Ava, Savi, and Alisa (Bandelier) at Tanoan Country Club

Coach Ciccarello and the Bandelier Jump-Rope Team

Kiva Gresham

2007 Track State Champs:
Maddie McPeak, Alex Darling, Asal Salehpoor

Curtis Beach, Coach Ciccarello, Olympian Sheila Burrell, and Grace Rich

La Cueva NM State Track Champs, 2011

NM State Record 4 x 4 Gold Medal Team, 2011:
Hattie Schunk, Mickey Brown, Carly Browning, Christina Clark

Coach Ciccarello and Curtis Beach, Gold Medal USA, Trinidad & Tobago

Whittier Play Day

Julia Foster giving back

Role Models: Julia Foster, Allie Alderette, Christina Clark, Kaylin Martin

Jumping At The Pit

Lobo Love

Halftime Jump-Rope

Mariah Rast and Cory Chavez, "Pit Jumpers"

International Balloon Fiesta

Orinda Martine On a Pogo Stick!

Banda, Coach Ciccarello, Whittney

Coaches Spencer Sielschott and Jim Ciccarello

Juliet, Coach Jarvis, Amethyst, Coach Ciccarello

Chaz Lewis, Tung Tat, Coach Ciccarello and Warrick Campbell at the Nob Hill 66 Festival, 2012

Val Boyer's Hall of Fame Induction

The Chicago Gang: Will, Coach Ciccarello, Julia, Sandy, Chad Clark

Los Padillas Jump Rope Show

Will and Laura Bernitsky, Coach Ciccarello

La Cueva Coaching Staff, 2007:
Coach Ciccarello, Coach Field, Coach Valencia, Coach Warfield, Coach Medley and Coach Martinez

Giving back: Christine Ostler, Coach Ciccarello, Aubrey Hererra

Neffi Quintana "passing the love" in the Philippines

Philippino Rope-Jumpers

Santa Ana Reservation

Christine Ostler teaching jump-rope

Rebecca and Steve at the 2012 New Mexico State Fair

2012 New Mexico State Fair

New Mexico Runners: Kaylin Martin, Coach Jim Ciccarello, Stephanie Brener

Viktoryia, Merdith Vargas, Coach Ciccarello, Dyani, Orinda

Our number-one distance runner was Lindsey Barr, a former softball athlete. Also helping us were Rebecca Warin, Sara Guylinger, and Maddie McPeak, a very good relay runner. We had a lot of promise but we would face some very imposing teams that year. As the season was developing, I could see that while we did not have much virtuosity, we did have diversity. Our job, as always, was to help all athletes reach their highest potential. The assistant coaches at La Cueva became very important: Ken Medley in the jumps; Eddie Hellenback in the distance events; Dan Ashcraft in the pole vault; Jessica Sanchez in the hurdles; and Sandy Beach Warfield with the sprinters. Our philosophy was now to "nickel-and-dime them to death."

Eldorado, Cibola, and Clovis were the teams to beat, though Gallup and Highland were also very talented. As the track season developed, we won most of our meets. Each week new athletes picked up a point here, a point there. In some ways I think this is the best kind of team, as all the athletes feel they shared equally in the victory. As the State Meet moved along, we stayed afloat. Despite a couple of problems in the prelims, we aimed to bounce back in the finals. We changed our order of athletes running in the 4 x 2 for finals, and where in the prelims we placed fifth; in the end we won the gold. This was a huge turning point for us.

As we went into the next-to-last event, the 3,200m run, we knew if Lindsey Barr won the gold, we would win the whole meet. All eyes were on her as the gun went off. She ran with as much confidence as I have ever seen a La Cueva girl run. At the end of the race she took first, broke the school record, and locked us in as 2004 State Champions. Lindsey and her teammates were very proud as they stood on the top step of the podium. The next day on the front page of *The Albuquerque Journal* sports page there was a picture of Lindsey Barr with an unbelievable smile, and the headline "Barr Raises Bears to Title."

PAXTON, MAMA BEAR AND GRACE

As satisfying as 2004 was, it was only a prelude to 2005. It is hard to win a State Championship, much less to go "back to back," two years in a row. In 2005 the competition was extremely tough. Highland had one of the fastest teams in the history of the game. Cibola still had the great Tressi Richardson, and Clovis had a good all-around team. We knew it was going to be a battle.

The regular season was interesting. Highland and Cibola dominated the sprints. La Cueva was strong in the hurdles and field events. Once again, the coaching staff added up potential points and realized we needed to diversify.

Two of our key athletes on this 2005 track team were daughters of former athletes of mine. Brianna Paxton (whose mother, Laurie Gilliland, ran for me as a Duke City Dasher 30 years before) became key for us in the discus and shot put. Alex Darling was the daughter of Christine Roybal, another of my former track athletes. Their moms, naturally, believed in the coaching staff, and loyalty from parents means a great chance to succeed with the athletes themselves.

As the 2005 State Meet started, *The Albuquerque Journal* stated, "This… will be a mad dash to the finish line." They added Cibola and Rio Rancho to the mix, predicting this would be to be the tightest team finish in years. We needed Allie Snell and Reece Cuddy to help us in the pole vault. Katie Candelaria had to perform well on the track. We had some great relay help from Maddie McPeak and Megan Hoffert. These two girls became most important running those relays, as they ultimately put us in position to compete for the blue trophy. We had a first-year javelin-thrower in Vanessa Strobbe, who had been improving weekly. She was ranked first in the city and second in the state. At the State Meet she got off a tremendous toss to set a new school and State Record. A Carlsbad athlete with a tremendous arm had one throw left, and passed Vanessa by a half of a foot. Vanessa had set a State Record… and held it for about five minutes. She finished second in the competition and her new record was listed as a past State Record.

That is the way of athletic competition. Vanessa's second-place finish was worth five points for the team, which would become important. We finished the prelims in good order, and qualified the athletes into the finals where we needed them.

On the second day of finals speculation about the contest became very interesting. The aforementioned five teams were all in, as predicted. Brianna Paxton set school records in the shot put and discus and won gold in both events. This double-victory positioned us for the team championship. Alex Darling and Allie Snell took second and third in the hurdles, respectively. With two events to go Highland had a seven-point lead. We placed second and fourth in the pole vault, giving us a one-point lead going into the last event. At this point, the skies opened up and rain and lighting poured, and everything stopped.

All teams were in the staging area and had to wait together. They sat across from each other for 45 minutes. The coaching staffs from both La Cueva and Highland stared at one another in the bleachers. Every team in the meet knew that our teams would decide the championship. Coach Elmer Martinez and I shook hands and said "may the best team win." We have always had a great relationship and were respect-ful of each other's programs.

At every State Meet the last event is the 4 x 4. Two of Highland's athletes were for-mer Whittier students of mine: Rayanna and Rochelle Johnson. Not many coaches have had meaningful contact with athletes on both sides of the competition. Of course I wanted my former Whittier students to do well—but I was a La Cueva coach and my first priority was to the blue and white.

In a long career of coaching, my stomach was still tied in knots. The coaches were all just as nervous as the athletes. It was cold and wet. All other team State Champi-onships had already been decided and the next race coming up would decide the 5A girls' team title. Not one person left the stadium.

The gun went off and Rio Rancho took the lead, with Highland in close pursuit. La Cueva was in sixth place. The positions did not change during the first three legs of the race. Our last runner, Katie Candelaria, took the relay baton and started to chase the field. We knew Katie was good, but she needed a super-race to catch up. As Katie started to pass people around the track, we could feel something happening. Coming off the last turn, she was in third and with 20m to go she passed Highland and almost caught Rio Rancho. Katie ran a time of 57.10 on that leg of the relay. It was the fastest time of the day—and it gave La Cueva the points we needed to capture the team championship.

The next day in an article by Harold Smith (May 15, 2005) *The Albuquerque Jour-nal* wrote: "Like a Mama Bear protecting her young cubs, Katie Candelaria brought her 1,600m relay team from the brink of disaster to win the Class 5A girls track and field title."

From this day forward Katie Candelaria has been known at La Cueva as "Mama Bear." A special and well-earned nickname!

Katie graduated and we went into 2006 intending to rebuild. Alex Darling and several good athletes were returning: Asal Salehpoor, an Iranian runner, was beginning to step-up, which was especially impressive, as her family lacked a background in American athletics. Asal had natural speed and a pleasant personality, so it was no surprise that her teammates loved her, and respectful to a fault, she was also a delight to coach. She had only been running three years, and her junior-year focus was in the triple jump. Asal could also run the 100m and a leg on the 4 x 1 relay. In addition to her superior academics, she was a smart athlete, and we could enter her in many events.

She had just one problem: a bad case of shin splints, an inflammation of the lower leg. It is painful and the best treatment is rest, which is hard to do during a track season. Asal, though hurting, still contributed. She was a great role model and always grateful for help from the coaching staff. Ken Medley, the jump coach, developed her to compete with the best jumpers in New Mexico.

The big story this year was Grace Rich. Grace was a senior who had transferred to La Cueva from St. Pius, a Catholic school on the West Side of town. Grace was an outstanding soccer player; she ran some track, but had never committed to it. That was about to change.

In the fall of 2005, Grace had been involved in a school prank. She and several others went to the Albuquerque Academy, St. Pius's main rival, and painted their school colors on several buildings and important statues. After much fanfare, discipline committee meetings, and administrative hand-wringing, Grace was expelled. This was a huge disappointment for her: she had always been committed to St. Pius, but had chosen a poor way to express it. She appeared before several committees of parents and administrators and apologized, but was forced to return to a public school.

Jessica Sanchez Field, one of my assistant coaches and a dental hygienist, called me that December and asked if I had heard about the new athlete we were getting. I had not. Coach Field was also Grace's dental hygienist, and the secret was out. I told Jessica to have Grace see me. Ironically, I was at the Albuquerque Academy working with Curtis Beach, in the off-season, when Grace found me. I knew instantly that our personalities would mesh. She was very pleasant and I could not believe what she had just gone through at St. Pius. Grace was very open and contrite, and hopeful that she could finish her senior season as an athlete again. My first thought was that the St. Pius administrators had overreacted. Myself, I always lean toward forgiveness and second chances. Like life, athletics is a series of mistakes, corrections and victories. Children make them constantly and adults should be careful in their judgments; the greater harm may be in a student dropping out, missing an opportunity to learn, and recover.

But Grace had another problem. A New Mexico High School Activities Association rule stated that an athlete could not transfer from a private school to a public school, and compete, without sitting out for one year. Being as this was Grace's senior year, she had to petition for a waiver. There was a hearing and it was decided that, because Grace did not voluntarily change schools, they would allow her to compete during the second half of the season. It was not a perfect solution, but it was one she could live with.

She began to train on her own. Grace wanted desperately to finish high school as a track athlete. Even though we were rebuilding, we knew that when Grace became eligible, we could use her drive and talents tremendously. While we waited, we kept working with and developing other athletes. When she became eligible she would be welcomed with enthusiasm!

Lindsey Harper was the runner to beat. That season, she went undefeated in the 400m and the 800m. As fate would have it, she ran for Albuquerque Academy, and Grace happened to train for the same events. Our girl could run from the 100m to the 3,200m—even the hurdles. Her best shot was in the middle-distance sprint events. They were on a collision course.

I certainly believe that Grace was on a mission to show the Albuquerque sports community that she should be considered as an athlete, not a vandal. While our schools were in different classes (Academy was in 4A; La Cueva 5A), there were several opportunities before the State Meet for the two athletes to compete.

When I first started training Grace, she was as motivated as Val Boyer. No workout was too tough for her. She led the team by example.

As Grace improved, so did the team. Grace would run so hard she got "butt lock," a spasm in the rear. She would fall on the ground, roll over, and when I said, "Grace, get up and run another," she would rise, walk to the starting line and run another (much like Val Boyer). Others followed her lead, and everyone got better.

In watching the workouts and timing Grace, I knew she was going to give Lindsey Harper a good race. In mid-season, two weeks before the Academy Invitational, Grace competed in her first two relays. She ran the best times of anyone. At her second meet Grace placed first in the 400m and first on the 4 x 4 relay. People were beginning to notice her on the track.

The Invitational was a two-day meet. In the preliminaries Grace ran in a different heat from Lindsey and both made the finals. So, the following day, lined up for the 800m, all eyes were fixed on them. This was perhaps the most exciting moment of the meet. Grace had been training hard, and Lindsey was undefeated. This would be the only time they would face each other in the 800m in a high school meet. In strategizing with Grace, we told her to stay one stride behind Lindsey. We thought Grace was the faster of the two, and, if she was close at the end of the race, her natural speed would work in her favor.

It seemed like the entire Academy was gathered to watch. Grace, the student who had been kicked out of St. Pius for painting the Academy campus, now wore the blue and white of La Cueva and was racing Academy's top runner.

Certain races define your coaching career. As they lined up, neither girl could look at the other. Every high school coach in Albuquerque had their eyes on them. The great Lindsey Harper and the challenging Grace Rich toed the line.

As expected, Lindsey took the lead and held it for most of the race. Grace stayed close to her hip. With about 10m to go, Grace blasted ahead. It was the fastest time of the year. Somewhere a pin dropped in the Academy stands.

On the other side, the La Cueva section was making up for them! Later, in the open 400m, the same tactic worked, and Grace won in the last 10m. Grace faced other 5A athletes, and Lindsey other 4A athletes, but the two did not meet again. Lindsey went to the NM State Meet three weeks later and broke two State Records. Both respected each other and showed great sportsmanship. In athletics we often achieve our best when we compete against the best.

There is a post-script to this story: later, in the finals, a protest was filed claiming that Grace had been in too many events. The coaching staff at La Cueva knew this was not true. Two coaches, the Academy coach being one of them, thought that Grace ran on an additional relay. She would be disqualified and her points and gold medals would taken from her. I went to the protest committee, and after discussion and a review of the film, the protest was dropped. They had confused Grace with Megan Hoffert, another great La Cueva athlete. Grace again had to prove herself, but this time with the help of her coaches. We would not allow her to be disqualified on an inaccurate protest. Grace had a great performance that day, and we meant for her to keep it.

La Cueva had a very successful season and we were predicted to be one of the top five teams in the 5A Class in the upcoming State Meet. This was a year in which the team points would be spread out. With the great sprinter Tressi Richardson (now a senior), Cibola was the favorite. Grace Rich won the 400m and the 800m. Alex Darling placed in the hurdles. Asal Salehpoor placed in the triple jump. With one event to go, La Cueva was in third place.

In order to capture the blue, we needed to win the 4 x 4 and hope that Clovis and Eldorado each finished lower than third. And we did win the 4 x 4, but Eldorado took second and Clovis third. The final team standings were Clovis in first, Eldorado in second, and us in third, separated by just a few points. But the first-place finish in the 4 x 4 put the La Cueva Girls on a high. Grace won three gold medals that day, and was the runner-up for high-point athlete of the meet. This was one of the most competitive State Meets ever. This team finish set La Cueva up for one of the greatest track seasons ever in 2007.

In the summer of 2006, after the State Meet, I worked with Grace and Curtis Beach to attend AAU track meets with the ATC. I have always spent part of my summer coaching ATC athletes. They went to several local, state, and regional track meets, trying to qualify for the 2006 USA Youth Outdoor Track & Fields Championships at the end of June. This meet served as a selection pool for the IAFF World Youth Championships in the Czech Republic. Both Curtis and Grace dominated the smaller, local qualifying meets, but they both would have to step it up in national competition.

Curtis won the gold in the decathlon and Grace won medals in the open 800m and 400m hurdles. I have always loved seeing Albuquerque athletes do well in national competition, since my first experience with the Duke City Dashers, watching Alice Watson win the 220-yard dash at Bakersfield, California in 1970. Now I had athletes who were not even born when Alice won that title.

The Tribune did a story on Grace that summer entitled, "Track and Field-Helping Others Keep the Pace" by Vanessa Strobbe (Thursday, July 27, 2006). Vanessa was a former La Cueva track athlete. She wrote a favorable article praising both Curtis's and Grace's efforts. She and Curtis raced frequently. Lining up on the track for a repeat 300m with Grace was no picnic.

She also asked me how I liked coaching as I was getting up in age. I told her my attitude was young. In the past I have dealt with health issues but I always tried to make a comeback. Working with young people keeps my attitude young.

My expectations are high. When I stay late, and ask athletes like Grace and Curtis to do extra work, they almost always respond positively. I can put in long hours and stay late because I do not have an immediate family, and over the years, the athletes have become my family. Countless times I have asked Curtis, Grace, and others to work and practice with the young kids. And like family, they have.

LUCKY SOCKS, DANIEL, JULIA, CHAD AND CHICAGO

In the summer of 2006 Curtis went to Indianapolis to compete in the 2006 USA Junior Outdoor Track & Field Championships. This was after a great high school season, in which he won the 110m hurdles, the 300m hurdles, and the long jump at the NM State meet. Though just a freshman, he was the high-point athlete.

I was also working with Daniel Gooris, a good friend of the Beach family. When Daniel was seven, I had gone to Los Lunas and put on a high-jump seminar for Mary Lou Gooris (Daniel's mom and a local age-group track team coach). After that lesson, Mary Lou expanded her knowledge of the high jump and officiated at local meets. Later on, the family moved to the Gallup area and Daniel would compete for the ATC, where we worked in the high jump and the hurdles. He would sometimes accompany Curtis to practice. Daniel turned out to be a great decathlon athlete, like Curtis, and he became a State Champion with Cibola.

Curtis and Daniel also became great rope-jumpers and would sometimes join us at the Pit. One year they both dunked the jump-rope in the basket at the end. Daniel even did a back flip with the jump-rope. People would call me up and ask, "Coach, who *were* those jumpers you had at the Lobo game? What other sports do they do?"

I remember these boys at the Junior Men's National Championships in Indianapolis, warming up. The other competitors all asked to borrow their ropes so they could warm up the same way. We must have been doing something right. Anyone who runs track for me will learn to jump-rope; its benefits are obvious.

In an *Albuquerque Tribune* article headlined, "A Foot (Pole, Shot, discus, and Javelin) in the Nationals," Vanessa Strobbe quoted Curtis:

> "When I first started track, I had lucky socks," said Beach, 15. "I had so many different, colorful pairs with different designs for every type of event. "Last year, I had to change my socks between almost every event for the decathlon. I just couldn't do it anymore." "Right now, I'm knocking on the door of specializing in an event, and I've narrowed it down to the 400m hurdles or the decathlon to try to make it to the Olympics." Beach's dreams don't stop at the Olympics. "I want to go as far as I can possible go," Beach said. "The highest I think anyone can go is a world record, and I'm going for that." Ciccarello has been working with Beach since the fifth grade and continues to do so five times a week. Ciccarello, the La Cueva girls' track coach who works with individual athletes in the summer, says Beach's dreams are not so farfetched. "I think Curtis is the best athlete New Mexico will ever see," he said.

About this time I had gone with Curtis and his mother to an age-group competition in Baltimore, MD. While there, I invited an old friend to the meet: Dave Tucker. As we competed at Towson State University, Dave spent most of the meet watching our athletes, and he was particularly interested in Curtis. (Meanwhile, Dave and Jeana hit it off, and their friendship continues to this day.)

Talking and visiting with Dave was special. I felt like not a day had passed since I saw him last. Dave was always positive and personable. He immediately gave Curtis feedback and kudos, and shared stories of old-time athletes and the Penn. Relays. I am always amazed by the number of people I meet who are motivators. He made the Beach family his friends, and has followed Curtis in all of his recent competitions. When you are a national competitor, you make friends across the USA. These friendships often last a lifetime.

Julia Foster was a former ATC athlete now competing with the Albuquerque Academy. Her father and uncles were former students at Whittier, where Julia became one of our top role models, jumping rope with the kids and racing them on the playground. One year *The Albuquerque Journal* did a story on her accomplishments, which I taped on the wall in the gym. Over time she became known as "the girl on the wall." Only after some years of visiting did she realize the effect she had. Sandy Beach Warfield took Julia under her wing, and Julia became the top 800m and 1500m runner in New Mexico age-group competition.

One summer we went to a national meet in Chicago. Julia was one of the favorites. As she came down the back stretch in her 1500m run, she was bumped into the inside of the track, and was disqualified. She did not make it to the finals, even with the fastest time of any athlete. Sandy wrote up a protest and Julia's dad paid a $100 protest charge, but it was disallowed. This was a heart-breaker, but she used the experience as motivation. She sent me a card one day:

Dear Coach,

Thank you so much for all your help and support over the years. I've really enjoyed helping out at Whittier and with the jump-rope team. It has helped me become a better person as well. I'll really miss helping out and seeing you at meets next year! Best of luck for the Bears next year and I'll keep in touch. You've made a great impact on me and I'll always appreciate that. The girl on the wall will visit as much as she can!

Always,
Julia Foster

Julia is a student and running track and cross country at Stanford University now. Her academics are superior, and she is part of a winning track program.

That same summer I was working with Chad Clark, a hurdler from La Cueva. Chad had just taken up hurdling and was learning quickly. We took him to Chicago to run against the big boys. This was an eye-opener; he was still learning and a bit intimidated. Though he came up short of the finals, he ran his best time ever, and this was a turning point for him. We paired him with Curtis, and he learned a lot that summer.

The summer club meets are different from the high school scene. Competition is out of state, and athletes must outperform themselves. We encourage them to take in some local culture. Over the years, our group had many unforgettable experiences in places like Los Angeles, Miami, Phoenix, Baltimore, Denver, St. Louis, Lincoln, Eugene, El Paso, and Provo. When athletes participate in school-affiliated meets, they seldom leave the state, as there are rules which limit out-of-state-competition, which the private clubs are not subject to. The excitement of traveling to a new city is a huge part of being a club member.

That summer in Chicago we had quite the experience. Our group was staying at a hotel 30 miles west of downtown. About 11:00 p.m., the coaches decided to turn in after a night of pizza, riding a tour boat on Lake Michigan, and other tourism. Sandy Beach Warfield was driving while I navigated from the passenger side. In the back seat, and being very quiet were Chad Clark, Julia Foster, and Will Romano, another ATC athlete. As we drove out of downtown, it was a rainy, dark summer night, and we could hardly see the road. We made a wrong turn and headed for South Chicago.

Following in another car were Karen and Leonard Foster, Julia's parents. I had to use the rest room. I asked Sandy to stop by an empty toll booth. It was pitch black. I jumped the rail and relieved myself behind a big box, with no alternative. It was surreal. We did not know where we were; other cars were parked on the side of the road; people were walking around; no street lights were working.

Before we knew it, it was 2:00 a.m.. All those bad stories of South Chicago came to mind. We were tired, cold, scared, and lost. We stopped at a gas station in a questionable neighborhood to ask for directions. The station's lights were off, and we saw only several cars with men in them, smoking and drinking. Both cars stopped and we rolled down our windows to ask for directions. Leonard Foster, a fast-talking lawyer, exited his car and began a conversation with the men in the darkened car. Leonard had another special talent: street language.

He joked with them and hopped back in his car. A couple of turns, over a few hills, and through an alleyway, and we were back on the freeway. We were back at the hotel, at 3:00 a.m.. Par for the course.

When I first started coaching track and field, every road trip was a big deal for me also. Even after 40 years, I still find out-of-town trips challenging and rewarding. The journey is more important than the destination, and leading young people to compete in athletics is ongoing. One never knows what the next trip will bring.

2007: A SPECIAL YEAR

Everything in the 2007 La Cueva girls track season seemed to come together. They went undefeated and took top honors at the New Mexico State High School Championships. This is rare; all teams have their share of injuries, bad luck, sickness, absentee members, or competition against other teams that have a great day. I knew the previous year we had trained one of the best teams ever in New Mexico, but I did not realize it was only setting us up for a remarkable 2007.

To have a great track season, a strong pre-season workout schedule is crucial. Not all students will work out August–December for a competition that begins in March. We encourage all athletes to do this; but, because of other commitments, such as school work, and social engagements, I have found only a few athletes who will accept the challenge. For those who make that commitment, the rewards are tremendous. In the fall of 2006 I received that commitment from three motivated athletes. Curtis Beach, Asal Salehpoor, and Alex Darling were ready to train the extra mile. These three athletes showed up at the track in the off-season to prepare. We met three days per week, for one hour.

Asal did sprint pickup workouts as her base. Curtis and Alex did hurdle drills. As I watched them work on their techniques, I knew that they were going to be the best hurdlers in New Mexico. They challenged each other each practice. I was particularly fond of one drill: I would start Curtis 20m behind Alex, and tell him to catch up before they reached the fifth hurdle. She could not see him as he chased her down the track. Later, Alex would tell me, "Coach, I could hear his breathing! He sounded like a locomotive chasing me!" Curtis came close, but never caught her. And both improved tremendously.

Meanwhile, Asal's pickups were getting faster and stronger. She also ran up hills and did short sprint ladders—a distance-varied series of short sprints. I would invite Coach Medley out one day a week to help her with triple jump techniques. Asal had always had shin sprints, which limited her practice time during the regular season. Because of this pre-season work, she had eliminated them.

Alex and Asal, now returning seniors, were ready to lead the team. They didn't boss their teammates, instead leading by example through hard and complex workouts. All coaches at all levels look for team leaders. It does not matter if you are a professional or an elementary PE teacher; you need the help of motivated people. The La Cueva Girls' Track and Field Team was lucky to have them.

The pole vault was a key event with seniors Michaela Ross, Megan Economedes, and a couple of up-and-coming vaulters in Lauren Finch and Samantha Bapty. Our hurdlers were strong with Christine Ostler, Amy Buffett, and Christy Barela. Janel Clark, who had been a potential strong hurdler, tore her cruciate ligament and missed the season. Laura Lavezo, Jessica Knewitz, and Carly Porter would lead our distance runners. Maddie McPeek, Bridget Wilding, Nicole Wessendorf, and Lauren Riley would help our relays throughout the season. Sofie Schunk, a freshman, would turn out to be a key runner in the 800m.

Our coaching was solid, and we tried to develop athletes for all events. This year we added coaches Chris Valencia (throwing), and Nick Martinez (distance). At La Cueva I was blessed with assistant coaches who wanted to work together to help the athletes achieve.

The La Cueva girls completely dominated the meets, scoring totals that sometimes doubled their closest competitors'. At the District Meet we scored 360 points, which is unheard-of in track and field. At the New Mexico State Meet, we finished with a score 30 points higher than Clovis, the runner-up.

Alex Darling became the state High-Point Athlete, with Asal Salehpoor trailing her. Alex accounted for 27.5 points and Asal had 18.5 for a total of 46, of the 87.5 points scored. Alex won the 100m hurdles, 400m dash, 300m hurdles, took third in the long jump, and ran the last leg of the winning 4 x 4 relay. Asal won the triple jump (missing the NM State Record by one inch), was third in the 100m dash, was second in the long jump, and ran on the third place 4 x 2 relay. Sofie Schunk, a freshman, was second in the 800m and ran on the gold medal-winning 4 x 4 relay. Also on that important relay were Christine Ostler and Lauren Riley. In the prelims Jessica Knewitz helped our team qualify for the finals. Michaela Ross finished second in the pole vault. This was a complete team effort.

At one point Alex Darling had to complete an extremely hard back-to-back competition. The finals of the 400m and the 300m hurdles were only 10 minutes apart. Alex won gold in both events. Doug Dorame, the Albuquerque High girls' track coach, said, "I have never seen a kid that tough… That double is one of the hardest tasks in track and field."

We also received many post-season awards. Alex Darling was selected as the New Mexico Gatorade Track Athlete of the Year. At the Albuquerque/NM Sports Hall of Fame banquet, the La Cueva Girls' Track and Field Team won several awards. Alex Darling was selected the Female Athlete of the Year, the team was selected Team of the Year, and, I was selected Coach of the Year.

A team had never been so recognized by the Albuquerque Sports Hall Of Fame. As an added honor, Curtis Beach was recognized as the Male Athlete of the Year. He had won five gold medals and scored 35 points to lead his team (Albuquerque Academy) to a New Mexico Team State Championship. He set State Records in the hurdles.

To see both Alex and Curtis as high point champions, as well as hurdle State Champions, was one of the highlights of the New Mexico State Championships. It brought to mind the pre-season afternoons they raced each other. Our labor was recognized for the entire state to see. Susan Vigil MacEachen was also inducted into the New Mexico Hall of Fame that night. Susie had been a Duke City Dasher when I was just starting out as an age-group coach. She had run on relays with Alice Watson as a 12–13-year-old in age-group track meets. I was proud to be part of her career. Later on, her daughter, Sara Belger, ran for me at Sandia. I was a proud teacher and coach, sitting beside the podium, with the finest athletes and coaches in New Mexico.

STUDENT-TEACHERS: SPREADING THE LOVE!

There was nothing more important in my career than being a mentor to student-teachers. If I could reach one teacher with my skills and techniques, and they in turn could pass those principles to their students, and I would have exponentially multiplied my effect. These young teachers picked my brain (and of course, I picked theirs). When they had become teachers themselves, they would contact me to share ideas.

In 1972 I had my first student-teacher assigned to me by Fred Hinger: Mel Lucero—now retired. Since then, I estimate with both junior and senior blocks, I have hosted more than 200 UNM student-teachers. After, Mr. Hinger I worked with John Gustafson and Gloria Napper Owen. There were also many graduate assistants who were part of the student-teaching experience at UNM. They moved on to other universities or went back to their home state to become involved with public education. They were all professional in their approach and contributed to a great program at UNM.

Because of that program, I have connected with thousands of New Mexico students who have passed on the love of movement and fitness. I am fortunate and proud to have worked with these young educators, who I now call associates and friends. Elementary PE in New Mexico has a bright future. Here are a few stories about some of them:

In 1972 a young Glenn Lucero came to Whittier. The students loved him and we established an enduring friendship. He went on to teach and coach at Highland, including their Girls' Track Team in 1980—barely edging out my Sandia team (by three points) for the State Championship.

Then there was Matt Henry, who came to Whittier in the early '70s. He had a great experience and went to West Mesa to teach PE and coach boys' track and field. Matt married Lisa Chivario when I was coaching at Sandia, one of my assistant coaches. I delightfully watched his family grow; his three boys, who were very young when Lisa was at Sandia, grew up to coach track, themselves.

Matt told me years later, "Ciccarello, when I was a beginning student at UNM, I was watching you coach those age-group kids (the majority of them African-American) from the athletic complex, overlooking UNM soccer fields, and I thought, I would like to work with him someday." Over the years we kept in contact and shared ideas. If Matt had not been at La Cueva in 1999, I don't think I would have started over.

Then, 30+ years after retiring from coaching at UNM, Matt accepted a job as an elementary PE teacher. One Saturday in 2012 Matt told me, "The elementary level is where it's at. Most people don't know the impact elementary physical education teachers have on young students."

Meanwhile, Lisa Henry has been teaching at Eldorado for over 20 years. She too has had a huge impact on students in Albuquerque. Lisa has not only been one of the best female track athletes ever in New Mexico, she has been a head track coach at Cibola, an assistant at Sandia, serves as an APS track official, computes and organizes track results, is married to one of New Mexico's finest coaches, and is the mother of three up-and-coming track coaches. The Henry family is certainly a prominent educational resource for New Mexico students.

Mel Lucero (no relation to Glenn) was at Whittier in 1974, and went on to a career at East San José Elementary. Mel taught for 27 years. I find it amazing how many of my student-teachers have retired, while I continue to teach. (Slackers!) Mel was a great golfer, and there were many days he, Lee Hays, and I would play golf after teaching. Today Mel and I share a barber. When we meet in the shop, we talk about the good old days and I always kid that he retired too soon. I did a jump-rope show at his former school in 2011 and saw a plaque with his name on the wall in the gym.

Dave Fleming was another Whittier student-teacher in the early '70s. After a position in APS, he started a jump-rope program at Apache Elementary. They performed at many elementary schools, and Manzano basketball games. Many years later, Dave became an APS track official at Wilson Stadium, and I always visited while he judged relay zones. We would talk about PE and the jump-rope teams. He never forgot his time at Whittier. Now retired, Dave still officiates meets.

Identical twin brothers Derrick and Dave Irion arrived at Whittier in the mid-'70s. (We had a lot of fun with that: the kids never knew which Irion was teaching them!) They went on to teach in southern New Mexico. Years later Derrick became a PE administrator in Santa Fe and he always tried to help Whittier improve. I believe it was because of his influence that we were allocated an extra PE teacher, paid for by the state, in 2007.

Norm Cacy did his student-teaching at Whittier in the early '80s. He was a Lobo basketball player and the students were taken with his height and fame. Imagine a 6'7" student-teacher working with a five-year-old student. Young athletes need to realize that they have a huge impact on little kids. Their size alone makes them statuesque in the eyes of a five- or six-year-old.

Also in the early '80s, young Kathy Guerin came to Whittier. Kathy was a former Manzano track athlete and ran with Val Boyer. Kathy ran on the 400m relay. She loved to race the students, and was also interested in gymnastics and loved to help supervise our program at recess. It was always gratifying when a former athlete came and learned to work with young people, paying it forward.

Kevin Stark was a Lobo football player who student-taught at Whittier in the mid-'80s. Kevin was a gentle and soft-spoken offensive lineman, almost 300 lbs. The kids did anything he asked of them.

In the early '90s, when I was first starting my jump-rope team at Whittier, we had a young lady do her student-teaching at Whittier by the name of Christine Castillo. She graduated and went on to become an adaptive physical educator at Manzano. Years later, a young student at Bandelier named Ciarra, who lived with Chris, became one of our best rope-skippers ever. Ciarra was very creative, and learned to do many complex combinations. Chris also became very involved with the Special

Olympics, and worked as a long-jump official at APS meets. She always knew how the La Cueva athletes were doing. We have stayed in touch.

Aaron O'Campo, a UNM football player, originally from Socorro, NM, student-taught at Whittier in the mid-90s. He taught the kids many useful skills in touch-football. He was most known for doing his "kick-up celebration strut" after scoring a touchdown. The kids would put a hand behind their head and kick straight-legged in front of them all over the gym. Aaron accepted a position at Manzano as a PE teacher and the head football coach. He has developed many outstanding football teams and competed for many NM State Championships. He now teaches and coaches at Centennial, a new high school in Las Cruces, NM.

Santiago Stockton was a first-grader of mine from the '90s. His mother Joline taught third grade at Whittier. Santi was a great soccer player and PE student. He went on to play for Highland, attended UNM, and came *back* to Whittier for his student-teaching. This was quite the experience for me. Santi was not only very professional, but on a *mission* to learn to teach Phys. Ed.. Being young, he could play soccer with the kids and demonstrate skills my age would no longer permit. They loved him. Maybe his dad had something to do with it, too; he had also attended UNM while I was there, and became an adaptive PE teacher.

Santi now teaches PE at Edmund Gonzales Elementary, and frequently calls. We meet for breakfast, talk new ideas, and he updates me on his classes. Having Santi as a student, student-teacher, and an associate PE teacher is a unique relationship not many educators get to experience, and his great attitude made him a joy to have around, both times.

Jamie Williams came to Whittier from UNM for his junior student-teaching block, then returned for his senior block. Jamie was from the Seattle area and had played high school and college basketball. Jamie and I hit it off right away. In the summer after his senior year we helped move my brother Frank back to New York City. Jamie and I drove the trailer—and played basketball in every state from New Mexico to New York. Now at MacArthur Elementary, he always checked in. We met for breakfast with several other elementary PE teachers, including Santi Stockton, to share ideas.

In 2001, Jamie and I travelled to Las Cruces for the NM Association of Health Physical Education Recreation & Dance Convention. This was a special weekend. Jamie was receiving the Elementary Physical Education Teacher of The Year award, and I the Professional Career Achievement Award. Though 30 years apart, our goal is the same.

Corina Bonilla did her student-teaching at Whittier in the late '90s. Her sister Rose student-taught at Bandelier while I was there. Both girls were from El Paso, and loved working with kids from the Southeast Heights. Corina went on to accept a position at Highland, teaching PE, and became the girls' track coach. As the head track coach, naturally Corina had a rivalry to keep up with La Cueva. Our relationship was always one of respect. Corina was particularly adept at working with low-income children. The bond that we developed during her student-teaching years remained excellent and we always exchanged ideas. In fact, some of my Whittier PE students found their way onto her track team.

Cameron Clark taught under me at Whittier in the early 2000s. Amazingly, his grandmother, Mrs. Dora Clark, was my first principal at Whittier, and his father, Blaine, was the boys' track coach at Sandia when I coached the girls there. Cameron was a very good runner and soccer player. When he taught my class the kids would chase him—as he ran backwards. He could do this with or without a ball at his feet. Kids are completely motivated when a young person can physically challenge them in a drill. Cameron could run, jump, dribble a ball, and exercise at a difficult level. Students would accept the challenge and try to stay with him. He went on to teach PE and coach at a high school.

Greg Gonzales also came to Whittier in the early 2000s. He had played basketball at UNM, and completed his junior block in PE with Stan Chavez at Osuna Elementary. Greg, Stan and I spent numerous hours discussing PE philosophy on weekends. Greg was a master at recording music, which we used in our classes, and he was current with it, which lead me to incorporate still more of it.

Greg got married, moved to Colorado Springs to work as a middle school PE teacher and basketball coach, and has since moved back to Albuquerque. Now he is teaching PE at Reginald Chavez Elementary School. He recently applied for a position at Jefferson Middle School, where I did *my* student-teaching 45 years ago.

Justin Sells was a great UNM soccer player. He also played professionally in St. Louis. When he came to Whittier in the late '90s, we were beginning a soccer unit. You can imagine how excited the kids were just to see Justin control the ball. He could do rainbow (over his head) and scissor kicks (between his legs). My favorite was an instep kick in the gym: he would line the ball up at the half line, center court, and kick as hard as he could. When the ball hit the mat on the wall under the basket it sounded like a cannon. The students were mesmerized. Coach Sells is now coaching soccer at the high school level.

Shortly after Justin came Chris Serino. He was a short soccer player. Chris would dribble all over the gym, in and out of orange cones, with full control. His tricks and juggling skills were amazing. Chris taught students that an athlete didn't have to be big to be great. He is now teaching elementary PE.

Jeremy Dunham, whose family came to Albuquerque from Cuba, was a student-teacher in the early 2000s. Bilingual relatable, Jeremy was also a successful Highland assistant boys' track coach. We taught track and field and many running activities. He was always in control, even when the kids were misbehaving. Though soft-spoken, he had a way to calm them down. Jeremy is now teaching at Zia Elementary, only two miles from Whittier. (Kids often move from Whittier to Zia.) Jeremy and I always share stories.

Norbert Gabaldon came to Whittier in 2005. When he did his student-teaching I was at both Whittier and Bandelier—and so was he! He was a former Highland and UNM football player, and very high-energy. He had punted for the Lobos, and at both Whittier and Bandelier we had a football unit. At Whittier, he would kick the ball over the gym roof, and the kids would be on the other side of the building waiting to catch it. They could hear the sound of his foot against the ball and knew it was coming their way. This was a 50-yard punt; to an elementary kid, I would imagine, those kicked footballs were coming from Heaven!

Norbert was also a creative personality. He liked to dance, play, act, and teach music. His biggest music contribution was Hip Hop and body movement. One day at Whittier, he put the kids to sleep with yoga and quiet music, talking in a quiet voice with the lights down low. When the classroom teacher came to pick them up, she remarked, "Coach, can you do this for me every day?"

I also got to know Norbert on the track. He coached the jumping events at Cibola and at Volcano Vista. He would always kid me about my La Cueva girls' team. I think that deep inside he would have liked to coach with me at La Cueva.

He had a lesson in which he set up mats on their ends and made a closed-tunnel maze. As the kids entered the gym, they had to navigate from the front door to the coach's office. He eventually accepted a high school position.

Justin Pillmore also did his student-teaching at both Whittier and Bandelier. He loved the more than 100 magic tricks Chris Jarvis and I would do, and he tried many new ones each Monday. In one, his shoelace appeared to be untied, and he would shake his leg, and the lace would tie itself into a bow. Justin also loved our jump-rope team and wanted to learn how to do the tricks himself. He eventually accepted a job at an elementary school in Pennsylvania, where he started a jump-rope team. He sends me pictures of his team performing at shows.

In the summer he puts on a clinic for five- to 13-year-olds. This summer camp for young jumpers has received much acclaim and has seen many views on YouTube, and Facebook. Justin was one of those overachieving student-teachers who elevated his game as he went into teaching.

Brian Stinnet followed Justin and he too loved magic tricks for motivating children. He was a very good basketball player and demonstrated many tricks. Brian took a basketball position at Sandia and taught elementary PE at Tommisita Elementary. His career in APS is just beginning.

Gavin Ferguson graduated from Valley High 40 years after me. He and I hit it off immediately, and he had a lot of fun at Whittier. He was a great baseball player and taught the kids many throwing and catching skills. He went on to teach PE at Grant Middle School.

Josh Perrault, also split between Bandelier and Whittier, introduced a new dance to our school. The "Cupid Shuffle" became one of our favorites, and after a while, I learned it, too. Kids love any kind of line dancing, and with a modern beat it becomes even more exciting for them. Josh went to Baltimore to teach, and has returned to teach elementary PE back in Albuquerque.

Oscar Calderon did his time at Whittier in the spring of 2011. Oscar was also a bilingual student, and could easily relate to our students. He presented *Dance, Dance,*

Revolution to the Whittier kids. This was another big hit—moving to music and reacting to on-screen images. Oscar was soft-spoken and easy-going. He loved to work with the jump-rope kids. He told me he wanted to start a jump-rope team wherever he taught. He has accepted a job at East San José Elementary, where, indeed, he is starting a team. The Whittier/Bandelier jump-rope team visited and did a show.

My former student-teachers instruct their students in similar activities as the PE classes we teach at Whittier/Bandelier. They have learned valuable lessons to help them become teachers. The trickle-down of positivity has always been my proudest achievement.

In February of 2012, UNM's supervisor of PE student-teachers, Dr. Gloria Napper Owen, asked if she could bring a group of aspiring physical educators to observe at Whittier. We are very proud of our PE classes and accepted this as an honor. Our five- and six-year-olds were excited when 25 UNM students walked into our gym. At the time we were working on a dance and rhythms unit, with some basketball skills. The 21–25-year-olds were enthralled to see these youngsters participate in physical and musical activity. Our kids were proud, and UNM students were learning that elementary children can do more than these young teachers expected.

In March, 2012, I received a letter from Gloria Napper Owen. This was their response to a great presentation by a group of five- and six-year-old students:

Dear Mr. Ciccarello, and Whittier Students,

The students in my Elementary Rhythms class would like to thank you for allowing us to visit you on February 23, 2012. You were awesome! We loved your creative rope, hoop, and ribbon routines! We learned that elementary students can be very skilled when they practice what they love. This was a moment of reflection for our students and will help prepare them for the future. Keep having lots of fun!

Dr. Napper Owen & Students of UNM

RESTORATION

Over the years it has become clear to me I do not control my destiny. In 2008 I was called into the office at Whittier. The principal, Cindy Bazner, informed me that I would no longer be working at Bandelier. There was to be a cut, and I would teach at Whittier full-time again. It was not my choice. I would miss the daily contact with the Bandelier students.

Whittier faced a different set of challenges. The students were on a 100%-free lunch program. Transportation to after-school performances was hard for Whittier students. For most of my career I have quietly transported students to extracurricular activities, when necessary, but with new APS liabilities and procedures, I had to scale back my efforts. I had been insisting that schools provide us a bus during the school day; no bus, no show. But when we had after-school hours we still had to rely on parent transportation, and Whittier parents could not always participate. Whittier kids missed many shows, simply because of money.

I do empathize with Whittier students' daily struggles. Most of the time, parents of kids in a low-income area do not have a higher education themselves, and often do not value the commitment they and their child must make to education, or work so much they cannot be on-hand to help. Low-income parents hope that the school alone will take care of their children's education. They know that an education will help, but do not realize it is not the complete picture.

My dad dropped out of school in the fifth grade and my mom never finished the ninth grade. Neither of my parents read to me or helped with homework. In all my years of athletics my parents never attended one game; I did not even know that was unusual. Now that I have taught and coached, I see parent involvement as paramount to a student's success. Most middle- and upper-class parents support their kids through their educational years, and those students have a greater chance to succeed for the rest of their lives.

In the last few years, I have only seen one function that the Whittier parents consistently attend: the cultural fair. The classroom teacher picks a theme, such as a country, and the kids present a small play about that country's cultural history. Their families invariably support with a huge turnout. This program's success at Whittier highlights the need to invite parents more into everyday learning.

As 2008 progressed, I was told that Whittier was adding another PE teacher. I had thought there was a budget cut and our program would be dropped. Instead, the state legislative branch had decided to increase PE at low-income schools in an effort to raise test scores. Finally, someone upstairs was listening!

In just a year, I was cut from Bandelier, had gained an extra teacher at Whittier, *and* we were given a $32,000 budget for equipment and supplies. This was more supply money than I had ever been allocated. Though the principal picked the new teacher, I was given input in the selection process. Mrs. Bazner interviewed several candidates; I was present at each interview. Meredith Vargas was selected; she was in the early stages of her career while I was entering the latter of mine.

Coach Vargas and I immediately decided to share the gym and new supplies, and doubled students' activity time. Being as I was the older teacher, we agreed that Meredith would teach on the playground and I would use the gym, though we would team-teach in the gym as often as possible. I would take the lead, with a nod to my experience and familiarity with the students. There were times when I would teach a double-class while Coach Vargas monitored and made sure the students were listening.

Coach Vargas would be a prime role model for the female students. This turned out to be a good fit for both of us. The students now had male and female teachers, extra class time, and because of the supply money, more activity choices. Coach Vargas also embraced jump-rope. She had the strongest hands I have ever seen. When I needed help fixing PE equipment, she took care of it. In return, I would make sure the students were cooperative and listening. She told me when she was growing up in Taos, NM, she did many physical chores around the house. She was always working outside, fixing plumbing, and learning about cars. Her dad taught her how to survive in this world with her own hands and wits. Our students benefited through our cooperation.

Meredith was married and had two daughters in elementary and middle school. At times she would bring them to Whittier for the day. Jacquelyn and Jamie were bright, motivated students, and were happy to role model. Coach Vargas was also coaching at Taft middle school basketball and volleyball. She showed an interest in track and field. Since she had been involved in high school track in Taos, I asked her to join me at La Cueva. She came aboard as an assistant coach in the throwing events, and became an important contributor to the program. Our daily contact at Whittier made it easy to plan our workout schedule at La Cueva, and we covered for each other at both schools.

2008 was supposed to be a rebuilding team; we had just graduated Alex Darling and Asal Salehpoor, the number-one and -two high-scoring athletes in the state. Not many high schools had girls who worked for the team like Alex and Asal. We would miss them immensely. We expected a good team, but we focused on developing new athletes.

In 2008 some new names rose to the top. Amy Buffett and Christine Ostler dominated the hurdles. Laura Lavezo, Jessica Knewitz, Megan Quimby, Jordan Grace, and Carly Porter were our best in the distance events. Bridget Wilding, Becca Denny, Lauren Riley, Nichole Wessendorf, and Nicki Ingram were our sprinters. Sofie Schunk was back for the 800m and relays. Michaela Ross, Lauren Fitch, and Samantha Bapty were outstanding pole-vaulters and ranked in the top ten. Rachel Ney was an up-and-coming discus thrower. Aubrey Diz and Alyssa Pfeiffer were good jumpers, and outstanding javelin-throwers. This group won the District 2 5A track meet, and finished fourth at the State Meet, one point shy of third. Our athletes were learning as they ran. At the state meet we also won the 4 x 4 relay, which was a most exciting finish to the year for this team.

That summer at the National Association of High School Coaches Banquet in Colorado Springs, I was the runner-up for the 2008 National Coach of the Year award. I was proud of having Alex Darling and Grace Rich attend and present a jump-rope clinic to the National Association of Coaches. I am blessed to have so many great athletes in my life who share my love of fitness, and track and field.

In 2009 we returned with many of the above and added Mickey Brown, Kaylin Martin, Christina Clark, Nicole Habbit, Caitie Petrofes, Cory Chavez, and Mariah Rast. Aubrey Herrera, a senior and first-year track athlete, turned out to be our team-player of the year. She was a sprinter who had good speed and helped the 4 x 1 and the 4 x 4 relay teams. Not a day went by that Aubrey did not thank me for the workout. In today's world, you will seldom meet someone who, sweating and heart pounding after a hard workout, would tell the coach that she appreciates his hard work.

Aubrey had not only the respect of the coaching staff but of her teammates. She was the first to congratulate someone who did well. Coaches do teach athletes to give a winning effort, but they are not there *only* to win. In the big picture, most coaches teach teamwork, caring, support. When we meet students who show respect to others and the sport, are great learners, give their best at practice and compete to their fullest, we have accomplished our mission. Though she never reached the top of the podium, she helped our team immeasurably.

As we rebuilt in 2009 we again had a great team. I feel blessed coaching at La Cueva, and as the years flew past, I became more attached to the athletes and students there. Athletes were beginning to accept the hard work my program demanded, and gave my coaching staff their confidence. Ken Medley and Sandy Beach have been with me the longest. It amuses me that we Valley graduates came together to lead this La Cueva girls' team.

We won most of our meets in 2009. At the City Meet we placed third. The District 2 5A track meet was a battle with Albuquerque High, but we prevailed and won our 15th straight District Meet. At the New Mexico State Championships, we placed in the top four. One of my fellow coaches at Alamogordo High was Doc Helm. His team received the third place trophy and finished one point ahead of us. He was so excited to have his team on the podium, he looked at me and said, "Ciccarello, you have had your share of time up there, and we are proud to finish in front of La Cueva. Thank you for the opportunity to compete against you." Doc always had a good attitude.

Our team slogan that year was, "If you can dream it, you can do it." Doc Helm and his Alamogordo girls team had a similar favorite: "It's about having a dream, and it begins with the team running towards personal and team success." Though hundreds of miles separated us, our philosophies were very close, and in competition we were as close as you can get. I respected Doc's program and his team's strong finish.

The La Cueva girls had again won the 4 x 4 relay and finished the season on an upswing. It is always nice to win the 4 x 4 relay; it is the last event of the State Meet. If you win that event, it fires the athletes up for the following year.

Another great team performed in 2010, with most of our athletes returning. Highland was having a great year, their sprinters and jumpers dominating most of the season. The coaching staff at La Cueva was developing many athletes in many events to counter Highland's speed. We have always developed the team around the 400m runner. When you have middle-distance runners you can cover the 400m, 800m, 300m hurdles, 4 x 2, 4 x 4 and the Medley Relay.

Meanwhile, we had been counting on Aubrey Diz to score big in the jumps and javelin. In an early meet, she blew her knee out and we lost her for the season. Likewise, Rachel Ney, our top discus thrower, was injured in competition at District. Carly Browning and Maggie Sabik stepped up for our relays.

The 2010 New Mexico State Meet was another exciting championship. Though Highland was the favorite, we were very close. We made one major mistake.

All coaches hate the sound of the relay baton hitting the track. We had counted on third in the 4 x 2 to put us over the top for the team score. We did win the 4 x 4 and the Medley Relay, Sofie Schunk, Mickey Brown, Maggie Sabik, Kaylin Martin, and Carly Browning all running great splits for the team.

We placed second, and it was a big pill to swallow. The coaching staff had planned on inching out Highland. It did not happen! We congratulated Highland and accepted second place. The Highland coaching staff and athletes were crying with joy. Corina Bonilla, my former student-teacher at Whittier, was a co-Head Coach at Highland. I gave her a hug. Sean Armstrong, also a co-Head Coach, was beside himself with happiness. Tears of joy were on his cheeks.

I know the feeling, and it is deeply gratifying. It had been 30 years since Highland had won a Girls' State Championship, and it was their turn.

My philosophy has always been to love the sport. It helps to take the good with the bad. Yesterday is gone, today is now, and tomorrow is a promise. You pick yourself up, you get back to work. As the track season ended in 2010 we celebrated our accomplishments and moved forward.

Back at Whittier, Coach Vargas and I kept recruiting new students to learn jump-rope. Mickayla, Christina, and Marissa were three promising lower-grade students that who worked hard at it. Jessie, the supervisor of the Whittier Recreational Center after-school program, would support the team and always excuse kids to attend a show. (It didn't hurt that she had a granddaughter on the team.) Students were moving, transferring in and out, and it was hard to keep a consistent group of jumpers. Bandelier, at least, had no such attrition.

I worked with kids at La Cueva after school for one hour, three days a week. This is a great time to teach technique-work, such as in hurdling. At the end of the school year in 2010, and into the summer we were prepping for 2011. I believe in off-season work for everyone—teachers included.

SURPRISE!

Never in my wildest imagination could I have predicted it. After 42 years, I was thinking about retirement—maybe even going fishing. Every day people would ask me, "Coach, when are you getting out?" They thought I was working for nothing. People would send me copies of the retirement pay scale and suggest I give myself a raise. Even Ken Medley, who is now retired 15 years, would tell me, "Keep feeding my retirement fund!" In the last couple of years the ERA fund had lost seven billion dollars. People like me, still working, were helping to rebuild it.

I thought it could not have been more obvious that I wasn't in education for the money. I wanted to be the best teacher and coach I could. My bills are always paid on time. I have a nice house, car, health benefits, and take vacations. I have two dogs, UNM Lobo basketball season tickets, more clothes than I need, a nice health club membership, and I visit with friends to share my life. I do not have an immediate family, but I do have my brothers; Frank lives in Florida and Rich lives in Albuquerque. "My wealth is my health," as the saying goes. I work out, eat well, stay active with others, try to be productive, and live a healthy lifestyle.

New Mexico students are my extended family. When you have taught 65,000 students, your life goes in another direction. I never imagined I would be one of the oldest in the business. My first year at Whittier I was the youngest in the lounge. Today, at 70, with arthritis and a bad back, I cannot play golf or hike, nor do the things retirees do. But I have an immense amount of experience in education I draw upon to be productive and help others. So when other people tell me, "When are you going to retire?" I answer, "When that day comes, I will know."

In the summer of 2011 Cal Guymon said he was going to nominate me for the New Mexico Sports Hall of Fame. I gave him some written material on things I had done, and forgot about it. After all, while I have been a good athlete, I certainly was not a star, and had no national athletic experience. I *coached* gifted young people to the podium. Cal assured me the nomination was not for my own athletic accomplishments, but for my contributions to education.

In the fall I concentrated on the Whittier/Bandelier jump-rope team. It is also the time when I can give individual attention to track athletes and work on special skills. Our jump-rope team was developing new athletes and performing across the state. We held clinics at Sandia and Pojoaque Pueblos, and performed in Santa Fe. At the New Mexico State Fair we performed on the main stage. We went to Los Lunas, and had a special trip to Los Alamos to teach jump-rope to their Cross Country team, led by Ron and Kathy Hipwood. A member of that team was the daughter of Teddie Sue Hogsett, a former Sandia track athlete. It was a great moment to have both mom and daughter join me on the gym floor.

We went to Wilson Middle School and the Pit for a basketball half time show, and did a UNM soccer halftime show, where UNM Mens' Soccer coach Jeremy Fishbein, was very proud to see his two daughters, Alisa and Gabriela, perform for the crowd. Jeremy has become a very good friend over the years. His daughters are excellent jump-rope athletes, which combined with their other gifts I'm sure will give them a leg-up in any sport they choose. We are proud that their careers started with jump-rope. The jump-rope team was improving with each trip we took.

At La Cueva, I spent some time with Kaylin Martin, Christina Clark, and Stephanie Brener, teaching hurdle skills. Cory Chavez and Mariah Rast worked on sprints.

We were certainly preparing for the coming season. I encouraged the athletes to lift weights and run on their own.

In late November Cal called. He asked if I had anything to do in the first week of March. I said, sure, the track season starts. He said, "No, I don't mean on Saturday." He then asked, "Have you got a tux?" Well, I have known Gary and Jan at Mr. Tux for almost 20 years, and I thought Cal wanted a deal. Nope! "You will need a tux when you sit at the head table at the Hall of Fame banquet."

Something was up.

"Chic, you were just voted into the Albuquerque/New Mexico Sports Hall of Fame."

I was speechless as I tried to comprehend what he had just said.

For many years I have gone to and followed the Hall of Fame and thought it was the greatest honor a person in athletics could receive. Now I was about to become a member of that distinguished group. Rocky Long, the former UNM football coach, and Curtis Williams, the former Gallup cross country coach were to be inducted the same night; I was to share the same podium with two gentlemen I had admired and followed closely for nearly 50 years. Three of my former athletes were already in the Hall of Fame: Val Boyer, Susie Vigil and Sally Marquez. I had attended at all three of those ceremonies. They were special affairs.

I particularly remember the night that Val was inducted, as I introduced her. The room was filled with former track athletes. It was a thrill to speak on her behalf. Since that night, there have been changes made in the format of the awards program. The Hall of Fame committee now uses a film clip for introductions.

As I invited friends and colleagues to the banquet, I came face-to-face with all of the loyalties I had built. Almost all of my ATC athletes wanted to share this evening with me. Not one person thought $40 too much to pay to come see their old coach inducted. Athletes from Manzano, Sandia, Highland, La Cueva, and former students from Whittier were going to come. When I told Val, she screamed.

All of my assistant coaches were going to come. My brothers Frank and Richard were coming. Cousins Jack, Jean, George, and Joy were coming. Nephew Anthony was to be there. Most of my former student-teachers were coming. Many friends, such as Stan Chavez, Joy Wofford, Roger and Cheryl Flaherty, Tom and Jackie Tice, Lee Hayes and Patty Taylor, Lloyd McPeters, Edgar Briggs, Earl Lyon, Dick Gallegos, Clarence Brooks, Mike Gallegos, Steve Clapper, Carl Leppleman, Joe Behrend, Marshall Bear, Kris Gracy, Chris and Melissa Jarvis, Meredith Vargas and her family were coming.

My former high school principal Earnest Stapleton and former Sandia principal Richard Romero committed. Cindy Bazner, the principal at Whittier and her secretary Linda Aragon were also coming, beside assistant principal Annitra Atler. The Hall of Fame committee informed me there would be over 250 people there—to support me. They said it was the biggest turnout of all time. *Oh, my gosh,* I thought, *I have to give a speech. How can I credit so many people?*

From early December to March, I worked out details out for the big night. I had to visit Gary and Jan for a tux, write a speech, interview with an *Albuquerque Journal* sports reporter, take care of tickets, film my introduction interview, and have a photo taken for the program and honor wall.

I took the photo at Milne Stadium on the coldest day of the year. Kim Jew shot the photo at 10:00 a.m., wearing a heavy winter coat and gloves; I had a light track jacket on. I was shaking so much he had to keep shooting. Eventually I held still long enough for him to snap a good photo. All I see in that picture is one of the coldest days of my life. It was only rivaled in Alaska, at the Portage Glacier. (But that didn't stop me from putting it on the back of this book.)

For help with my speech, I called on Tom Tice, a speech pathologist. He said "not to thank everyone in the whole wide world." At the risk of not taking his advice now, I have to say Tom saved me from getting beeped off stage like an actor receiving an Academy Award. Tom had experience talking to large groups and his advice paid off: the speech was, to us, close to perfect.

The night at the Albuquerque Marriott Pyramid was like no other. I had a beautiful black tux. I sported a fresh haircut. Lori Monceballez brought me a red rose for my lapel. I had taken a substitute day at school. My phone was ringing off the hook with various questions. I had house guests from Florida, Roger and Cheryl Flaherty, who helped me fit into that tuxedo. Cheryl made sure I looked "spiffy." When we got to the Marriott it was buzzing. There was no way I could have a conversation with everyone there to support me. I was overwhelmed.

Having seen many such banquets before I knew I had to hold my cool. I also promised myself I would have fun. Rocky and Curtis looked good. We were sitting at the top step of the podium, surrounded by committee members and local media. As we looked out into the audience we saw only the bright lights. I soon realized, though, that beyond the glare there were many smiling faces looking back at us. "Coach, Coach, look at *you!*"

The evening started off with awards for Athletes and Coaches of the Year. In front of me was Julia Foster, receiving Female Athlete of the Year. Next to her was Steve Alford, UNM Lobo basketball coach, receiving Coach of the Year. As the program continued, I was struck how many great contributors to New Mexico athletics were in that room. Stan Whitaker, Hall of Fame president that year, was involved in most of the festivities. Stan was a State Champion track athlete at Sandia when I was coaching in the 1970s. He is now a judge, as is Val Boyer. JP Murrieta from Channel 4 Sports was the Master of Ceremonies.

When we got to the inductees, Spencer Sielschott introduced Curtis. I listened to Curtis speak about Gallup and all of the support he received there. He had a very successful career as his boys won 14 State Championships and his girls 11 titles. Curtis also was voted National Cross Country Coach of the Year in 1996.

It was fitting that Cal Guymon handed me the plaque. He was the first person I met in Albuquerque, and my longest friend here. As I stepped to the podium the audience *roared*. I knew I was among friends, and it was easy to move forward. I spoke briefly. (I'd promised the committee I would not go over 10 minutes.) I wanted to inform, entertain, and enjoy the moment.

I gave credit to certain individuals. There was no way I could mention everyone there for me that night. The film clip was perfect. My talk centered on how great it was be to be an educator and how blessed I was to have worked with such great athletes and students. Afterwards, I had people tell me my speech was the highlight of the evening. Mission accomplished!

I may never have another night like that in my life. It was a culmination of many things. Now approaching my twilight years, I realize that the people in my career have given me more than I gave them. As a coach and educator, I have had a good life and became involved. I did not make a lot of money, but I made enough, and I made a lot of friends. When I stood at the podium that night at the Marriott and saw the friendly faces, I knew a warm feeling inside. Would it not be great if everyone could at some point in their lives know that feeling?

TRACK 2011: A SPECIAL YEAR AND MICKEY BROWN

The 2011 Track season began the next weekend. We went in with high expectations, as we had been rebuilding since 2009. Now, we hoped, was our time to shine. Sometimes you have a great year, with superb athletes and no injuries; others, times you owe some favors to Lady Luck.

I have always taken the long-view. My excitement is to help kids excel and develop teams to compete. There are no guarantees, so I always find something to feel good about. Sometimes it can be the team effort, or a single championship event, maybe an over-achieving individual. The best, though, is when the team shines as a unit. We knew we would have a good 4 x 4 relay and several 400m runners, and our 300m hurdlers were in place to shine. The 800m was a question but we also had a plan for that event. Dewy Bohling had come to us with many years of experience to coach shot and discus, and with his contributions, the coming season seemed especially bright.

When the athletes first reported for practice we were looking for team players. I noticed a ninth-grader by the name of Venitra Fields with good speed. Also running was a senior, Sam Bowe. Both of these girls showed promise immediately.

At La Cueva we have never been blessed with short-sprint speed. Cory Chavez and Mariah Rast were seniors with good speed and knew our work ethic. For a successful season, the athletes had to dedicate themselves to fast repeats, with a burst that would give them the endurance and race speed they would need. This is not always easy, as personalities sometimes determine how hard a team will work. Returning for her senior year was our great 400m runner Mickey Brown. She turned out to be the leader we were looking for.

I asked her to write a summary of the 2011 track season. I asked, "How important is your participation in track and field to you as a student and an athlete?" She begins her story as a sophomore:

> I never imagined that track and field would be my ultimate outlet. I was the type of girl who thought that volleyball would be my ticket into college. But during my sophomore year of high school, I began to see that volleyball was not for me. I decided to join in on the track program at La Cueva and see what happened.
>
> I always loved to run, so I didn't believe that making the team would be too difficult. I met the coaches and to be honest, I was a bit skeptical; Jim Ciccarello seemed a bit "older" than most coaches I had worked with, and I questioned his ability to "do work" on the track. Once our few weeks of preseason started, my mind quickly changed. I was working harder than I had ever had. Circuits, abs, and repeats became everyday words, and I had to learn to love them too (even though I still cringe at 300m–600m–300m–600m workouts on Monday).
>
> My first season on the team was average, to say the least. As Coach Ciccarello predicted, I was to be a 400m runner. He has some sort of skill to be able to pin-point exactly what event you are built for. It's almost like a sixth sense. After running in my first meet, I knew that he had predicted right. As much as I hated that race, I also loved the rush of speed for that specific length of time, and I loved the burning feeling of accomplishment once I crossed the finish line. My first time in the 400m was a :65, and boy did I have work to do.
>
> Now, see, as a sophomore, I was the type of girl who really just kind of went with the flow. Training was what it was, and I did the workouts, but I didn't really put in the effort that I should have. I did minimal work, and just got by with what I had to do. I loved running in relays, so I made sure that I was at least doing what I had to make those teams. When state came around, my emotions were off the walls.

I was confident, and had no doubt that this race would be one to remember. I was not the best in the city, but I was close enough to scare the other girls. I was on Cloud Nine, thinking that I was going to place high; needless to say that when the race was over and done with, coming in third in the prelims and not even making the podium with a seventh place (out of eight) in the finals was a heartbreak. I took it all out on the relays to come. I believe I had run some of my fastest times of the year in those relays, thanks to knowing how to release my anger in a positive way on the track. We took places in them as well, so I was somewhat satisfied with the results, but still wanted more self-accomplishment. I competed for the first time in the Great Southwest that year, and had a blast. It was practically a joke that I could compete with some of those girls, but it was so much fun.

Coach Ciccarello somehow knew that this would be a changing point for me as an athlete. He talked with me almost every day about how hard work will pay off on the track and in running great times. I just couldn't give up and had to keep working through the workouts day to day and not let anyone stand in the way of what I was trying to accomplish.

I completely quit volleyball my junior year, and began focusing on the next track season. I did some off-training in the fall, and started official preseason in winter. I was lucky enough to compete in a national meet with professional athletes when our school was invited to a trial run for the 4 x 4 relay. We won and were interviewed about the experience, and got to meet so many professional athletes, including my idol, Allyson Felix. It was definitely an eye-opener into what I wanted to do as a runner.

I worked harder and I could definitely tell because it was starting to take its toll on my body, but I was not going to let shin splints stand in my way. Coach Sandy reminded me that working hard was all fine and dandy, but I need to know my physical limits. I thought I knew them, and just kept running and running. I had to get better. I had to improve my times.

Unfortunately, shin splints did start to play a major role in my workouts. I had to cut some of the hard workouts short, do minimal work, even as I needed them.

It was the worst feeling in the world to have to watch my teammates do the workouts that I so badly wanted to participate in. I always tried to do extra, but never was able to measure to what I really needed to have a beneficial workout. I had to completely stop running the week before state, and all I wanted to do was be on the track practicing handoffs for the relays and running the 200m repeats with my girls. I was even wearing a walking boot for almost 2 weeks (which on its own was embarrassing enough), but I was not going to let this minor setback get me down from winning the championships.

When it came down to the race, my nerves began to get the best of me. Questions raced through my head: "Would not running this week affect this race?" "What if my leg gives out?" "What if I can't do this?" Coach Sandy Warfield could tell that I was distraught and told me not to think about it, and just run. I should have listened to her then and there. My heart was pounding at the starting line. The crowd echoed through my ears and then I heard the gun go off. I took off strong, a little slower than what I anticipated, but not terrible either. I was in the lead for the first 300m. And the last part of the race is where it hit me. The crowd's overpowering cheers, and the fact that a girl in lane 5 was gaining on me, and also in lane 1 and lane 3 they were closing; were all working against me. It was a heated race, and I was beginning to crack. I got fourth. I cried. I wanted so much more out of myself, and was utterly disappointed.

I tried to reassure myself it would all be okay, and when people asked me how I was, I lied and told them everything was fine, that it was just a race and that I would get over it. But running was my passion, my life. Who was I kidding? I was even lying to myself at this point.

Only my coaches could tell that it was really eating me up inside. Coach Brandon Back even asked me the same question, and I gave him the same answer, and he actually responded by saying, "Bull. You are going to run this relay now and show everyone in those stands that you have so much more drive and heart, and to show these other runners that they had better watch out, because you are going to run them down one by one." Now, I really pondered what he told me, and took it to heart. He was right. I was angry, I was hurt, and more than anything else, I wanted to prove everyone wrong and show them that this girl came to show what she got, and she was not leaving until she was sure that those fans understood that.

The following relays, the 4 x 2, the medley, the 4 x 4, I got first place. We got second overall as a team. I like to think that my running contributed to that. We were four points from first. Senior year—it had to be then. I had so much more to prove.

I also competed in the Great Southwest that year to help better my chances with competition. I didn't come even close to some of the girls with their times (again). It was a great experience and opportunity to meet so many people I am still friends with today. I was starting to make my mark as a runner and getting to know everyone else who loved what I had a passion for.

Over the summer I went to an orthopedic doctor to help me figure out how to work with my shin splints, and then to physical therapy. I was getting stronger. I took weight-lifting with Coach Back more seriously, and did everything I could to get involved with the running world. I became the manager of the cross country team, and loved working with everyone there, especially Coach Nicholas Martinez (who became one of my biggest fans and my number-one guy, besides Coach Ciccarello, for support). I was more involved and ready to make this season one to remember.

I even practiced indoors and competed in the Great Southwest Indoors Meet. It was rather small compared with the one held outdoors, but still nothing to take lightly. I ran the 200m and the 400m, and the 4 x 4 relay and placed in all of them. While practicing indoors I also met a world-renowned runner from France who told me that I had potential and wanted to see where I ended up. I was lucky enough to practice with her and knew that I was in for a long road ahead, especially after trying to keep up with her; I am pretty sure I puked for the first time that day due to running so hard.

I wanted personal-best times. I wanted to take Amy Warner's name off the La Cueva school record board. She had run a 56.5 and I was running low 58s. I had a lot of work ahead of me, but I was determined.

Now for anyone in the Albuquerque area, you know that La Cueva was ending up in the news, and not in a good way. Girls on the volleyball team were caught smoking pot (glad that I was not on the team anymore), and our football team was a caught drinking on the bus—and about a year before all of this, the baseball coach had hired strippers as a team "reward." We were in some major trouble. It had reached the point that APS had considered cutting all of our sports completely. I was ready to transfer because I needed to be able to run to have any chance at a scholarship for college. Our sports programs were put on lock-down, but we were still able to compete under a heavy watchful eye.

Our 2011 season was off to a golden start. Our team was closer than ever, and we were all working harder. Every day Coach Ciccarello would tell me "Mickey, you're the girl," and I always believed it. I was the girl to push the limits and do whatever it took. I was now the "top dog," and I knew that the team looked up to me. Now, in most cases, it is hard for me to take charge; I am a very passive person. But I took coach's challenge to be the best leader I could.

I worked my butt off at practice, and as Ciccarello told me to, I lead by example. I did the "cherry" workouts and was getting better as the weeks passed. I was number one, but I was not number one alone. We were all number one, as a team. People noticed. People believed in us. We were unstoppable.

We took meet after meet by storm. To my surprise, I was being interviewed, and talked about. I loved the attention, but also had a great fear of it. I had to stay true to myself, and remembered some advice: "Never let a loss get to your heart, and never let a win get to your head." I began to live by this, and my coaches emphasized that I could not let the "publicity" get to me. These coaches, who I had come to love, were looking over me like parents. And when I received this letter, the first people I showed were Coach Sandy and Coach Ciccarello. They had helped teach me every word this man had to say about me:

Dear Principal Resch,

On four occasions this spring, I have served as a track official for APS, in charge of the girls high jump. La Cueva has competed in all four of these meets. I am just writing to say that one of your student-athletes, Mickey Brown, is everything that is right about high school athletics. I could give you the details that make her a dream from an official's standpoint: knowledgeable of the event; always checking out and back in when she goes off to another event (and she does a lot of them!); polite and respectful to her fellow competitors. But besides all of that, she just strikes me as being as nice a person as she is a tremendous competitor. I was thrilled to see her be the high point scorer at APS Metro Championships.

I know that it has been a tough year for La Cueva sports in the news. I don't have a dog in that fight, but I do want you to know that for me, at least, Mickey Brown is the face of La Cueva athletics. For that fact, the La Cueva administration and Track and field coaching staff can hold their heads high. As should Mickey!

I don't know what Mickey's collegiate plans are, but I enclose my card in case she should enroll at UNM. I would be happy to serve as an informal advisor to her.

Sincerely,

Fred Carey

Needless to say, I was speechless, and almost teary-eyed. I was doing it right. Everything was paying off. My coaches created this runner to be a good, reliable person; a person of great character. I could not thank them more.

Now back to getting ready for State. As the race came closer, so did our team. For the first time, all of us sprinters, hurdlers, throwers, and distance runners were interconnected. We talked about strategy, and how prelims were the main focus. And I took this time to tell each girl how much they meant to me as a teammate and my senior year as one to remember. Now all of us seniors cried because we all felt this way about our team. We did everything together and were all practically like sisters. We had girls who had to step up to the plate and take the challenge to get us into the finals at state, and I would not trust anyone more than my girls. Not only did they do it, but did an excellent job of it.

My own race was finally at hand. I was nervous, but not like the year before. I was ready for this. As I waited to reach the starting line, the 4A race was about to begin. One of my good friends from Los Alamos was getting ready to run.

When the gun goes off the one thing every runner dreads to hear is a second gun, indicating that someone false started. It boomed through my ears. It was my dear friend. That's when the nerves kicked in; I was almost in tears for her. She was projected to win, and was out of the race in a blink. When I went to hug her she told me "Win this for me, girl. This is your race. I have seen you work year-to-year for this, and this is your RACE. Take it." As I walked to the blocks, my heart pounded and I kept repeating what she said in my head until the gun went off. I took off. It was a close race between me and a girl I had to love named Amber Lala. We were the top competitors for the race.

It was a photo finish. We sat on the side of the track for a half an hour. We cried together when they finally announced that I had won the race by .02 seconds. And not only did I win; I took Amy Warner's name off the board. I ran a 56.14! I was ecstatic. The rush of being at the top of the podium was like nothing I had ever experienced. When I scanned the crowd, I found my coaches and smiled at them, knowing that they helped get me here, to this very spot. But my day was not over. I had three more relays to run.

The relays went just as well. My 4 x 2 time was about .2 seconds away from beating a 30-year-old State Record, and even though our Medley Relay took second, we were still doing well. The meet itself came down to the last race, the 4 x 4 relay, my favorite race. Now, we were a little concerned about who was to run this relay for us. One of our key girls, Hattie Schunk, was at a soccer tourney, ending right when we had to check in for the relay—about an hour drive back to the stadium. Hattie ran in, one minute to spare. All of our hearts were pounding out of our chests. All we had to do was stay ahead of Cleveland High and the championship was ours. When it came time to race, it was like the whole stadium was quiet, like the fans knew the pressure that was at hand.

The girls that we were racing against became our good friends. This was due to the type of team I made sure that we were. We supported everyone, because we knew that everyone worked just as hard as we had. These teams all knew that it came down to the final race, and wished us the best of luck as we all got ready for the race of a lifetime. The gun was up. And the race began.

Christina Clark got us to third, which was good, but considering that Cleveland was in first we really had to pull together. Hattie pulled us into second on the second leg and it was Miss Carly Browning's turn to work—she ran the race of her life. She took my breath away. She pulled us in to first within the last 150m of her leg. As she came in, I said, "I'm not leaving you," (which was our team motto, especially on our relays) and, I was out like a bullet.

I kept hearing footsteps behind me, so I kept running harder and harder. When it came down to the last hundred meters, all I had to do was keep my position. As I looked up, I saw the time clock and realized that we were going to beat our school record, which made me run even harder with excitement. I crossed the finish line, threw my arms into the air knowing that we had not only won the race, but won the meet, and beaten the school record.

It was a good day, which became an even better day once we found out that we had broken another 30-year-old State Record, as well. I came to discover that the girl behind me was almost 50m back, so I don't know whose steps I heard, but I am glad I heard them.

Coach Ciccarello always used to tell us that no victory ever compared to winning a State Championship, and he was 100% correct. As much as I loved standing on the podium for my 400m, it didn't even compare to being there with the team that I had loved.

I now run for UNM with a full-ride scholarship. I never thought this is where I would have ended up. I have so many more opportunities ahead of me that I could have never even dreamed, had it not been for the coaches that pushed and supported me every step of the way. I now get to compete with top athletes from across the country on a regular basis. It is all a dream come true.

I still dream of competing in the Olympics, and running at the professional level. Whether or not I get there will be a determination of fate, but I know that no matter where I go in my running career, my coaches are behind me every step of the way. As Nicholas Martinez told me "We are your support group." I think about all the times they had me run just one more 300m or finish those 200m's at 30 instead of 32; their push always made me better, even if I did whine and cry about it, or when they used to joke with me and told me to quit pulling at my shorts all the time. They helped shape me into the person I am today, and I can never thank them enough. Sandy Warfield, Brandon Back, Nicholas Martinez, and Jim Ciccarello changed my life, and there is no way that I could ever repay them. In the words of Jim Ciccarello, "That Mickey Brown, she likes to run." Only thanks to you, Coach. You helped me to find the love of my life, and helped me discover who I was as a person. I can never thank you all enough.

Sincerely yours,
Mickey Brown

Mickey wrote a letter most 18-years-olds could never do. As I read it, I could feel her joy and defeat. I had to share the letter in its entirety so you could feel her passion for the sport, and also her appreciation for her educators. The tone of her letter is what this book is about. As much as the La Cueva coaching staff gave to her, she gave right back to us. I have only a few notes:

We had other athletes who overachieved this track season. To win a New Mexico State Championship does take a total team-effort. All schools that have been in that position will always have some athletes step up and help the team.

Alyssa Pfeiffer would do anything for this team. There were times we would ask her to run in the prelims of a relay and then replace her in the finals with a faster kid. She was also a long-jumper and a javelin-thrower. Alyssa was an all-around athlete and because of that was very important to this team. Ranked 12th in the javelin going into the State Meet does not normally bring points to a team, but Alyssa scored two points for the team, as she found a way to finish fifth at the State Meet with a throw of 116'.

Alex Mantos, a young triple-jumper/long-jumper was ranked 10th in the long jump and had a great meet. She placed sixth and scored a point for the team.

Cory Chavez and Mariah Rast, two very dedicated short-sprinters, have run the short relays for several years at La Cueva. Both athletes ran outstandingly in the 4 x

1 relay, finished third and scored six points. Mariah, running last, almost anchored that team to first in a very close race. Mariah may not be the fastest athlete in the state, but she has courage and never backs down in competition. The last position on a relay team usually means you run against the other team's fastest athlete. When I asked Mariah to run the last leg of that relay she responded, "Sure, coach, whatever's good for the team!"

Christina Clark was another like this. We asked her to run first on the 4 x 4 relay, knowing that she was in fast company. Her response, "I will keep it close for my girls, Coach." Little did she know that she was about to become a New Mexico State Record-holder. After that race, Chad Clark, her brother, the former La Cueva star hurdler, now running for UNM, came up to me and said, "Coach I am so proud of my little sister. In high school, as well as I did, I never was part of a State Record-setting relay team."

Jordan Grace scored four points in the 3200 and kept us close in the team score.

Hattie Schunk placed second in the 800m and was very near to winning the gold medal. She scored five points for the team.

Carly Browning is an unsung hero as she was a relay girl (where most of the points are) who ran her best for her teammates. On that 4 x 4 relay at State she came from behind and put La Cueva into first place, as Mickey Brown took home the blue ribbon and a new record.

Venitra Fields was our ninth-grader who not only placed in the 100m dash but ran on our 4 x 1 that almost won. She also ran fourth on the winning 4 x 2 relay.

I called Stephanie Brener our "Secret Weapon." She was a hurdler who had been battling shin splints all year and had to sit out some of the meets. Stephanie was an Irish River Dancer, and put a lot of stress on her lower legs from pounding on the floor. She ran in JV meets early in the season. As her three-step approach in the 100m hurdles got better she became a threat.

Kaylin Martin was top-ranked in New Mexico in the 5A 100m hurdles. In the prelims she pulled her hamstring over the fifth hurdle and did not run again at the State Meet. There is a lot of luck in athletics, both ways. If Kaylin had not hurt herself, we could have won the meet by 20 points.

So when Stephanie Brener qualified for the final of the 100m hurdles we had a chance. We had a motivation-talk, and asked her, "Can you help us out with the loss of Kaylin Martin?" Her answer was, "Okee-dokee, Coach, I'll see what I can do." Well, little Miss Secret Weapon finished third and almost won the 100m hurdles! Mickey Brown told me, "Coach, she is from this point on just 'The Weapon.'" We were closing on Cleveland and the meet was getting interesting.

Samantha (Sam) Bowe was a godsend for this team. She was a senior in her first year of track. Sam had been a gymnast. We knew right away to teach her the pole vault. Sam had such a strong body she looked more like a college girl. Coach Back, the La Cueva boys' track coach said, "She is the strongest female athlete I have ever seen at La Cueva." She never mentioned running to me—but, well, I have an eye for runners. I knew she could sprint. I had to use some trickery to get her on the track. I enlisted the help of her brothers, who I knew had run track. After talking to her dad (a very good track and football athlete in his youth) I knew we could get her to run.

She agreed to the 4 x 1. We ran her in the third position on that relay to hide her. There was no doubt that she was the fastest kid on our team. As the weeks went by I started to move her into different events. One week she would run on the 4 x 2 and the next the Medley Relay. We finally ran her in the 100m dash and she won that event in a small four-team meet.

With Samantha and Venitra on the relays we were doing well. Both of these girls were fast and had about the same speed. Samantha spent most of her practice time at the pole vault pit, but I was winning her over to the running also. At the District Meet she qualified for the State Meet in both the 100m and the 200m. Now we had some hard decisions to make, as Sam could only run in four track events, but was qualified in three open events, and could help us run on three relays. We decided to hide her again on two of the relays and run her in the open 100m dash.

She not only made the finals, but placed third and scored four points. In the pole vault she placed second with a new La Cueva record of 10'6", and scored five points. Her third leg on the 4 x 1 was a scorcher as she handed the stick off in first place. But it was in the 4 x 2 that she made her mark. We did not run Sam in the prelims, saving her instead for the finals. This event was a critical part of the meet. We were ranked seventh going into the final.

We put Sam at the first position out in lane 8. With the stagger she could not see anyone behind her; she was the type of athlete who did not want anyone to catch her if she had the lead, and we wanted her to run scared. At the time Cleveland High had a huge lead and was one of the favorites in the 4 x 2. The odds-on favorite was Mayfield High School, with the great Jenna Banegas running the first leg against Sam. Jenna was the State Champion in the 100m and the 200m. Sam, still new to track, did not really know how fast these runners from other schools were. We did.

On the 4 x 2 just following Sam we had Carly Browning, Mickey Brown, and Venitra Fields. If Sam could stay close to Jenna Banegas, we had a chance.

Usually the stadium gets loud for a relay race. Not this time. The gun went off and here was an eerie quiet. People could not believe what they were watching.

Samantha bolted off the curve, smoked the straightaway, and handed the baton off with a 12m lead to Carly Browning. Sam's split time for that run was a 23.20, which would have smashed the State Record for an open 200m. The Mayfield and the Cleveland coaches were speechless. Our team ran a 1:42.26, missing the 30-year-old State Record by only .2 seconds. The La Cueva girls were now in the thick of the race for the team title. When I asked Samantha about that race she answered, "Coach, I was in Lane 8, and I had to run by the pole vault pit, and I didn't want the pole vault athletes to think I couldn't run!" From this point on, all my pole vault sprinters will run the first leg of the 4 x 2!

In her letter Mickey described the 4 x 4 race. As I watched and celebrated with the athletes and coaches, I was wondering, is this the greatest victory ever?

Coaches are often asked about our best team. Blessed as I have been over the years with great teams and athletes, it's impossible to answer… but I had that warm feeling again, and it took all summer for it go away. Everywhere I went people asked me about those relays and Mickey Brown.

After 40 years and a boatload of fine memories, I realize that sharing these moments with my students and fellow coaches was a lifelong journey. There is no best. They were all great. They were all the best.

2011 was quite the year for this old dog. My teaching and coaching seemed to come to the forefront. As I am writing this story, I am reliving those moments as if they were yesterday. Next to some of the stories in this book, they were!

Here is a letter I received from Christina Clark, a member of the new La Cueva State Record 4 x 4 relay team:

"Running takes heart, dedication, and training. In order to be the best you need to train like the best, or even better than the best. While your opponent is sitting at home watching television you need to be at the track running repeat 600m's. Some people may be born with talent but if you can outwork them you will always come out on top." This was said by a very wise person I am proud to call my coach.

Now imagine a man in his upper-60s, early '70s. His hair is white, with random speckles of gray, and a mustache to match. He wears a pair of thick glasses that take up most of his face. He is sporting a baseball hat, a towel around his neck, a long-sleeved T-shirt and a pair of blue jeans with his tennis shoes. This… is my future coach.

I was a freshman when I first met him. I knew a little bit about him, since he had coached my brother four years earlier, and since I had never officially met Ciccarello, on that first day of practice I introduced myself. He studied me, and with a stern face said, "How hard are you willing to work to become the best?" My reply was, "As hard as you need me to work." He broke into a smile and said, "You are a Clark. I am going to like you."

Since that day, four years ago, a relationship has formed between a coach and an athlete. How can it not? I train with him during the summer, during the off-season in school, and then during the regular track season. He knows exactly how to push me and what works to make me run harder. My coach "tells it how it is," as he would say. When I am not running my best, he makes sure that I know it. When there is a girl who is faster than me, who is training harder than me, who is stronger than me, my coach is the first one to tell me that I need to pick it up. This can be extremely frustrating, but I respect his honesty. He is not one of those who will sugarcoat things. He is open and honest. If you ever ask him a question about yourself… he will tell you the truth. This can be both a blessing and a curse, but you always know what you are going to get.

During practices Coach Ciccarello is always paying attention to the effort being given. On those days that I do not feel like giving it my all he refers to his favorite saying: "Run with the big dogs." I have heard Coach say this at least once every practice. He even had a shirt made. (And I am pretty positive it is his new favorite, considering he wears it most days now.) Hearing him yell, "Run with the big dogs!" used to scare me. I did not want to be a "big dog," I just wanted to survive. For Coach Ciccarello, it is too easy to just survive. You have to push through your fears and what holds you back, and become the big dog.

Through Coach Ciccarello I have learned how to become a better athlete, but more important, I have learned to become a better person. He reminds me to appreciate every moment of my youth because it does not last forever. He reminds me to always respect my parents and elders because although I may not agree with them in the moment, they are only looking out for my best interests. He reminds me to lend a helping hand to those in need because one day that could be me. He reminds me to enjoy life because eventually it will be gone.

My coach may be showing signs of getting old. He may be further losing his hearing, developing arthritis, and forgetting small things. He is still my inspiration. Coach Ciccarello makes me want to work hard not only for myself, but also for the people around me. Meeting my coach those four years ago changed my life. I will always remember the lessons that he has taught me, the support that he has shown me, and I will always remember to "Run with the big dogs."

Sincerely,

Christina Clark

It is letters like this that help me to keep going that extra year. As long as I can inspire young people to excel I can overcome the effects of aging. I now use my wisdoms to accomplish that task. Each generation of athletes makes me a better educator. I myself am an old dog. But I still learn new tricks!

TRACK 2012

As we entered the 2012 track season we were thinking potential back-to-back wins, which requires both excellence and luck. We have had a repeat before, but as we entered 2012, we now lacked both Mickey Brown and Sam Bowe. We had to develop new athletes and help improve most of those returning. This would be a tall order. Across town, in Rio Rancho, the Cleveland girls were ready to make a charge for the state title. They had the senior team to do it. Eldorado, as always, would be our other primary challenger.

Our preseason went well. New athletes tried out. Alexa Romano, a ninth-grader, looked promising. I remembered her from many years ago, at the ATC, as a 10–11 year old age-grouper. She was a very strong runner.

Kaylin Martin was back in the hurdle events. Our sprinters were Maggie Sabik and Venitra Fields. Christina Clark and Stephanie Brener were ready for hurdles and relays. Carly Browning would be the 400m/800m runner we needed, and Hattie Schunk was a favorite in the 800m run. Akuadsuo Ezenyilimba looked very strong in the discus. Allie Mady would place well in the shot put.

The coaching staff liked this team's potential. Sandy Beach Warfield decided to spend more time with her family, and Alex Darling has taken her place on staff. Sandy wanted to follow her son Seth's high school basketball career. Coach Nick Martinez would again have the distance runners. Coach Dewy Bohling would handle the throwers. Alex and I would train the sprinters and the hurdlers. It was nice having a former New Mexico State Champion like Alex Darling on the coaching staff. She could run with the athletes at practice.

We were qualifying athletes to the State Meet every week, which would give us flexibility there, but developing new athletes was also a priority. We lost two close meets to Cleveland. Eldorado was also close.

Meanwhile, our number-two sprinter, Ari Eddings, blew her knee out in a soccer game. Hannah Hawash, our top javelin thrower, tore a ligament in a basketball game. Venitra Fields, our number-one sprinter, strained her hamstring. Carly Browning, whom we counted on for the 400m/800m, also had a hamstring issue.

On the bright side, Alexa Romano, was developing into one of the best 400m runners in the state.

As we entered the State Meet we felt like we had a chance, but we needed luck. The coaches hatched a plan we hoped the athletes would execute to perfection. We ran the preliminaries and set our team up for the finals. It was going to be a three-team race: Cleveland had the edge; Eldorado and La Cueva would be close.

The hurdle events were a key scoring race for La Cueva. The 300m and 100m hurdle events were both a photo finish. Both events were almost a dead heat. Kaylin Martin (La Cueva) and Gina Okoye (Eldorado) had some of the year's most exciting races, with Gina taking the 100m and Kaylin 300m. Gina was first awarded the gold, then was disqualified for not having brought her leg over the hurdle properly in the 300m. This was controversial, and eventually, the order of finish was changed. Kaylin was awarded the gold 45 minutes after the event.

We were expecting gold in the discus throw, but Akuadsuo Ezenyilimba had a bad day. She had three scratches out of bounds and did not score. She did take fourth in the shot put.

Alexa Romano won a gold medal in the 400m run with an excellent time of 56.89. This is one of the fastest times ever for a ninth grade track athlete.

The big story came for us in the Medley Relay. We had hoped to run Carly Browning, one of our top 800m runners on this relay, but because of a hamstring strain we asked Jessica Cuadra to run the last leg. Jessica was a 2:40 800m runner during the regular season. We had to gauge her confidence.

Jess looked at us and said, "Coach, I will do my best and I think I can run well for the team." After consultation with Coaches Martinez and Darling, we decided she was the runner we wanted. The coaching staff was confident she would go hard. We committed our changes and hoped for the best.

Jessica Cuadra ran a race that I consider to be one of the most over-achieving performances by an athlete of all time. Jess was a senior in her first track season. She had to run against two of the best 800m runners in the state. Venitra Fields and Stephanie Brener ran the first 200m's, Kaylin Martin the 400m. The first three girls ran great and Jessica had a 10-yard lead when she received the baton. Two outstanding 800m runners were ready to chase her down. Up in the stands the coaches' hearts were pounding.

During the first 400m the Eldorado runner passed Jess, opened up a 15-yard lead, and it did not look good. Jessica at that point turbo-charged and moved up directly behind her. With 150 yards to go, and the fans in the stands going crazy with excitement, Jess passed the Eldorado girl. She had run a split of 2:24 for her 800m, 16 seconds faster than her best run in an individual event. This was the only gold medal that La Cueva won in a relay event at this meet. Jessica's coaches, mother, family, friends and team members were amazed.

The La Cueva girls had a couple of other noteworthy performances. Our 800m relay won a silver medal. Hattie Schunk placed second in the 1600 run. Maggie Sabik placed third in the 800m.

In the end, Cleveland and Eldorado placed first and second. La Cueva took third, two points behind Eldorado. For a rebuilding year it was good. Many other teams that day would have loved to have taken home the third place trophy. And the coaching staff was proud. We have a particularly great memory of our overachieving Medley Relay team. Jessica Cuadra's run is part of the great track tradition that has been established at La Cueva.

During this 2012 track season two school records were broken. Akuadsuo Ezenyilimba broke the discus record, formerly held by Brianna Paxton, with a throw of 134'1". Kaylin Martin broke the 100m Hurdle Record formerly held by Sina Pleasant, with a time of 14.41.

Hurdles are close to my heart, and record-breaking especially so. At Manzano Christine Brockhoff set two new school records, as well as breaking the New Mexico State Record. While at Sandia High Shannon Ryan not only set the school record but also broke the 100m Hurdle Record. Hers is the longest-standing NM State Record in the books, set in 1980. At Highland, Natanya Jones did the same, breaking both school and the NM State Record in the 300m hurdles.

In 14 years at La Cueva I have had many great hurdlers who went on to become New Mexico State Champions. Alex Darling holds the La Cueva school record in the 300m. Though we had great hurdlers we had not been able to touch Sina Pleasant's 100m record, so when Kaylin Martin broke it in 2012, she was as proud of her performance as any athlete I have coached. Kaylin and I had a special relationship. I used her quickness to laugh to motivate her. Every day I would quote someone from 50 years back. She would look at me with that 'Da' look and then show me how fast she was, as if saying, "Quote this!" We had fun and got better every day. Just recently, the day before she was to catch a plane to start at the University of South Florida, she sent a short letter:

> Focus. A simple word has a big meaning behind it. From the first day of track practice my freshman year Coach Chic has been trying to teach me to live and breathe the word.
>
> He will do anything to get me to learn focus. He uses quotes, funny sayings, and just stares at me. Ask anyone who knows me and they'll tell you I'm a social butterfly, so focus didn't come easy to me. One of my favorite memories of a "focus" lecture by Coach was at practice on a hot day in the off-season. I was practicing hurdles on the track while nearby on the football field the La Cueva boy's football team was running plays. As a large and I mean LARGE, lineman makes a tackle, Coach turns to me and says, "Kaylin, if you do not FOCUS and run over those hurdles, I'm going to have him tackle you." Coach would then walk over and talk to the biggest football player he could find, turn around and point at me. I swear he was smiling as he looked at me. Well, that was the best visual motivation I could ask for; after all, I wanted to make it to State in one piece. Coach always knew how to keep practice fun and every memory I have with him is full of laughter. He's taught me that you need focus throughout all aspects of your life, not just track, and for that I cannot thank him enough.

Kaylin Martin
La Cueva Record Holder 100m hurdles

Kaylin did not know I had learned that little trick from Asal Salehpoor, a great sprinter, who was dating a huge lineman on the football team in 2006–07. To get her to sprint faster I would walk over to that footballer of hers. We would have a motivational talk. He was more than happy to chase her down the track. Coaching is more than repeats and hurt every day. You got to have fun along the way!

MAGIC-MOTIVATION

I always look for new techniques. In 1959 my biology teacher at Valley High (Mr. Bishop) did some magic tricks to motivate the class, I knew that someday I would use that approach. Mr. Bishop activated my imagination when he opened a brown paper bag and pulled out a zippered banana, ate it, and pretended this was normal. Since that time I have always valued magic. Now I see through the tricks—but done right, they will focus a group and challenge them to focus.

You can never be effective with most children unless you have their attention. Some teachers command students' attention and respect just by walking into the classroom. In some cases it is natural; they are tall, strong, young, blessed with Hollywood looks. Or they are older and distinguished, with a shock of gray hair, modern in dress with all the current trends. They have a special presence about them. They are very articulate and can express themselves easily to a group. Some teachers have none of the above, and play the hand they have.

When I was young the students gravitated to me. I ran and jumped as they did. When I taught high jump I could hear the kids *oooh* and *aaah* as I cleared the bar. Most high school athletes jump over 6' in the high jump, but to an elementary kid, an adult that could clear 4' was a *star*. At practice I would run backwards faster than the kids could run facing forward. Demonstrating basketball shooting I could rip the nets with my outside shot. Young elementary students thought I was an NBA star. My favorite was hitting a volleyball with a bat. When I hit one on the roof of the cafeteria, the children were speechless. When you do something spectacular— then show them how to do it—they listen! Positive responses motivated me. I would get excited if a kid could clear the high jump bar at 3'. The first time a kid ran a 6.9 50-yard dash, I thought I had an Olympian.

It did not matter what level I was at; if he achieved the skill I was teaching, the moment was special. A kindergarten kid was just as important as a high school senior. Some teachers and coaches only want to work with those who excel at the state and national level. My own personal motivation was, and is to this day, to help all students achieve to their own best potential.

I've seen many ways to motivate. Foremost, of course, is to recognize them when they do well. Next is magic. Even as a young teacher I did simple tricks, like taking my finger apart and putting it back together. Thirty years later people would come up to me (in a grocery store, wherever) and ask me to show that trick to their children. Over the years I added to my stable: moving my ears and hair, making animal sounds, counting 11 fingers my hands, and wiggling my nose. The day I pulled a bouquet of flowers out of an empty vase the kids were amazed, and completely focused. One of my favorite tricks was to take a 3' needle and push it through a balloon without popping. They were all precious tricks that demanded focus. I was tricking them into learning, and the tricks were all easy to master.

Chris Jarvis at Bandelier joined in the fun. He would take elastic bands and make them jump from one finger to another, or turn a penny into a dime. At the time, Gloria Napper Owen was sending student-teachers to both Whittier and Bandelier. All of the student-teachers joined in, too, Justin Pillmore notably with his self-tying shoelace trick. A new generation was inheriting our ideas.

We had these students so motivated they would go home and practice. They would ask to demonstrate tricks to the class. This helped their self-image and gave students a chance to verbalize and stand up in front of the class.

Cal Guymon was aware of some of the things I was doing in the classroom:

> I have known Jim Ciccarello most of my life, having met when we were both 15 and starting school at Valley High School in Albuquerque. We first met at a football scrimmage on a Friday night at Milne Stadium. I am not sure how he got there. Norm Ezell invited him to sit with us. At the end of the game he needed a ride home, so he rode home with us. That was the start of a very close and long-lasting relationship.

> Following high school Jim went into the Air Force and I went on a mission for the Mormon Church. After my mission, I came home and got into College, first at St. Joseph's College and then UNM, studying Physical Education. I wanted to coach and teach. When Jim came home, his family no longer lived in Albuquerque.

I was now married and was managing some apartments near UNM so I held an apartment for him in the fall of 1966. Jim also majored in Physical Education.

After college I obtained a job at Valley High School and Jim took an elementary teaching position.

Jim was a natural for Elementary PE. Many teachers use Elementary PE as a stepping stone to mid-school or high school; not Jim. He has always felt he could have the most impact on the younger kid and that he has.

Very early Jim learned how to do some very basic magic tricks. I'm not sure where he picked them up, but he has always incorporated them in his teaching. He has expanded on these tricks and still uses them today, and although the trick is simple, like giving the impression that he is pulling the outer joint of the thumb away from his right hand, he mesmerizes the kids. It is a beautiful thing to watch the looks in the kids' eyes. Jim uses many techniques to educate.

Over the years, I have observed Jim in action. He will start the class with a trick, which focuses the kids. I have been able to observe a lot of teachers in my life, and without question Jim is the best I've ever seen. Kids who have attended Whittier have been very fortunate to have had such a great teacher.

As good as the tricks are, the real magic comes from the kids themselves. It's his ability to get them to believe in themselves, to build their confidence, and to give them all the opportunity to be more than they thought they could be.

Not all kids who attended Whittier remember their teachers, but I doubt there are any who do not remember their PE teacher. It has been my great privilege to have known him most of my life, and I'm a huge fan. Keep working the magic.

Sincerely yours,

Cal Guymon

I have known Cal for 53 years. He taught PE and coached for several years in the early '70s, then joining the FBI, where he stayed for over 20 years. He and his wife Gail are two of my dearest friends. They have two daughters and six grand kids. I have performed magic for all of them.

When I attended UNM I took many classes in sports psychology, coaching philosophy, athletic administration, and coaching principles. It was not until I was *teaching* that I learned my approach and personal involvement with students is what really matters. I may read all the literature about motivation I want, but if I don't practice it—it does not exist.

Some of the brightest students I went to college with graduated with high honors. They had command of psychological principles and could ace any test put before them. Many years after we were teaching in the school system some of UNM's brightest dropped out because they could not control their classroom. They would ask how I could stand the noise and the unmotivated students. My answer remains simple, "Our job is to take them to the next level of their potential. We *must* get their attention."

Unfair as it may seem, some people walk into a room and command immediate attention. But to be effective over time with a large population, she also needs to care truly that students succeed. She needs to get excited when kids do well, forgive mistakes, and be there for the student when he needs help. Every teacher needs to commit to his students.

Many teachers study their subject, and become so informed they know more than any student in the classroom. Students sense this, and over time they lean on this educator to help them through difficult situations. A teacher must be fair, genuine, involved, dedicated, forgiving, helpful, patient, and above all, excited for the student to reach beyond himself. It is what makes a great educator great.

CICCARELLO'S RULES FOR EFFECTIVE MOTIVATION:

1. Know your students' names. Every single one.

2. Talk to all of them, individually and as a group.

3. Get their attention. Use whatever positive means you have to get them to listen. Most times when kids mingle they do not pay attention, so sit them down while you stand. Let the number of students determine your approach.

4. Look each of them in the eye. It is the basis for connecting with your students, making them feel recognized and important.

5. Do not talk over them.

6. Project your voice.

7. Give them positive feedback. All people respond to positive feedback better. I often say, "Show me a good look!" Acknowledge that look with a hand pointed at them and reward them with, "Great," "Nice," or "Good Job!"

8. Spend time with all individuals. Give of yourself.

9. Be forgiving when they make a mistake. Give second and third chances. Be firm and fair.

10. Give all kids opportunities. Everyone wants to feel like they have a chance.

11. Show humor in your daily approach.

12. Give breaks. Give a kid a time-out once in a while. Try to understand family problems and give a kid a break when it's necessary. Kids know when you don't support them, and when you do.

13. Be there for them when other adults are not. Work to help your kids, appropriately, outside of your program (such as writing letters of support for jobs or scholarships). Reach out. Give them help when they need it.

14. Know your chosen field and study hard. Attend workshops.

15. Study successful motivators. There is not a successful teacher or coach I have studied who has failed to improve my teaching.

16. Respect all students physically, mentally, emotionally, and spiritually.

17. Welcome students back to visit after they have graduated or moved out of your program. Reconnect.

18. Embrace positive over negative. Again and again and again.

Follow these rules and I guarantee students and athletes will listen and buy into your program. If you don't care, not only will they sense it, *they will internalize it and pass it on.* Your total program will stall. For a short while, you may be successful, with coincidentally great talent. But in the long run, to have a great program, you need to reach all students.

"You can't win without the horses," as the saying goes. I never truly understood or appreciated it until I got older, though I don't completely agree with it. I prefer, "Outwork them." Sometimes the race goes not to the best, but to the one who had learned to persevere.

Many times I have seen teachers or coaches at a program with high quality students never reaching their potential. *You need both talent and leadership to reach the top.* Sometimes it happens by circumstance. Most times we need the power of outside motivation. In the long run it is the leadership, and most important, the motivation given to our students, that will determine the height of success.

SHINING EXAMPLES

APS has many contributing educators who go above and beyond normal duties.

Sandy Beach Warfield, Patty Marquette and Barbara Andersen had developed a strong PE program at LBJ Middle School. We were invited to jump rope to music. Everyone loved and benefited from it. The LBJ kids joined in, and the staff said they would make jump-rope a big part of their fitness program.

At the same time Sandy told me, "Ciccarello, your kids really like music. Why don't you have them do the "Cha, Cha, Slide?" I had never heard of it, so Sandy explained the dance and sent me a CD.

Our kids liked it so much it was the most requested music activity in our PE program for the rest of the year. We decided to try other line-dances, and incorporated the "Cha, Cha, Slide" into our jump-rope show. Now we do a basketball routine to the "Cha, Cha Slide," which the students love!

In the late '60s I visited Don Francinci at Barcelona Elementary, and watched with amazement as his kids did tumbling and gymnastics. Don's approach to gymnastics became the basis for my elementary extracurricular programs.

Don was also a welder and frequently made playground equipment. He taught me how to fix game balls and outdoor equipment. Of course, while I studied his craftsmanship, I also picked up on some of his disciplinary methods, some of which I still use today.

Stan Chavez, a longtime PE teacher at Osuna Elementary, became a very good friend. He spent more than 27 years at Osuna and another 10 at Georgia O'Keeffe Elementary. After watching him teach jump-rope, I knew I had to pick his brain. Stan has never been threatened by sharing professional techniques. We talked about discipline, drills, music activities, movement concepts, fitness stations, cognitive development and movement activities.

Luther Garcia was a PE teacher at Los Padillas, then Lowell, starting in a classroom and landing in physical education. He came to Whittier to observe me. He always had kind things to say about my program. Coach Garcia was on a mission to become the best PE teacher he could be. When I observed him working with students, he was gentle and reassuring. I learned from him the art of compassion.

Eloy Moya followed Luther Garcia at Los Padillas. Eloy always invited us to perform. Though his school was in a low-income area, with commensurate test scores, he went above and beyond to meet his students' needs. When we performed for the Los Padillas student body, the audience was laser-focused. Eloy took pride in that. He checked in by phone when we were en route, and would call the student body to the gym when we were about 10 minutes away. When we arrived they were waiting, in rows. Eloy would also buy ropes from us, and asked to include the Los Padillas kids in our show. The Whittier/Bandelier students would perform. Then Eloy would call his students to the front to show off their newly-acquired skills.

Gabe Mora, a special education teacher at Los Padillas, was also part of the show. Gabe believes in fitness and special activities. Gabe raised the transportation money, scheduled the show, assembly time, and coordinated everything else.

Bill Pichette taught elementary PE in the 1970s in Rio Rancho. I got to know Bill after various PE meetings in our district. He was always upbeat. I spent many hours with him and Stan Chavez exchanging ideas. (Green chile over eggs, tortillas, and a Sunday morning cup of coffee make for a perfect atmosphere of exchange.) Bill, who is now retired from public schools, is entering his second career at a local parochial school. I received this letter from him recently:

> In my many years (37) as a physical education teacher I've been privileged to teach many thousands of children. This has been an honor, as they have let me into their lives, then and now. My kids range from 4-year-olds to grandparents. My adult kids talk about their experiences in my classes as the "good old days" of playing crab soccer, tumbling, earth ball, and field soccer. Through the years I always tried to make my classes fun, as well as reaching my goals and standards.
>
> As a PE teacher I was entrusted with many children. This is a gift, and an honor I take very seriously. Math, English, and other academic studies are very important, but only the love of physical activity can give a person a long and healthy life. In my early years I was one of the first PE teachers to appear in UNM's Pit at a halftime show. The kids played soccer, earth ball, and demonstrated tumbling skills to the audience. Everyone from the superintendent of schools to parents in APS schools has witnessed my programs.
>
> Jim, Stan and I through the years have learned so much from each other. Back in the day, we would get together once a month to trade secrets and ideas. I believe this is one of the reasons we were so successful in those early years. We would fight for our profession. As a group we would stand up for our program when many administrators wanted to cut us out. John Gonzales from Arroyo Del Olso was also part of this group to save Elementary PE.
>
> I would hope that the new crop of young PE teachers will continue to fight for their programs. Being a PE teacher is the best job you will ever have. If you're good at your job the kids will never forget you. Nor will they forget the activities. We have the best and most impactful job elementary education. Most students remember special times and days within the PE program when they were young.
>
> It changed their lives. My response is, "Don't ever forget that!"
>
> Sincerely,
>
> **Bill Pichette**

There were many women doing great work in PE. Marilyn Carpenter, Kay Morgan, Amy Suman, Ulirke Kerstges, Patty Rotunda, Doris Merzweiller, Brenda Loudermik, Paula Jackson, Lyn Atler, Ann Paulis and Pam Powers, were some I met running great programs at the elementary level. APS is a big system and I did not always know everyone in the district. I hope to meet them all before I retire.

At the high school level I always had respect for Joe Vivian. Joe was a wrestling coach and PE teacher for many years at Cibola High School. Joe had some of the best rapport with students I have ever seen. He was outgoing and friendly toward everyone, and devoted as much time to his PE classes as his wrestling program. He was the leader of high school PE programs.

Other physical educators wanted to participate in our meetings. Soon, we had Luther Garcia, Norbert Gabaldon, Chris Jarvis, Jeremy Dunham, Sandy Beach Warfield, Mike Anderson, Amy Suman, Jamie Williams, Santi Stockton, Zeb Marciando, Joe Buck, Greg Gonzales, John Gonzales, and many others joining us. By tradition, we would meet at the Frontier. This informal gathering was one of the more valuable experiences of my career. I have attended many professional conferences and learned less than I did from my peers at those breakfasts.

The middle school programs were also very important to us. 100% of Whittier students went on to Wilson, and about 50% of the Bandelier graduates, so for many years I worked with the Wilson Middle School PE staff and coaches. Over the years, the Wilson staff changed. I did my best to stay in contact.

Liz Green and Butch Stackpole are two of the longest-active middle school teachers at Wilson. I immediately saw their professionalism, and knew they had the interest of the students at heart. Having a very organized program, they were always adding equipment and activities. Where elementary kids prefer movement, music and jump-rope, middle-schoolers prefer team sports and weight-lifting. Liz is strong in volleyball activity and Butch in fitness and weight-lifting. They complemented each other and I appreciated their willingness to collaborate with me.

We would take students from Whittier/Bandelier to Wilson several times a year. We have a large Native American population at Whittier. Wilson now shares grounds with the Native American Community Academy (NACA), so when we perform many of our kids can meet their future teachers and have an idea of what to expect for program activities in the coming year.

Without a doubt, Wilson was the most exciting show of the year. Our kids would perform knowing their older siblings and friends were in the audience. This was always a "happening," and before the show was over, we had the entire Wilson student body on the gym floor doing a routine with us. The principal, Marco Harris, was so into it he himself would challenge an elementary kid to a rope-jump "mirror game." It just so happened that Mr. Harris's daughter, Sierra, was a student on our team and could do many outstanding tricks. Marco could never beat his daughter, but he made many new friends with his own student body for being such a good sport.

More than 500 students got on the gym floor to do the "Cupid Shuffle," without a single discipline problem. It was like a flash mob. Mr. Harris even joined in! We were motivating another (entire) student body and adding to the esteem of our own students at the same time.

Butch Stackpole recently sent me a letter with his take on the value of the elementary and middle school activities, geared to prepare students for high school:

> The Highland cluster of schools, part of APS's 90,000+ students, is located in the Southeast Heights. This area is known as the "War Zone." Many of the children that reside in this area are usually from minority families.
>
> Prime examples of how a disciplined Physical Education and athletic program has benefitted kids are the stories of Bobby Newcomb and Jarrod Baxter. Both were students of mine at Wilson Middle School. Whittier is the main feeder school into Wilson, while Wilson feeds into Highland. Both became extremely successful students and athletes. Both received college football scholarships. Bobby was a multi-position Quarterback, Wide Receiver, Punt/Kickoff return man. Bobby was a star player for the Nebraska Cornhuskers and Jarrod was a star running back for UNM. Both played in the National Football League. Bobby played for the Arizona Cardinals and Jarrod for the Houston Texans. They both were exemplary role models and became outstanding citizens.

A large part of their success came from the discipline acquired from the PE and athletic program during their early development years. Physical Education programs like Whittier's and Wilson's are indicative of many throughout the country. The PE teacher is such an important person in these children's lives.

They are role models to many of the kids who come from poor, unfortunate, misgiven and unstable homes. Since most children are inherently good, PE programs expose these kids to systems of fairness, firmness, and fun. Many of these kids who attend Wilson cause trouble at school or in the neighborhood. However, when they walk into the gym they are completely different: they know what is expected of them. They are safe from outside influences and can hardly wait to see what activity we have for them that day. I'm sure this is the case in many schools.

I've known Coach Chic for over 30 years. He is the most dedicated professional I know. Kids are his forte. He has coached high school track and field and has turned out many outstanding athletes and outstanding students.

Coach Chic sends us kids who show a great appreciation for physical activity. They are well-versed in most team and individual activities, especially jump-rope. They are extremely dedicated to the discipline it takes to be an outstanding jump-rope athlete. They are amazing in what they can do with a jump-rope. His jump-rope teams have performed for many a celebrity. Whether at the New Mexico State Capitol for our legislatures, or at halftime at UNM basketball games, his kids make an impression on you.

Coach Chick's program of being firm, fair, and fun has made an easy transition for his students to middle school.

Sincerely yours,

Coach Butch Stackpole
Physical Education/Wilson Middle School

Over the years I have met many outstanding PE teachers and been part of their programs at their schools. About 25 years ago I was invited to visit Van Buren Middle School. Dick Strong and Penny taught PE there.

Penny was very inspiring—she was completely deaf, and gave directions through hand signals and eye contact. Van Buren's students could at times be hard to control. Her special charisma won them over. Any time I think I have a hard time motivating students, I remember Penny's refusal to compromise. Dick, meanwhile, was tall and stern. He took charge and made sure students did their work in a respectful manner. He was best at teaching basketball. The kids at Van Buren knew the expectations and followed their leadership. We did a couple of PE demonstrations for them, and some of our kids eventually attended Van Buren.

In the far Northeast Heights sits Eisenhower Middle school. Tim Henry (brother of Matt) taught there. Tim was great at his job. He worked with kids who had different issues than the kids in the Southeast Heights. This bunch had a sound education even before they came to the school; they just needed good leadership. Tim was very personable and well-liked, and his program was well-rounded. One year we received a standing ovation at his school.

Just like teachers, there are some administrators who will go the extra mile. Ed Briggs was a principal at Grant Middle School. After 13 years at Grant and a total of 33 years in APS, Ed finally decided it was time for his own wife and family.

One year Ed invited our jump-rope team to perform for his after-school program. It was to be at night and was part of his school/community concept for which Grant was known. He spent an enormous amount of time at community events to provide the kind of visibility needed to make the concept work. He introduced us to an audience of every age-group imaginable, and provided food for all. After the show our kids each received a brand new rope. Ed always found a way to take care of everyone.

It is always a joy to meet an administrator who shares my faith in extracurricular activity. Some administrators promise and do not follow through. Ed was one who walked the talk. He often worked into the evenings.

After working at Highland and Manzano, Ed was quoted in a school newspaper as saying, "High School gave me the insight to what Middle School [students] needed…. The district intends to establish more middle school programs. They realize how many kids we're losing nationally and locally in middle school. If those fifth-graders come in here and disengage in middle school, high school is gone. Everybody has individual needs, and we need to meet them."

Grant, under Ed's direction, has hosted powwows, youth basketball games, hosted YMCA leagues, bluegrass band practice, church group meetings, Asian fine arts club meetings, health clinics, and of course, jump-rope presentations!

The payoffs for students at Grant and the community are enormous. The facilities are used, not vandalized. Students handle conflicts at the school, not in the neighborhood. Extended families play and spend time together. Multicultural inclusion is a given, not a slogan. As Ed said, "We have families that are facing everyday social problems together in a wholesome atmosphere."

In fact, our superintendent, Winston Brooks, after visiting the community center at Grant, NACA and Wilson said, "The 'one approach fits all' model does not work. This integrated service delivery model supports student achievement—including increasing school attendance, decreasing risky behaviors before and after school, and decreasing disciplinary incidents at school." The administrators in our middle schools and the top officials agree: keeping kids engaged in extracurricular activity has community-wide benefits.

When I started coaching at Manzano in 1976 Ruth Jackson was the APS athletic administrator. Ruth worked for all female athletes and supported coaches and teams alike. She had a vision to help all programs and was on the ground floor of Title IX. When I needed equipment or supplies Ruth was there. Through fairness and professionalism, Ruth had the respect of everyone in high school athletics.

At the time, El Richards was an athletic administrator for the state of New Mexico. Along with Ruth, El was a crucial example of how female administrators would help and support high school athletics in New Mexico. They did the groundwork to foster girls' athletics. They had been helping female athletes before Title IX was enacted in 1972 with a non-abrasive but firm attitude. Working beside them were James Odle with the New Mexico Activities Association, and Gil Miranda, with APS. New Mexico's rich athletic history is largely due to the work of these early dedicated administrators.

Our current athletic administrators have to work with disappearing funding. Ken Barreras, the current APS Athletics Director, oversees a much bigger program, with special interests groups nipping at the budget. APS is trying to build a third stadium, as politicians take both sides. Games and meets, team travel, even uniforms and equipment are all being scaled back. With Julie Sanchez, Ed Drangmeister, Ron Warren, and Rich Gerrells, Ken has to make some hard financial decisions. Nothing right now is predictable.

Coaches' salaries are not very good. There will be fewer qualified people to coach our kids if we don't come up with the money to pay them. At the other end, we are making it harder to *become* an APS coach with ever-increasing standards, paperwork and liability.

Athletics is too valuable to young people for these problems to go unsolved. We must pursue new organization of extracurricular activities for our public school students, especially as we look to the future.

Despite the importance and rarity of high-quality track officials, they are often underpaid and ignored. It is important to have people work a track meet to ensure great and fair competition, helping—not hindering—the athletes. Good officials are fair, polite, alert, approachable, dependable, knowledgeable, and positive. They must officiate without creating an atmosphere of power. Most times, track officials are former track athletes, helping out by staying close to the sport they love. Sometimes they are parents. In age-group track and field, you will find parents who do it year after year because their child was involved. Some of these parents become outstanding officials.

- With over 30 years experience, Dan Dehart is the best track official I have ever seen. He started in age-group track when his daughter Ann was competing. In a long-distance race you only needed Dan—no one else; he could time and place 20 runners. Too many timers could mix up the lap count and put runners in the wrong place, and Dan could time the entire race with no mistakes. As his reputation grew, he also officiated and timed high school and college meets. When big AAU meets came to town, he was always at the finish line. Dan knew the name of every kid who ever ran on the track in New Mexico.

- Elmer Baty, who had three daughters in track, (Jewel, Marcy, and Melanie), was 6'7" and he could see everything over the heads of other timers. He became the head timer at Albuquerque high school meets. Elmer was an outstanding basketball player who loved pickup games on road trips. Tragically, he died of a heart attack, in California, playing in one such pickup game. People always told me, "Elmer is one of the finest human beings I have ever met." When we lost him, a void was created that's never been filled in New Mexico track. At the Albuquerque Relays his daughters now present a plaque in his name to the winning team of the 4 x 2. It is a special honor to go to mid-field.

- Ed Coleman ran track at UNM, and he and his wife Carol taught PE for over 25 years. They officiated, timed, seeded, announced, and ran APS meets. They were easygoing, listened well, and worked easily with the coaches and officials.

- Ed never let a big ego get in the way of making a correction on the track. There were times when the weather was harsh and Ed would call the coaches to the 50-yard line. Sometimes he would suspend the uniform rule, so that athletes could dress warmly. He would turn the hurdles around, so that the wind was to the athletes' backs, which afforded the athletes an easier race and a better time. Ed was always for the athletes and fair competition. I could always approach Carol with a concern in the press box.

Here are a few (only a few!) of the starters I have respected through my career:

- Leland Pierce worked most of the APS boys' track meets. He had a lot of experience and confidence. He was steady and professional.

- Jim Bear worked for the Duke City Dashers when his daughter Tracy was running. He started age-group meets, high school, college, and AAU for over 30 years. Jim was professional and easy going. His voice projection at the start of the race was such that the athletes always were ensured a fair start.

- Originally a track parent, Rick Miller started with the age-group track program and then moved to the high school. He was a starter at the High School State Meets. Rick was very good at preventative officiating, fixing an illegal baton or uniform before the race. Rick would always come to La Cueva to give practice starts to the athletes the week of the State Meet, but that stopped when he became a track coach at Rio Rancho. I chided him, "Rick, you stopped because you didn't want to help that stiff La Cueva competition!"

- A former UNM track coach and elementary and high school PE Teacher, Mark Henry also had many years coaching track at Highland and La Cueva. Because of his experience running, and coaching track and field, I think Mark understood the value of making the athletes feel at ease.

We also had many outstanding relay lane judges:

- Dave Fleming. Dave officiated and did the relay zones for APS meets for many years. He was always alert and gave the kids instruction when needed. If an athlete was confused, he would hold up the race to make sure they understood the marks of the track.

- Stan Hays. Stan, a Valley student, graduated a couple of years before I did. He also worked the relay zones. He was very professional and monitored the rules.

- Gary and Hallie Spitzburg worked at Milne Stadium during both football and track seasons. They opened the stadium and helped to get the track ready for the meet on those cold and windy Spring mornings. Like many officials, APS could not afford to pay them much, and they worked for love of the sport and helping athletes achieve. Over the years many former teachers and athletes would work the track meets despite harsh weather.

- Matt Henry knew the relay zones as well as anyone.

- Buddy Robertson did the relay zones in addition to being a great meet referee.

- Wayne Prentice became a high jump expert over the years and always knew how to place the athletes in the event of ties. This event can get complicated because of all the missed attempts, and Wayne kept track of everything. He would always pick on me: "Ciccarello, do you know how many kids qualify from the high jump to the State Meet yet?" He loved to tell me how to break ties, and called me the "old man of track and field."

- Jerri Robertson, Buddy Robertson's wife, worked the track meets for more than 30 years. You could always find her at the finish line, stopwatch in hand. She also would recruit fellow teachers, family, and friends to administer beside her, including her good friend Gail Guymon. Gail wanted to go visit her grand kids, but Jerri would say, "Now Gail, you can go visit when the meet is over." If I ever needed to know a time of one of my athletes, I would go visit Jerri as she knew all the times recorded. If I was pleasant and cordial, she would give me a time I asked for.

- Matt Henry. When he retired from coaching at UNM, Matt became a meet manager. He and his wife Lisa would seed the meet and put the heat sheets together. I think the whole Henry family was involved in that process. Matt was like Buddy Robertson and Ed Coleman: he was there for the athletes. His decisions were always fair and he enlisted coach input. With his experience at the high school and college levels, and AAU meets, Matt became an outstanding manager. Matt was also an outstanding runner and coach. Not many people can do all that.

- Therese Dorwart was a great runner for the Duke City Dashers, but an even nicer person. In her early years she ran for the legend, John Baker, and then for Pat Cox. I worked with her as a Dasher when our team went out of town to compete. Many years later she became a teacher and administrator at Eldorado. When she went to teach and coach at East Mountain High, she helped develop several State Champion athletes. One year she invited our jump-rope team to perform, which was a treat. They provided hot dogs and hamburgers. We jumped while the high school students ate lunch on the sidewalk patio. We then taught the high school kids some tricks. Therese believed in activities and athletics for all students.

- Steve Baksa was an announcer and track and field historian. He knew everything and everyone. Steve taught PE for over 30 years at Belhaven Elementary.

- George Provolt was a former APS educator. Now a retired teacher and coach, he has worked at Del Norte, La Cueva, Manzano, UNM, and several other APS schools. George can coach many events in track and field, and is especially adept at the pole vault, and worked with athletes from all over New Mexico. Beginning or seasoned, he gave you his time. When Curtis Beach and Daniel Gooris were pre-teens, George and I would marvel at their dedication to practice. After running hurdles at La Cueva for an hour or more, both would meet George to practice pole vault. He was also a competent carpenter.

- The New Mexico Activities Associations runs the sports programs for all state high schools. Sally Marquez, a former Manzano track athlete, was an assistant executive director there, who has helped and supported athletes for many years. She is now their Executive Director. Gary Tripp, the former head executive director administrator, has also been deeply involved and helps teams throughout New Mexico.

He has recently resigned and accepted the Principal position at a high school on a Native American reservation. Dana Sanchez, a former Whittier student, was a commissioner of officials at the New Mexico State Meet. (Dana's sister and her parents, Tom and Helen Pappas, were among the most supportive families in Whittier's history.) Robert Zayas, an associate director, would call me to make sure my times and entries were correct for the upcoming State Meet. The NM Activities Games Committee would do this for all athletes who were to compete in the State Meet (close to 4,000 athletes). This is an extraordinary commitment on their part. Robert has since relocated to New York and works for their activities association

- In the same office is Rudy Aragon. Rudy in his early days was an outstanding athlete and coach; baseball was his focus. Chuck Aragon, the great Notre Dame runner, was his brother. One day Rudy asked if I would like to bring my jump-rope team to the State Basketball Championships. Of course! We practiced our skills and they appreciated the show. Rudy also asked me to give a jump-rope lesson to his son Isaac, who played basketball in Rio Rancho. This went well and Rudy always appreciated the extra time I gave to help his son. At the 2012 State Track meet he published a feature story on my career in the official program.

- Professional writers and sportscasters, by recognizing young athletes in public spheres, also motivate them to become better athletes. People love to watch and read about athletic accomplishments, and local writers extend the work of coaches and PE teachers, seeding pride into the community. I remember with respect the writings of Leroy Bearman, Frank Maestas, Paul Logan, Roger Ruvolo, Matt Lindsey, Jim Wagner, Carlos Salazar, and Phill Casaus. Today we have Rick Wright, Mark Smith, James Yodice, Harold Smith, Will Webber, Glen Rosales, Katie McKernan, Kevin Hendricks and Ken Sickenger. This lineup changes from year to year. We are grateful to each of them.

- In 1959 I met Henry Tafoya. Henry was a little kid in the North Valley who loved to go to the Valley gym and watch Vikings basketball, which I had played. He followed my basketball career, and he kept in contact.

Henry later went into radio and TV broadcasting. When he covered a Lobo basketball game, he and his announcing partner, Keith Griffin, always checked on the halftime show. When Whittier performed, Henry covered it live. "Henry T," as he was called, did this with little league baseball, youth soccer, boys and girls basketball, and all other sports in Albuquerque. He even called his radio program *The Kids Show*. It did not matter if the student was five or 18; Henry gave all kids respect. I believe Henry Tafoya was one of the most important voices a young athlete could hear, and Albuquerque was lucky to have his support in the local media. He never made much money; his payment came in the enrichment of families.

• Joe Behrend is a sportscaster for the Lady Lobos basketball team, and, incidentally, my next door neighbor. When the Whittier/Bandelier jump-rope team performs at a Lady Lobo game, he always gives the team a great radio introduction. Joe has a magical voice that makes the radio seem visual.

One day he asked me to give his nine-year-old daughter a jump-rope lesson. Maria, is an up-and-coming tennis player. She practices several days a week at the Albuquerque Tennis Club. Joe and I believe that if she learns to move her feet more quickly she will improve her game, and she is now adding jump-rope to her practice routine. When she has developed some great skills and combinations we will bring her to the Pit to take part in the halftime show. (Her tennis partner Mikayla Herrera has now joined her, to be part of the jump-rope experience. Both girls plan to up their game.) I know that the night that happens, Joe will add some extra "Magic" to the airways.

All track meets are a culmination of work. As we show up at Milne Stadium or Wilson Stadium on a cold Saturday morning, we see track officials already there. Many I know; some are new. There is no way to know all of their names, but I *do* know they want to do a good and fair job. There may be people working the meet I haven't named here, but we could not run it without them.

Officials come from all walks. Some are teachers, or were runners themselves. Sportscasters, writers and administrators are also often former athletes. I am proud to know so many educators and athletes dedicated to helping young people excel.

TRUE STORY!

Over the years, as I talk about education and track and field, people always prime me for stories. If you stay in one profession long enough you will have many to tell, and often the true stories are the more interesting. Here are a few short ones:

- My team and I were at a track meet at Milne Stadium in the early '70s and were set to run a 4 x 1 relay. Rhonda Adams was running first. As the gun went off she took off like a rocket and was in first place in the middle of the first turn. All of a sudden she turned and ran back. Rhonda had taken off so fast she left the relay baton at the starting line.

- In 1973 the ATC was traveling to Phoenix. We always needed to raise money for these trips. Age-group programs gather money from anyone who will give. My former Valley track coach, Jerry Apodaca, now former NM State Governor, always told me to call if I needed help raising funds. There was many a time the Governor would call during a PE class. The people in the office would freak out, and I would say, "Tell the Governor to hold until I finish teaching this class." Sometimes he had to wait for up to 20 minutes, but Jerry understood and waited diligently. The office staff could never figure out our connection.

- When you go out of town you always count your athletes—and hope to return with all of them. One year while I was coaching at La Cueva, our bus was pulling out of Santa Fe. A little outside Albuquerque, we realized one of our athletes had gone to the rest room to change, and never got on the bus. It was a windy, cold and snowy day. Lucky for her, she was able to hitch a ride with a boys' track bus. My staff and I had worried to death. She later told me it was her favorite road trip of all time.

- On a trip to Clovis, NM, we had the misfortune of riding a yellow bus. Normally you get a Coach, with fancy seats—which the boys had. 100 miles outside of Clovis the bus broke down. Of course we were in a hurry.

We made many phone calls. It looked like we would be about three hours late, which would mean missing the scratch meeting, and most of the meet. We stood outside with blankets and pillows, when behind us, over the hill, a bus appeared. It was the Rio Rancho Girls' Track Team—also headed to Clovis. As they sped by us, I got on my cell and called their head coach, Larry Chavez. After a little negotiation, he agreed to pick us up.

It speaks well of Larry, as Rio Rancho happened to be our chief rival that year. You can imagine the looks on the faces of the Rio Rancho girls as we hopped on their bus. It was a silent ride to Clovis. Larry and I were friends, but the athletes did not know this, nor did they care!

It got worse. In a very close track meet that went down to the last event, the La Cueva girls won by one point… over Rio Rancho. And we had to ride their bus back to Albuquerque. At about 2:00 a.m., just south of city limits, we had to decide who was to get off first. La Cueva was closer to the freeway.

Larry made it clear if Rio Rancho didn't go first he'd have a riot on his hands. Rick Miller, another Rio Rancho coach, and a good friend, added that he would never again give our athletes free practice starts. This added another 45 minutes. My kids were tired, cold, and hungry. They never understood why we went out of the way. Larry and I still joke about it, and I told him someday we will return the favor, but not the trophy. Rick has never started any La Cueva girls again.

- In my 50s and 60s, though I could not run with the young players, I could still shoot fairly well. At my gym I always played HORSE with young kids, in which one has to repeat the last shot—no running and jumping. I made shots over the backboard and from behind the basket. I even sunk one off the air conditioner.

I played many ex-Lobos like Hunter Green and Kelvin Scarborough. We would play these games at Midtown Sports & Wellness Club. My favorite competition were the young and upcoming athletes. Josh Jenkins, Alvin Brossard, JC Lovelace, Jordan Mahboub, Alfred Sanchez Jr., Jaylin Dominguez, Curtis Beach, Bre Rhode, and Dominique Dexter. Even high school kids I did not know would challenge me. Jake Flores, Kelsey Kouri and others at the front desk would encourage members to take me on. The front desk employees would always give me the nicer, softer-covered ball, and my opponents the older, rougher-skinned one. I was 50 years their senior and beating the shorts of them. They enjoyed the challenge, and I stayed in shape. They all grew up to be outstanding players. I cherished those moments. My love for basketball never waned.

There are three athletes who did give me a run for my money playing HORSE. Ron Nelson, one of the best shooters in Lobo history, was so good I avoided him. Dickey Gallegos, a former Appliance City club player, would shoot a hook from half-court that no one could duplicate. Clarence Brooks was an ex-Albuquerque High basketball star who played above the rim. We all had fun, but I was selective about who I challenged!

- In 1976 I was with Val Boyer at the Olympic Trials in Eugene, OR. This was a big meet for her, and she was nervous and excited. Val had qualified for the 100m and 200m dash. The night before, always meticulous, she had organized everything in her track bag. Her track uniform was clean and in order. Her spikes were new and in place. She had a great warm-up and was ready to go. When she reported for her preliminary event with all the big stars on the track, she realized for some reason, her number was in the bag—in the stands. I was on the other side of the track, trying to get a photo of her coming off the curve. When I realized what was going on, it was too late to get to her bag. Panic! A track official saved her, borrowing someone else's number, and writing hers on the back. On a national stage, at the biggest track meet of Val's young life, she was running with a hand-written number.

Not many coaches have the opportunity to work with such a motivated athlete. The following story I have only told a couple of times. I assure you, it's true:

Val attended ASU on a full-ride athletic scholarship. When she was a freshman she came back to Albuquerque to run in the world-renowned JC indoor track meet in 1978. This meet always attracted Olympic Champions and other world-class athletes, and was at the time regarded as the best indoor invitational in the country, a springboard to the coming outdoor season. The banked wood track at the time was 176 yards long. We ran our age-groupers on this track when they had a special invite to local clubs. Val had run on it for years as an age-grouper with the ATC. The previous summer Val had run on the USA Junior team against the USSR juniors, and had been voted Most Valuable Athlete. She was in good shape, with international experience. Albuquerque was excited to have her in the 60-yard dash against some of the world's finest sprinters. The local media loved it: 'home-town girl returns to face the best in the world.' Entered in the race from Brazil was Esmeralda Garcia, a two-time Olympian and future holder of the world record in the triple jump. Garcia was the top-ranked sprinter in the world at the time, with the fastest indoor time for the 60-yard dash, and a gold medal in the Pan American Games 100m dash.

Val was 19 and returning to compete. When she was introduced in her lane, the sold-out Tingely Coliseum went crazy. Maybe it was nerves, maybe just her first real competition in a while, but she had a slow start and Garcia zoomed start to finish. But this is just the beginning.

Val felt like she let the home-crowd down and was quiet most of the evening. Every year, following the JC invitational, there was an Albuquerque Olympette Invitational for age-group runners, with an open division for world-class runners. We had entered Val in the 220-yard dash for that meet a week earlier. The 220-yard dash is seldom held indoors because of the distance and measuring practicalities. Sunday morning, I heard from the meet director that Esmeralda was staying an extra day and had entered in the 220-yard dash. When I called Val and told her she would run against Esmeralda one more time, the phone was silent. If you knew Val, this meant something big was going to happen.

The meet started at 8:00 a.m.. Val was there at 7:00 a.m., warming up. The 220-yard race in the open division was to be run at noon. She went into a trance I had never seen before; there was no talking to her. Remember, these two world-class sprinters were about to compete against each other *for the second time*. It was a given that Garcia would take the race. Not for me. I knew Val Boyer!

For a runner, it is difficult to pass on the 176-yard wooden track. Val knew that if she could be first to the white line coming off the bank, she had a good chance to win, and with the outside lane, she could generate more speed coming off the curve. The gun rang over the Coliseum like a cannon.

Compared with the night before, the place was empty. But with the gun all eyes went immediately to the first turn. Val hit the white line first and immediately cut one stride in front of Esmeralda. You could hear their spikes pound the wood. Val had eyes for the finish line only. Esmeralda tried to make a move on the straight-away, but Val held her off, pumping her arms furiously.

Val crossed first, the great Brazilian sprinter one stride behind. The time was a 24.41. There were only a few hundred people there to see it, when the night before there had been thousands. The fans that showed for the *Saturday Afternoon Special* got what they came for. It was the best race of the weekend. But there's more.

Val was happy to avenge her defeat. She had reached back and over-achieved, and was satisfied. Garcia was gracious in defeat and knew without question that Val was a quality runner. The following week I picked up a newspaper and read that Frieda Hancock of the Colorado Flyers had just broken the world record for the indoor 220-yard dash in New York City—with a time of 24.39. The old record was a 24.42. Val had broken a world record herself the week before in the Albuquerque Olympette Invitational. Because it was an age-group meet, and they did not antici-pate anything newsworthy, the local meet management did not have official timers. People there knew that the race was a special moment. We did not know we had witnessed an unofficial world record!

The 2008 Albuquerque City Metro meet must have had one of the most exciting hurdle races of all time. I had been coaching Curtis Beach and Chad Clark in the 300m hurdles. Curtis was competing for Albuquerque Academy and Chad for La Cueva. Also in the race was Rolo Trammel, a great Highland hurdler. As the meet moved toward the final of the 300m hurdles the excitement was palpable. Curtis was the favorite and Rolo was picked for a close second. All three hurdlers were undefeated and it was time to match up.

When they started the race, every person in that stadium had their eyes on it. Clark took the lead, running the best race of his life. Coming off the final turn, all three hurdlers were faster than the State Record pace. With one hurdle left to negotiate, Chad had a three-yard lead. His leading leg hit the last hurdle and pushed it into the next lane. Chad fell down and rolled over. Rolo's hurdle also was hit and moved as he fell down. *Curtis* now hit the track, as they had bumped his hurdle, too. Rolo was the first to recover, and crawled over the finish line to win. This race was caught on film and someone put it on YouTube, where it became the most-watched race on the site's history. If no one had hit a hurdle, all three boys would have been under the State Record. They never rematched.

- In 1973 the ATC went to the age-group nationals in California. We were driving in private cars. Parents were driving some of the athletes. In a small town in Arizona, one of our parents' cars was overheating. She got so frustrated she stopped at a gas station, bought a used car from the back, and continued on, leaving her original on its own. She never received a penny for the car she left behind.

- On the same trip, parents in another car asked me to settle down some of the kids. At a rest stop I warned the athletes that we would not tolerate misbehavior, and if they did not stop, they would not run.

When we checked in our hotel we had another problem in one of the rooms. Three girls, 14–15-year-olds who happened to be the highest-ranked 4 x 1 relay team in the country, had threatened another girl with being locked in a closet. When I got to the room, they were feisty. After much consultation and consideration, I suspended them from the meet. This was one of the hardest decisions I have ever made; to this day, I second-guess myself. I never had trouble with that group again. Another athlete on that relay had flown in with her parents. It was her only event, and she did not run. Her parents never let her run again.

- In 1999 I went back to the Northeast to attend a fitness clinic, and rented a car to visit my old neighborhood. It had changed considerably after 42 years. We went to the Marion Projects in Jersey City, a federal projects program that was built solely for low-income people. As we took photos of my former grammar school, a white van pulled out of a driveway and hit us.

The rental car was damaged. At first we were stunned, and we quickly realized we were hit on purpose. It was an attempted car-jacking. We reversed and cleared out of the neighborhood. When we reported it to the Jersey City PD, we were told, "You should never go into that neighborhood alone…. The police department only responds to calls from the projects when we have four units available." We were lucky to get out of my childhood neighborhood in one piece.

- When I first started teaching at Whittier Frank Monceballez was teaching sixth grade. He had three daughters and a son who ran track for me. Lori, a nine-year-old at the time, was always asking about fitness and health. I told her if she wanted to be healthy at 30 she had better stay fit, because her metabolism would start slowing. As the years passed Lori never stopped working out. When she got into her 30s and 40s she would work in my yard, mowing the lawn, cutting bushes, fixing sprinklers and hauling away the trash. She had stayed fit all these years. She still calls me "Coach," and it was not until she mowed my grass at 50 that she learned my first name.

- Manny Smith's reputation for paddling was known throughout APS. His son Mark became one of Albuquerque's better sports writers. Mark covers the UNM men's basketball team, and always seems to have a good attitude. I often wonder, "Did Manny ever use that paddle on the young Mark Smith in the early years?"

- At the State Meet in 2000 we had a great 400m runner in Amy Warner. Eldorado had the equally great Donnita Harmon. We were locked up with Manzano in a very close meet. In the finals of the 400m dash, there was only one empty lane. Donnita, the top-ranked qualifier, was warming up in the grass area and could not hear her call to report to the starting line. As the starter was about to fire, his gun jammed. As he reloaded, Coach Kathy Brion from Eldorado got Donnita back into her lane, and she won the race with a new State Record, Amy in second. This was the same year La Cueva won the meet by ¼ of a point because of Allision Haar's four-way tie in the pole vault, edging out Manzano.

- At Sandia in 1983, I was on my way to a meet at Milne Stadium. I stopped at a light at Lead and University, and a Volkswagen Bug was passing me. A girl in a red track uniform was standing on the back fender. She had her hand on the carburetor and was trying to keep it open, to keep the engine running. I got closer and realized it was one of my Sandia girls. They were going about 40 MPH! This girl was slated to run on one of our relays. I immediately caught up and made them pull over. I helped them fix the car and we all proceeded to the stadium.

- Ten years earlier, at a track meet with the ATC, we had a parent excitedly cheering for Sandy Beach. With his accent, "Go Sandy Beach!" was coming out, "Go Sandy B*tch!" We had everybody in the stands wondering *who* and *what* Sandy Beach he was encouraging!

- I was traveling alone to an international track meet, in Ostrava, Czech Republic. Leaving Chicago, a lightning storm started. Our flight was delayed two hours. When I got to Warsaw I hurried to Terminal One (the international terminal), looking to connect to Krakow, and then on to Ostrava. Only the counter staff spoke English. I was at the back of the line with about 100 Russian travelers heading to the Ukraine. They were pushing and shoving, yelling in Russian. Everybody was mean and disrespectful. I was frustrated and thinking I would miss Curtis Beach's first day of the decathlon, wishing I had gone with Jeana and David Beach on an earlier flight. When I finally got to the front of the line I found out that I was in the wrong terminal and that I had to relocate to Terminal Two, the domestic-Poland terminal. I missed my flight.

  This was a legitimate but costly mistake. By the time I got it resolved, I was told to wait on a bench for a seat on a 2:00 a.m. flight to Prague, with a possible connection into Ostrava on a small private jet with a team coming from Africa. As I waited in Prague, they told me it did not look good. That meant that I would not get into Ostrava until noon the next day.

  But I had an angel looking out for me. A young Czech Republic attendant who spoke perfect English found me at 2:00 a.m. She was as nice as she was beautiful. I had just given up when she said, "Hurry, we have one seat left!" I was the last person on that plane, and the happiest passenger onboard. At about 5:00 a.m., I connected with the Beach family in Ostrava and did not miss Curtis's competition, though I needed about two days' sleep! Returning to the USA, I traveled with the Beaches. There were no problems.

- "Crash Jordan" Foreman is a very good tennis player who graduated from Sandia. His mother, Elaine, is an up-and-coming APS track meet timer. He is a good friend of Curtis Beach's, and at one time showed promise in the 300m hurdles. We would do hurdle drills on the track and at one time I thought he would be a top-shelf hurdler in New Mexico. He wanted to be as good as Curtis, his role model. Jordan tried to match Curtis's splits in the hurdle drills, and if he was close enough, he would just run *through* the hurdle ("crashing" into it). Once, in his exuberance to match Curtis (who had five years' experience on him) he took a nasty fall and broke his arm. From that day forward, he became "Crash Jordan"… and never the quality hurdler he sought to be.

- At Whittier in 2008 Josh Perrault had come to student-teach. He was a young, excited UNM student, and very trusting. He planned to start a new job, and new life, which he was inaugurating with a brand-new motorcycle and helmet. It was a beauty. He said it cost about $12,000. On his first day he taught a dance unit.

  Meredith Vargas was leading a soccer game during recess outside and saw a man with a helmet get on the motorcycle and leave. When Meredith came in later she asked, "Coach, did Josh leave already? I know our kids are tough, but I thought he certainly would make it through the first day." I shortly ran into Josh, who breathlessly told me his motorcycle had just been stolen. Josh received an A for his student-teaching, began teaching in APS in 2011, and still keeps in contact. His motorcycle was never recovered.

- In 2009, when the track season was over, I gave a couple of lessons in hurdling to Laura Lavezo. Laura was a distance runner for La Cueva. She wanted to enter the Steeplechase event at the Great Southwest Classic, a special postseason meet for high school athletes. Laura had only a few lessons and wanted to give this event a try. It spans about two miles, and involves several hurdle barriers and a water jump. At the first water barrier, Laura slipped and fell in. She completely disappeared. Athletes behind her, clearing the hurdle, stepped on her as she tried to get her head above water. Being the good sport she was, she picked herself up with a big smile and finished the race soaking wet. I don't know if Laura has run it again.

- In 44 years, I caught six to eight colds annually. Young kids carry the most potent germs you can believe, and they are always generous with them. One year I caught Pink Eye from a fourth-grader. I was required by APS to take a two-week break before I could return. My right eye has never recovered full vision.

- In the summer of 2010 I took a small group of jump-ropers to the Santa Ana Reservation for a clinic. I thought we would be in a gym. Instead we were on a cement slab by a cow pasture. The entire community came, some sitting under a tree in the shade. The elders introduced me to the audience and I started to teach.

In the middle of my presentation, three dogs came up and got in the way of the ropes. I had a boom box, but no electricity. All of a sudden a pickup truck drove onto the cement, an elder got out and said, "Coach, you can use my truck radio to play your music… and don't worry about the dogs—they just hang out here." Before the afternoon was over, I had all of the kids, and most of the elders, jumping rope on a cement slab in the middle of a cow pasture. It was about 95° and the cement was hot to the touch. As we were leaving, the elders invited us indoors and fed my jumpers a three-course lunch.

- The biggest show involving food was in 2004. Luther Garcia had invited us to perform at Los Padillas Elementary, which is surrounded by farmland. We had a great time, and when the show was over Luther invited us into a portable building for a special treat. I thought we would get the usual water and cracker snacks.

  Instead, it was as if we had entered a supermarket. There were fresh vegetables and fruit everywhere, and eggs and milk. Our kids were free to take whatever they wanted back on the bus. As they boarded, they were happier than I had ever seen them as they showed me the treats they were taking to their families: gallons of milk, sacks of oranges, apples, and veggies. When we arrived back at Whittier the principal and secretary said, "Coach, next time, please invite us to chaperone!"

- Kiva Gresham was one of our best rope-skippers of all time. She was very creative and invented many tricks. One time we went to Hodgin Elementary, and after Kiva did her usual dazzling performance, a first-grade boy came up and handed her a dollar bill—his lunch money. As we got on the bus, I told Kiva, "You are now a professional athlete and your high school and college careers are over."

- An Nguyen was a classmate and friend of Kiva's from elementary through high school. Like Kiva, An was athletic, and returned to help Whittier kids improve their physicals kills. I received a letter many years later from An. He explained to me that he had always felt that fitness and health would make him a better adult. He works as a zookeeper in Oregon now. Most future zookeepers need to work out 3–5 days each week for their job. Strength and endurance are needed. An has stayed in shape using the same motivation he learned in elementary school. His dream of being a zookeeper has been realized because of his physical fitness.

- We always took students to La Cueva to jump rope. The year-end senior assembly was one of our top shows. And seniors always pull a prank on the faculty: one year, they released two wild pigs in the administration building, as teachers and secretaries alike flew onto tables.

In 2003, we were performing for the entire student body—about 2000 kids. Right in the middle of one of our favorite tricks, the gym was flooded with bouncing little super-balls. The seniors had started to throw them at the freshman across the gym, who were in return throwing them back. Our kids were on their hands and knees picking up balls and putting them in their pockets and shirts. Our elementary kids thought this was hysterical. The older students got in trouble. The principal apologized. On the bus home, the elementary kids were proud to show everybody off all the super-balls they had recovered.

- Play Day at Whittier is held in the last week of the school year. We usually have track and field events followed by small, non-competitive games. In the late '80s, I decided to add a game of tug-of-war. We dug a big hole and filled it with water. Albuquerque is hot in late May, so water events are always popular.

The fifth-graders that year were a mischievous group with a lot of energy. After the last tug of the day, they began to lose control, dragging anyone they could into the hole. First they got the custodian. Then they went after teaching aids. Soon they were dragging seasoned teachers into the mud. When they went after the principal, I about lost my own composure. They chased her into the building and she had to hide until the last bell rang. The next day the principal informed me that there would never again be a tug-of-war with a mud hole at Whittier—while she was in charge.

- When you enter an APS building at night or in closed hours, you are expected to call security. Sometimes I schedule a nighttime show, which departs from and returns to the Whittier gym. At times, I get distracted and forget to call security. One year I forgot entirely. That night, after all of our kids were picked up, I heard a commotion from the gym lobby. Security had arrived—with their dogs. A big German Shepherd had pinned a parent against the wall. He was scared to death and told me he would never drive for a jump-rope show again. The next day my gym keys were taken away for one week.

- One day I was hosting a race in the gym. It was a simple line-to-line race, one direction across the gym floor. Bryanna Brown, a second-grader, ran so hard she hit the wall—with her head. At the time it looked serious, and she received stitches. There was blood on the wall and silence in the classroom. Kids may get loud and rowdy, but when one of them gets hurt, the silence is astonishing.

  That night we had a PTA gymnastics demonstration in the gym. Bryanna was on our team, and showed up, ready to go, with a bandage on her head. The blood was still on the wall—we could never completely wash it off. I used the stain as a teaching tool, to keep kids in control. Whenever kids run too hard inside, or are out of control, I take them to the wall and tell them about Bryanna Brown. Her legend is now 15 years old and kids always look for the stain. With their imagination working, they still see it, even after several paint jobs.

- All athletic teams have fundraisers to help support their programs. At Sandia in 1980, we bought 1,000 stuffed Teddie Bears to resell. Mr. Granados was the activities director at Sandia and kept them in his office, in a metal filing cabinet. They arrived in December and we were going to sell them when the spring track season started. One day in March, I was informed that the Teddie Bears were gone. Head coaches are held responsible for all equipment and supplies. No one ever found those Teddie Bears, and I had to use my home insurance to cover the replacement cost. The next year we had a spaghetti dinner. There were no attempts to steal the spaghetti.

- When we teach PE in the gym we sometimes get surprises. At the end of each class day we blow our whistle to line kids up and put away equipment. One day, after a football lesson, Meredith Vargas was standing next to me as we blew the whistle. The kids were told to put the balls in the barrel. As the balls were flying toward the barrel, a shoe hit Coach Vargas in the eye. The kid who threw the shoe said he did not have a ball, so he just took his shoe off and threw it with the balls. It took a couple of weeks to heal. He could not explain why he threw it.

- Twenty years earlier I was teaching a playground soccer unit. This was on Valentine's Day and the kids were excited about the afternoon parties. A third grade teacher was standing next to me to pick up her students. When I blew the whistle to line up, one of the kids took an extra kick: the ball hit her squarely in the face and broke her glasses—and her nose. Before the ball hit the ground, she yelled, "There will be no Valentine's party today!" The class was their quietest all year. I never found out if they had a party after all, and she never picked up the kids from PE again. Student leaders led them back to class the rest of the year.

- Stan Chavez told me a story about a second-grader named Justin, from his time at Osuna Elementary:

  The kids were playing kickball. Justin would tell them to run to third, second, first, and then home. When Coach Chavez tried to tell him this was backwards, Justin would tell coach, "No Coach, the correct direction to run the bases is from left to right." Every kid followed his instruction, and ran hard around the bases. One day at the Frontier Restaurant, I met Justin, now 35 years old. He told me, "Coach, I was a rascal back then, and everybody would follow me no matter what." Leaders are born to lead—even when it may be wrong!

- My life has always included dogs—I am particularly fond of Labrador Retrievers. They are very loving, loyal and good with children. I usually name them to mark a time in my life: my yellow Lab was named Scarlett, after Scarlett O'Hara. (I was running the Lobo Movie Theater, and everything was about movies.) After 13 years, she seemed to take on some of Ms. O'Hara's personality; she was very spoiled and an indiscriminate lover of those around her. Many years later I acquired two more Labs: Banda (black), for Bandelier, and Whittney (chocolate mix), for Whittier. People have told me, their personalities match the kids at the schools they were named after.

  Once in a while I bring them to school. They are friendly and well-trained. The day I bring them, I tell the kids whoever is quietest and the nicest can sit in my chair and hold the puppy on their lap. Invariably, we will have the best behavior of the year. One day I picked a kindergarten student. This puppy, while sitting on her lap, gave her a big lick on the face. The kids went crazy with laughter. For several years that kid kept asking when I was bringing Banda back.

- Kip Koech was a student at Whittier in the late '90s. One day he said he wanted me to meet his dad. Peter was very humble and very quiet. He just happened to be the Silver Medal-winner in the Steeplechase in the 1988 Olympics! He had competed on the Kenyan team. I invited Peter to make a motivational speech to our classes: he brought his silver medal and gave a demonstration in the hurdles. The kids were speechless. For several years, every kid at Whittier wanted to run the hurdles. I myself was further motivated to coach hurdlers. Kip's mom, Molly, has been the school nurse for over 15 years. Kip went on to Harvard and graduated with honors. When he speaks to my PE classes, he always tells the students how important an education is for every student.

- When I teach jump-rope at Whittier, I always have $2 ropes for sale. Kids put their names on them, and take them home for practice. Most times, I receive pennies and nickels. In February of 2012 a first-grader handed me $200 in big bills. She wanted one rope. At the office we discovered she had another $800. This was enough money to buy every kid at Whittier a jump-rope. Needless to say, her parent was called, and the issue was resolved behind the principal's closed door!

- In the late 2000s at La Cueva, I was introduced to the Trujillo family from Los Alamos. They wanted to work with the hurdlers and sprinters. Amanda and Victoria were the daughters of Ron and Peggy. They were friends with Steve Alderette, a parent of two other runners at La Cueva (Allie and Brittney). The girls were so motivated to learn that they would drive two hours each way, all week, for a practice session. Both girls became excellent runners and helped lead Los Alamos to a couple of State Championships. They were one of the most appreciative and respectful athletic families I have ever had the pleasure to meet.

- In 2012 the La Cueva coaching staff assigned Carly Browning the task of looking after Venitra Fields. As a freshman the previous year, we could never find Miss Fields. The final call for the 4 x 1 relay would be made with Venitra nowhere in sight. We would find her under a canopy in the stands, with her cousin or friend, not realizing her event was about to begin. This assignment extended to track. In the middle of our warm-up we would ask Carly where Venitra was at that moment. After a while, she always knew.

- I went to the Olympic Trials in Eugene, Oregon, in the summer of 2012, to watch Curtis Beach try out for the USA Olympic Team. His brother, mother and I were sharing expenses. We rented a brand-new Toyota SUV with less than 100 miles on it; it was a beautiful automobile. Luckily, Jeana had arranged for us to stay at a nearby house. At the time Portland hotels were running over $200 per night, and Jeana had met this family on her many track trips.

  Jeanie Fisher owned the house. The morning after our arrival, she was backing out of her garage, and forgetting she had company, backed into the SUV. It was a $1,000 fix. While they were working we rented another car—from another company. All they had available was a huge Ford pickup truck. Jeana had trouble parking this truck everywhere we went. The final expense was the rental for two vehicles, the repair, and the extra gas for the truck. So much for saving expenses!

  Later, Jeana and AJ Beach and I were in the stands as Curtis performed perhaps one of the most genuine acts of sportsmanship in competition ever seen on a national level. The decathlon is 10 individual events scored as one; it is a true total test of speed, strength, and endurance. Curtis's best event is the last—the 1500m run. He needed to finish third and meet the 'A' standard, but with a low-scoring high jump, and no score in the javelin due to an injured elbow, (he pulled out of the event to avoid risking further injury), he was effectively out of the competition.

  As the 1500m was about to begin I saw a determination in Curtis's eyes. The gun went off and he took off like a rabbit, opening a huge lead. He was on his way to a World Record. At the halfway point he started looking around. Ashton Eaton was on pace to set a World Record for the total ten events, if he could finish in 4:16. Curtis was on pace for this 1500m to finish in 3:54, a World Record for the 1500m itself. He slowed and waved Eaton on to pass. In the last 50m Eaton sprinted by. Eaton may have set the Record anyway, but Curtis showed the world an act of sportsmanship never seen before on a national stage.

  The US Track and Field committee decided that the sportsmanship he showed was so impressive they flew him to the 2012 London Olympic Games, all expenses paid, and presented him a special award as he met with Eaton. Curtis is on their radar as a potential USA decathlon representative in 2016 Rio de Janeiro. In New Mexico we have seen his attitude before. Now others have seen it, too.

- In the summer of 2012 we did a jump-rope presentation at the Nob Hill 66 Summer Festival. As our kids were performing, I noticed four men waving at us. Warrick Campbell, Tung Tat, Charles Lewis, and Jacob Jaramillo—former students and members of our jump-rope team—were asking to join in. They jumped on stage and proceeded to wow the crowd. Warrick and Jacob, in particular, were outstanding as they did the "Butt-Bumper," our favorite.

- Pete Simon at a young age developed Tourette's Syndrome. In elementary and middle school he was always a strong athlete but never had a chance to compete. He would have been one of the top football and track athletes at Del Norte, but because of his condition the coaches had a difficult time keeping Pete on the varsity team; he distracted players as the coaches talked. Additionally, because of his head movement and tics, Pete's neck grew from a 14" to a 26" in one year. One day, at the indoor track meet at Tingley Coliseum, Pete had a chance to meet the great Houston McTear, one of the USA's fastest indoor runners of all time. At one time he held the World Record in the indoor 60m dash. In an unofficial challenge after the indoor meet, Houston just barely beat Pete in a 50-yard dash. Houston later said, "This white guy with Tourette's is one of the fastest guys I have ever raced."

- Sisters Susan, Madeline and Carol Muraida attended the Albuquerque Academy and "race-walked" for the ATC. They could compete on a USA National Age-Group level. They came from a solid and respected family. One time, as we prepared for a halftime show at the Pit, the sisters sang the national anthem at the start of the game. Their voices were every bit as good as their feet.

- After teaching at Bandelier, Lee Hayes taught in several remote Alaskan villages. I went to visit him many times. One year he taught in the island village of Yakatak. There is not a lot to do in Yakatak for recreation. The locals fish, play basketball, and socialize at the airport bar. There are only a few flights a week in and out, and when a plane lands most of the village is there. After debarking from the plane Lee and I spent several hours at the airport.

Several locals at the next table were listening to our conversation about Lobo Basketball. They asked if I played. I said sure, but only HORSE these days. They laughed and asked if I wanted to play Jimmy from the village. Little did I know Jimmy was a 27-year-old superstar, the island's basketball legend.

Lee had the keys to the gym and set up the match. The whole village showed up! It was a great match, and I beat him at the end with a left-handed free throw, perhaps only because he had a few drinks in him still from the airport. He was very gracious and afterward invited me to his house to meet his family. Later, he took me into the garage and said, "I want to give you something to remember our match forever when you return to the lower 48." He opened a freezer and packed King Crab, Salmon, and Halibut into a big box. I was speechless. This was the peak of great respect, all because of a game of HORSE. On my return flight Alaska Airlines lost the fish. Five days later they found it in an airport hanger—rotten to the core. They issued me a $500 round-trip ticket to return to Alaska.

• Lee later retired and moved to Bisbee, AZ after retiring. He brought his Siberian Huskies with him.

Louis Schiffman was a friend of ours from the gym. He loved dogs and liked to walk Whittney and Banda when I was out of town. Lee invited Louis to care for the dogs for a week. Lee had 13 dogs leashed to a pole on his ranch. Louis flew out on a Friday and returned on Sunday. He said, "Coach, those Huskies are *not* like your Labs. When I tried to feed them they attacked *me* more than the food!

Lee later told me, "Jim, those Huskies are part *wolf*." Louis has never returned to Arizona.

RIVALS!

Coaching track and field has always encouraged great competition. Here are a several stories of our great rivalries:

- I started the ATC with former Duke City Dashers. Because they were older, with girls in the open division, and we dealt with age-groupers, it was light competition. The real rivals were from California—the Rialto Road Runners and Long Beach Comets. Mary Decker, with the Long Beach Comets, and Wendy Koenig with the Colorado Gold, were fierce competitors. They both went on to make Olympic teams.

  The two clubs became natural rivals. AOC had the great Carol Hudson and Lisa Chivario. As our girls matured and ran in the open division, the rivalry with AOC increased. Other clubs soon joined the fray: the Boca Grande Track Club from Roswell, Police Athletic League (PAL), Supremes Track Club, Albuquerque Tumbleweeds, Farmington Fleet Feet, Alvarado Track Club, Albuquerque Indian School, and the Barcelona Elementary Track Club all competed fiercely, too.

  As we improved, our rivals came from further away: the Colorado Flyers, Boulder Cinderbelles, Phoenix Flyers, Valley of the Sun Track Club, Phoenix Track Club, Southern California Cheetahs, Blue Angels, El Paso Track Club, and the San Diego Cougars. We even had a healthy rivalry with Wilt Chamberlain's Wonder Women. Wilt's teams were always fast—but our teams could run beside them.

  At Manzano our main rivals were Alamogordo, Farmington, Roswell, Del Norte, Belen, and Los Lunas. They all had motivated coaches and athletes. Coach Marilyn Sepulveda's Alamogordo team was a tough match in every meet. She developed her team into one of New Mexico's top girls track teams ever.

- The age-group program was completely different from high school competition. My coaching philosophy had to change; the team score had to be emphasized over the individual. The southern schools, led by Alamogordo, understood this better than most. We had some catching up to do. And with catch-up came new rivals.

- When I coached at Sandia, Cibola became a team to reckon with. Our Shannon Ryan always had to compete against Manzano's Reator Golston. Shannon's rival in the hurdles, also from Manzano, was Tanya Thompson, a former DCD teammate. They were two of the best athletes in the state; rivals push each other to excellence.

- In 1985, at Highland, we had a great rivalry with Eldorado. There my friend Jimmy Knop put some great teams on the track. The "Blonde Bomber," Michelle Schmidt, ran for him, beside some other sprinters. Sandra Crowe from Alamogordo and Anne Frost from Farmington were outstanding hurdlers. Susan Kreis and Natanya Jones from Highland gave them all they could handle in the hurdles.

- In 2000, when I started with La Cueva, Manzano was our close rival, coached by John Flores. John was a quiet man, very knowledgeable and very dedicated, and no matter the outcome, he was always a good sport. As a former coach of the Manzano team, I took our competition seriously.

- Other serious competitors were Clovis, Highland, and Eldorado. Clovis has always been the strongest girls track team in New Mexico. Over the long haul, Eldorado, Manzano, and La Cueva have been Clovis's primary opponents.

- Amy Warner of La Cueva and Donnita Harmon of Eldorado were fierce rivals in my first year at La Cueva. They had great races in the 200m and 400m sprints. One day at the Academy's Harper Invitational, they ran a fierce 200m race. Amy's photo-finish victory formed our rivalry with Eldorado. Her 24.39 time was the fastest 200m's ever recorded in NM.

- La Cueva and Eldorado are only a few miles apart, and Kathy Brion's team was our toughest local contender. The kids knew one another well; some even attended middle school together. We both take pride in the 4 x 400m relay, and while we often have an edge on them, Kathy Brion coaches a close race every time.

- Tom Mescall was a former St. Pius and Norte Dame track athlete. He was a NM State Record holder in both the 110m hurdles and the high jump. I would work out with Tom at my gym, and we would talk track for hours. When I introduced Tom to Curtis Beach he became excited about the multi events as he himself was a decathlon athlete. Tom was very impressed with Curtis's jump-rope skills.

As Tom met some of my La Cueva athletes he always offered them coaching tips, showing them great sportsmanship, despite being a rival. Many of my rivals over the years always had respect for their opponents.

- Coaches Dorme (Cibola) and Ray (Clovis) always put strong teams on the track. Cibola had the sprinters; Clovis, the jumpers and throwers; La Cueva the middle-distance runners. Team scores usually came down to the last event, and only a few points would separate several them.

- La Cueva and Highland also had a great rivalry. Highland had the jumpers and sprinters, La Cueva, the 400m runners. As ever, the last event defined everything. The rivalry with Highland was such that the team score would be very close.

Today our biggest rivals are Rio Rancho and Cleveland, coached by Rick Miller and Tim Flores, respectively. In 2011, when we barely beat Cleveland, Coach Flores came over to congratulate me. The following year I made sure I returned the courtesy, when Cleveland won their first team championship.

Both schools have strong teams, and their schools are growing. Big schools, good coaches, and great athletes make for a strong rivalry! Sometimes the difference is very small. Over time competition can become tradition. New Mexico has many fierce athletic rivalries, and we are proud at La Cueva to count so many. It means we are working hard and doing something very right.

GENERATIONS

I am always excited and proud to hear a student tell me, "Coach, you taught my mom…" or "Coach, you taught my uncle!" It's a reminder of accomplishment, as well as aging. Many of us evaluate our lives watching our families grow. We become grandparents and enter new stages of our lives. Cal Guymon and Roger Flaherty are grandparents. They are excited to spend time with their grandchildren. Cal has six grand kids: three in Las Cruces and three in Rio Rancho. Cal and Gail are always visiting. Roger lives in Florida and he spends many hours in the air traveling to Albuquerque, to visit his grandchild.

I never did marry, and have no nuclear family; instead, my family became the children I have taught and coached, and their families, over the course of 44 years. I've taught more than 65,000 students in Albuquerque and my opportunities to stay connected with them have multiplied many times over.

At the supermarket, people introduce their children and say, "This is Coach Ciccarello; he was my coach in elementary school." I always welcome a chance to meet the children of former students. This happens everywhere, from movie theaters to health clubs, and of course in my own classroom.

When I first started in the late '60s, my oldest students were 13 years old. Today, they are 56. While I don't celebrate getting older myself, I do embrace a 56-year-old saying they remember me fondly. Sure, some of the fondness is embellished, but I'll take that over never reconnecting with them.

When I remember their names and details about them, they beam from head to toe! I don't understand how I can remember it all, but I do! This year I am having some trouble memorizing names; maybe my brain is full. I cannot recall my first second-generation student. At Whittier it happens so much I can't tell you all of their names. Hopefully, this won't make for an embarrassing encounter in the Express Lane in 15 years.

The Romero family was a true example of how a neighborhood school works. Delia had been a quiet, cooperative young student in the early '70s. Her brother Phil came back years later to offer martial arts expertise to our students. Delia's two children, Levi and Anita, arrived in the early 2000s; Levi was a fast runner and loved to run in Play Day activities. Delia's mom, Martha, was a teacher's aide for more than 15 years, and while her kids were there, Delia served on the PTA and in the front office. Whittier had a great reputation for this kind of community. When she heard I was writing about this book, she sent this letter:

It's been four decades since I met Coach Ciccarello. I was in second grade, my first year at Whittier Elementary, when he became our coach. My future husband was also in second grade at Whittier. There are so many fond memories of elementary school… I still remember the day he became our coach. In 1970 Coach Nicely introduced him to every class. One of my most fond memories is when the school had gymnastics night. The students got to perform for the parents. I liked to tumble. My favorite part was when we got to make the human pyramid. I was always small for my age and didn't weigh very much, so I was picked for the top. Everyone would get on their hands and knees, shoulder to shoulder, and I climbed over them to the top.

When everyone was in place, Coach would make us look up and smile. Then he would blow his whistle. That was the signal to collapse the pyramid. We would put our arms and legs out. (It was like a big dog pile.) This was a controlled fall for all that were involved. When I was a child I loved to jump rope. Coach had the big fat white jump-ropes for us at recess. I could jump for hours if they would let me. For Play Day I would sign up for the jump-rope competition. I always received a blue ribbon. I also took part in the classroom tug-of-war. Each class, by grade level, would tug against each other. The grand finale was the tug-of-war between the sixth grade and the teachers. This was a big activity for the sixth-graders. With all the PE we had in our daily routine I believe it made us stronger as we became adults. I have joined a cycling team and have had a few half-century rides and a full-century ride under my belt. I think all my rope-jumping I did as a kid gave me the necessary stamina.

Have you heard how life comes full-circle? Well, it's true. My own children were students at Whittier and Coach Ciccarello was their coach, as well. When my daughter was in first grade I started working for APS, and Coach Ciccarello and I became coworkers. I was an auto EA sub for Whittier. I worked in kindergarten and Special Education, and would take the kindergarten class to PE and stay to monitor their progress. Coach would have the kids jumping rope, and I would join in right along with them. The kids would stop and say, "Look at Ms. Delia! She can jump-rope!" It was a blast. Thanks for the memories, Coach!

Delia Jimenez (Romero)

There are several more names I remember, whom I would like to share with you:

- Anthony Burrell was a student at Lowell in 1969. He was a track athlete who competed with my boys' team there. Many years later, I had his son Drew in my PE classes at Whittier. Drew turned out to be one of my best jump-ropers. He is the only PE student I ever had who could do a "5-Under," in one jump, turning the rope five times before he hit the ground. Most professional athletes cannot do that. At Highland Drew became one of the best high-jumpers in state history. I see him once in a while. He is studying to be a hair-stylist. I still see his dad at Lobo bas-

263   GENERATIONS

ketball games. He always seems to have extra tickets, and loves to share with his old coach.

- When I started with the Duke City Dashers in the late 1960s/early 1970s, Julie and Lisa Andrews, twin sisters, ran long distance races in track and cross country. They were great athletes with good family support. As they grew up they were always friendly when we ran into one another. Their brother Doug's wife, Stephanie, heard about my Whittier jump-rope team.

- Even though their daughter, Sidney, did not attend Whittier, her parents brought her to a couple of jump-rope practices to see what she could learn. We gave her a T-shirt and took her to the Pit. Sidney had a blast, returned to Osuna Elementary and recruited other students. Sidney became one of the better jump-rope athletes in the Albuquerque area. As a teenager she has won National Competitions and is considering competing globally.

- Christine Roybal was a nine-year-old running with the ATC. She came up through the age-group program and later ran for me at Manzano. After high school she married Brian Darling, and had a daughter. Alex became one of my runners, and after graduating from UNM, she became an assistant coach on my staff at La Cueva.

- Mary Lynn Griffin was a runner with the ATC and a PE student at Whittier. She later became an assistant coach on my staff at Highland. She had two daughters who attended Whittier—Erica and Bryanna Brown. Both were great rope-skippers and became team captains.

- Melissa Eakin ran hurdles for me at Highland, and years later her daughters Sam and Alex were in my Bandelier PE class, and members of the jump-rope team.

- Sandy Beach Warfield, of course, started with the ATC at age nine. Her daughter Stephanie ran for me at La Cueva, and I gave running and basketball lessons to her son Seth. Sandy coached with me at Highland and La Cueva. Curtis, Sandy's nephew, I've discussed plenty. I taught the high jump to AJ, Curtis's brother, and worked with Sandy's brother, Ron Beach, in track and field when he was an age-grouper. I feel like a member of their extended family.

- Ann Bernitsky ran for me in 1980 at Sandia. Years later I coached her nephew Will in the hurdles. I also coached Will's siblings, Laura and Alex, in the hurdles and high jump.

- Marcie Baty ran in the early '70s in age-group track and field. Her daughter, Amber Battle, whom I taught skills in the high jump, turned into one of New Mexico's finest runners.

- Tammy Meade was a sprinter at Highland in the mid-'80s. Her son later attended Whittier.

- Denise Mueller, a great runner at Sandia, later had a daughter who ran at La Cueva. I used to call Denise "19er" as she always wore that jersey to practice. She never forgot the nickname.

- Laurie Gilliland ran cross country while I coached with the DCD. Her daughter, Briana Paxton, led our La Cueva team to several State Championships. Briana was the best thrower we ever had and holds several school records. Thirty-five years separate these teams, both with these outstanding athletes. Brianna once told me, "Coach, thank you for taking a chance on me… you helped me when no one else would."

- Teddie Sue Hogsett, a 400m runner at Sandia, later moved to Los Alamos. While giving a clinic in jump-rope to the Los Alamos Cross Country Team, I taught her daughter Jennifer how to skip rope. We have been to Los Alamos several times and Jennifer always tells her teammates I coached her mom.

- Shannon Ryan, one of my best hurdlers at Sandia in 1980, moved to Denver, CO. I have been giving her daughter track workouts by email.

- Karen Browning ran for me at Sandia. Two of her daughters, Cassidy and Carly, ran track for me at La Cueva, and her third daughter, Katie, will attend La Cueva soon.

- Fred Mady was a great shot-putter at Sandia in the early '80s. In 2011 his daughter Allie ran and threw the shot put for me at La Cueva. His other daughter Madison was throwing the javelin for La Cueva. Both girls are exceptional athletes.

- Julia Foster ran track with the ATC and jumped rope for Whittier. Her dad, Leonard, and his brother, Kevin, also attended Whittier. Julia went on to become a great runner at the Albuquerque Academy. She is now enrolled at Stanford.

- I used to give Val Boyer's son Stephan basketball lessons. When I visited Val in Arizona I would give track lessons to her daughter, Justina.

- Mellissa Allen was a PE student in the '80s, and her daughter Amethyst is presently one of my top rope-jumpers at Whittier. Mellissa was on the gymnastics team and her mom, Sue, was a big supporter. In 2012 Sue, now a grandmother, is the jump-rope team's biggest supporter. Amethyst is one of the school's top athletes and students.

- Greg Smith and his sister Tanya were Whittier students in the '90s. There were both outstanding PE students and participated in jump-rope activities. Greg attended through fifth grade, and has great memories of playing "Wall Ball" at recess. Greg's daughter, Isabella, currently at Bandelier, is a member of the jump-rope team. I see Greg regularly at my gym. When I first met him he was a little guy, about 3'4' tall, and weighed about 60 lbs.. Today in the fitness room he is 6'4" and well over 200 lbs.!

- Nora Ortiz was as thrower on the Highland track and field team, and an outstanding shot-putter. Years later, her children, Rashad and Asha, attended Whittier. They were perfect role models because they knew if they misbehaved I would have a talk with Mom. Many years later they also ran on the Highland track team. Rashad would sit next to me in the stands at UNM and remember his early days at Whittier. Both competed against La Cueva athletes.

- Laurinda Zubiate ran track at Highland in the '80s. Her daughter Micah ran for me at La Cueva in the 800m and the 400m. Her niece, Jordan Grace, ran the 1600m and the 3200m for me, also at La Cueva. Her son Gus ran the hurdles there, where I would give him tips.

- Tom Gentry was an outstanding student-athlete while at Whittier. He ran on my little track team. His father Bill was my athletic director at Highland. Bill was a very successful football coach at both Highland and at Eldorado. Tom's two sons, Sam and Zach, played football for Eldorado and they were students' of mine in jump-rope. They credit jump-rope for their quick feet. This is extremely important for quarterbacks, as they must elude onrushing defenders.

• This teaching of subsequent generations is wonderful. Most times you have their undivided attention. They know you are helping them as you helped their parents.

SUPPORT AND UNSUNG HEROES

A successful PE program or extracurricular activity program does not happen without peripheral support. School administrators help your program grow, funding activities, equipment, supplies, uniforms, and coaches' salaries. As our economy changes and funds become scarce, we need to find new ways to generate money for these programs. In the 2000s, we had periods of zero-allocation.

At the elementary level I had to ask parent-teacher groups to help buy uniforms and ropes. I shared equipment with other schools if I knew their PE teacher.

I could not afford a bus for field trips, and the administration did not want teachers to drive students in personal cars. It was a Catch-22. The more I scheduled shows, the better I got at organization. I would ask the host-school to pay for a bus. Groups, including friends of mine, would donate for T-shirts and jump-ropes. Former athletes like Dolores Archuleta Black are always an asset to our efforts. The Whittier kids over the years never had to purchase one shirt. When a kid was ready to perform, she received her uniform.

Parents not only had to drive their children but sometimes had to pay to attend the show. One year we performed at the Pit, and UNM charged $12 at the door. They were only there to see their kids perform. Some of the Bandelier parents, and almost all of the Whittier parents, did not come; several left and came back to take their kids home. I was using all my connections to get them in the door. I had a couple of extra tickets from time to time, and I knew a ticket-taker who let a few in for free. One night we had 40 kids scheduled to jump. Many of their parents could not see them, while 16,000 other people, with the means, could.

As we look to 2013, with new liabilities we face more restrictions. Not only is funding a problem, we now have to worry about litigation.

High schools have seen cuts everywhere. Athletic teams do not take overnight trips unless absolutely necessary. Track meets have been cut. In some sports the number of teams and available transportation has been reduced.

Over the years I have worked for many outstanding administrators: Desi Baca, Reginald Chavez, Manny Smith, Dora Clark, Doug Carmichael, Nell New, Pat Woodard, Agnes Redmond, Cindy Bazner, Nikki Dennis, and Glenda Armstrong in elementary, and Richard Romero, Keith Whethersby, Joann Coffee, and Todd Resch at the high school level. Supportive principals, athletic directors, and main office administrators are critical to the function of extracurricular activity.

Buddy Robertson, APS's Athletic Director from 1977 to 2002, is perhaps the best administrator under whom I have worked. Many have described him as honest, decent, friendly, hard-working, and family-oriented; I simply call him *professional*. Coaches need top-down support. While he could not make everyone happy every time, Buddy just did what he perceived as the "right thing."

So, what is the "right thing?"

In 2000, when I began as La Cueva's head track and field coach, I inventoried our uniforms; we were missing most of our warm-ups. When I went to Buddy and asked for replacements, he could have pushed me off until the next order, but he somehow came up with an emergency order for warm-ups only. As a first-year coach at La Cueva, this gave me deep confidence in the program, and let me focus more on the start of the season. Buddy has said, "I always figured my job was to help the coaches, because the coaches were the ones who made the kids happy, and the kids were the ones who made the parents happy." This formula is trickier in practice. Everyone has his own interest in their kids or team. Buddy somehow looked out for all programs, equally.

Buddy also said, "I never tried to close the door on people even if I didn't agree with them. I never expected people to always agree, so I tried to listen." There were times when, as the head track official, he had to arbitrate protests. Whenever I had an issue on the track, I found Buddy Robertson. He always made the most equitable decision. Once I had a kid whom the timers and place pickers had missed in a preliminary race, and was not qualified for the final. She had finished second, completely overlooked. The finish line camera was not working that day. The officials were baffled. Buddy put the athlete in the final in an open outside lane (8). She won the next day.

The community had so much respect for Buddy's arbitration that a phone was made available to call him whenever a question or conflict arose. Everyone abided his decision. He let coaches go onto the track to help a kid mark steps for a handoff on a relay. You may think this was a small thing, but this allowed for the coordination of athletes, coaches, and officials for a better meet. Of his success, Buddy always said, "I was lucky!" Those of us who worked with him know better.

When I started at Whittier, the PTA would always allocate money for special programs. Into the '90s and the 2000s they decreased in numbers, and that changed. Bandelier still had a viable PTA, and the resources to provide transportation and uniforms.

Julie Sanchez is a young APS administrator a good friend of Sandy Beach Warfield. She had always wanted to run with my team, but younger and on the other side of town. Now she is an APS administrator. She told me recently, ""I might be the only girl who did not run for Coach Ciccarello." I myself wonder, "How did this happen?"

She then left me with something as simple as it is true: "Coach, in my whole experience as a student and educator it does not matter where you go to school... *you get out of it what you put into it!*"

A new teacher should always meet and greet the secretary, nurse, cafeteria manager and custodian. Without them, any school would grind to a standstill. While I cannot remember all the great people I have worked with, I can mention some who have contributed to success of my program.

Our secretary at Whittier in 1970, Mrs. Overbury, was serious and diligent. She watched out for all staff. Annette Perno, who came to replace her, was outgoing and friendly to everyone. When the Teachers' Lounge became filled with treats and goodies, and she always contributed. (I found myself gaining some weight.)

Doris Dobbins and Maria Maestas were two very helpful secretaries at Whittier. They were followed by Jeanette Brito and Pasty Trujillo, who covered all the little things. Over the last decades teachers have been asked to complete more administrative work. Our secretaries remind us when forms are due—a simple, invaluable act. Patsy's brother was a custodian here, and her children also attended. They were unquestionably part of the Whittier Family.

Today we have two very helpful secretaries. Linda Aragon is in the front office and watches out for me and Coach Vargas. She keeps us up-to-date with administrative duties, and sells jump ropes from her desk. Icely Stanley, the side office secretary, helped to organize a bake sale at Wal-Mart to raise money for T-shirts. Icely's granddaughter attended Whittier and participated in PE and jump-rope.

Secretaries are like moms: they get littler credit but do all the intangible things. When a kid gets hurt and the nurse is unavailable, they go to the secretary. Secretaries will wipe a kid's bloody nose—while answering phones. They pick up supplies for the staff or principal. They are the first stop for visitors, and the first line of support for an uncooperative photocopier. They deal with disgruntled parents and misbehaving students. Secretaries are essential to running a school.

If you want a clean working environment, make sure you meet the custodians. They also find equipment for you, and will move it on request. Not only this, but they are usually friendly about it. Most custodians are fun to be around and they appreciate respect from the teachers.

When I first went to Whittier, Sam Jones was a custodian. Sam took night classes at UNM and eventually became a teacher. He and I always talked about the Lobos, sports, and current events. Sam was diligent and helped everyone.

Della Flores cleaned at Whittier for 20 years. She had two sons who loved the Dallas Cowboys. I would spend hours talking football with Della and her kids. Monday morning was always a reflection time. If Dallas lost, Della was depressed; when the Cowboys won, the gym floor was spotless.

Della was there during the Cowboys' great years, so the gym often looked good. She also liked to make *tamales* and red *chile* for the Coach. Every couple of years I would fly to Dallas and catch a Cowboys game live with Roger Flaherty. Della always wanted to go to Texas Stadium herself, and could not wait to hear about the experience. Knowing I was single, she used to tell me, "Coach, put me in your will and leave me one of your cars, and a little cash to go to a Cowboys game."

Freddie Trujillo, the custodian at Whittier for about 15 years, and even at 50 had the attitude of a 30-year-old. Not only did Freddie do his job well, he did side-jobs. He would clean and perform repairs at my house. When I moved, he brought his truck and helped load and unload. One day I asked Freddie if he could help me move a refrigerator. He looked at me and said, "Stand back, Coach." He then bent over and put the fridge on his back and walked it over to the truck, by himself. He would do more work in 15 minutes than most people could in hours.

Freddie had three weaknesses: food, drink, and women. On Monday morning he always had a story to tell about going fishing with some gal, eating and drinking. He was a great fisherman. One Saturday he took me and my dad to a ditch in the South Valley and said, "Coach, there's a big one in those weeds." A couple of minutes later he pulled out the biggest fish I had ever seen. My dad was speechless, and though he tried, Dad could not catch even one small one. Freddie always carried a can of worms in his truck. Leaving work, he would catch a fish for dinner.

Now at Whittier we have Gregorio. He came here from Mexico and is about 40. He keeps our gym spotless. I made friends with him by letting him drive my sports cars. I have always liked nice cars, and I share them with friends, sometimes for a date. He drove my Caddie XLR Convertible one day and had a grand old time. Whenever he took one of my cars for a drive I noticed the gym was a bit cleaner. The fancier my car, the cleaner my gym!

An Nguyen and Kiva Gresham were good friends in elementary school. I could always count on them to come back and help the Whittier kids on Play Day. They would line the kids up and help them understand the rules for the Play Day. An and Kiva were two of the smartest students we ever had at Whittier. They are both college graduates and come back to Whittier to advise the students on the importance of education. They are perfect role models.

Also giving back were Jason Richardson, Rachel D'arcangelis, and most of the students from Wilson Middle School and Highland High. On Play Day they would show up at 7:00 a.m., unprompted, and start lining the field with marble dust. At the end of the day they would haul in the equipment. Most times I would feed them lunch and soda or lemonade at the local 7/11. My work was cut in half because of their dedication to the school and the Play Day activities.

Midtown Sports and Fitness is a big part of my after-school daily life. I work out after track practice. Nell Kane, a manager at the club, told me, "Coach, this club would not be the same without you." I have met many former students while working out. One day I was soaking in the hot tub with three men in their early 40s. They were related and all had attended Whittier some 30 years before. They had fond memories of Play Day in particular. Their names were Hafiz, Faisuh, and Aleem. I invited them out to help run the 2012 Whittier Play Day, and put them in charge of the starting line. The kids, in their enthusiasm, were always trying to jump the gun. These three gentlemen were about 6'3," and over 200 lbs. each, and after they directed the kids to wait we had fair starts to every race. Three former Whittier students were giving of their time to the new generation. That love of Whittier and PE activities (such as Play Day) is now a 44-year tradition.

Kip Koech and Luke Lagattuta were soccer buddies at Whittier. They went on to be solid competitors at Highland. The day they would come to teach soccer the kids were on their best behavior. Both spent time coaching and teaching. They would work soccer, basketball or football activities.

Julia Foster, Curtis Beach, Christine Ostler, Grace Rich, Aubrey Herrera, Allie Snell, Reece Cuddy, Mariah Rast, Christina Clark, Kaylin Martin, Cory Chavez, Chad Clark, Daniel Gorris, all helped the Whittier children in similar ways. Students who graduated from Whittier always felt an allegiance to the school.

Multi-level teaching is one of the best techniques to reach a young child. Many times I would be teaching a PE class and one of my former students would just *appear* at the door. They were always welcomed and always participated in the day's activities. A former student is a hero to current students. Luke Lagattuta later became Highland's head soccer coach and always volunteered at Whittier. The following letter I received from Luke regarding his experiences there:

Hey Coach Ciccarello,

I have so many fond memories from my days with you at Whittier.

First, and foremost, there was nothing I looked forward to more on any given day other than PE and/or recess. Being able to play sports, run around, try to impress girls, and try to one-up another student in a competitive arena was my safe-haven. I loved doing anything active. You made that an integral part of elementary school.

Yes, learning how to write cursive and memorizing multiplication tables was important, but so was learning how to shoot a basketball and throw a baseball. I give you (and my parents, of course) a great deal of credit for laying the foundation of a healthy, active lifestyle. Not only did I play some fun and creative games, such as Tether-ball, "Wall Ball," jump-rope, and gymnastics, but you made it an enjoyable experience for kids of all ages and skill levels. I was fortunate enough to possess good coordination and athletic abilities, so being able to showcase this was truly influential in my growth process.

I remember that when we learned something new or played a new game, I would try to get ahead by practicing more after school, at my caretaker's, down the street, or at the yard a block from my house. I remember the elation I felt when the gym was rebuilt. It looked like a state-of-the-art athletic facility to my young eyes. To this day, I still remember being so afraid to jump on the springboard and flip unto a padded mat for gymnastics, but when I summoned up the courage, it was one of the best feelings ever.

I formed many friendships (and even some rivalries) in that gym, and especially on that dirt soccer field. I remember I wanted to own that playground like a king owns a castle. I always strived to be the best at any game we were playing at the moment. Of course, that was never the case, especially with the jump-rope team, which was something I never fully got the hang of, but you were always supportive, no matter the case. You were encouraging, yet not to the point of coddling. You were challenging, yet not to the point of setting up failure. You struck a critical balance that has remained in my head to this point in my life, and I believe I am a better-rounded person as a result. I am almost 24 years old and I think that without your influence and dedication to PE and coaching at such a young age, I would not be sitting here now writing about these fond memories.

So thank you, Coach. I'm not sure you realize how much I appreciated your time and efforts, and I'm sure, presentations to help a younger child.

Luke Lagattuta, Whittier 1999
Head Coach: Highland High School Boys Soccer
Staff Coach: Rio Vista Soccer Club
Manager: International Indoor Soccer Arena

Neffi Quintana is a retired teacher now in his mid-80s. He also was a former boxer and a referee in boxing for many years. I met him at the Midtown Sports & Wellness Athletic Club. He was aware of my jump-rope team. One day he asked to buy some jump ropes. "Sure" I answered. "What's up?" He then informed me that he takes annual trips to a poor section of the Philippines to give boxing lessons. He does this for his Catholic Church, which supports depressed communities overseas. I came up with 25 ropes, a CD of music to jump to and a video of Kiva and Curtis for demonstration.

Neffi later informed me the presentation was the highlight of his trip. Now he asks for new ropes every year. Just recently he told me that his church wants to expand into Puerto Rico, and of course, he wants to teach jump-rope there also. Someday I plan to join him on one of these trips.

I need to mention Mark Romero, the great track athlete from Valley High and UNM. He was the New Mexico High School 800m State Champion, and won the same event at the NCAA championships. His time of 1:48.25 in the 800m is the fourth-fastest in UNM's history.

I have known Mark since he was an age-group track athlete. He always gave his best. His best story is how he treats his son, Mark Anthony. Mark Anthony was born with arthrogryposis multiplex congenital, or simply arthrogryposis, in which certain joints do not develop correctly, limiting movement. Mark Anthony has been in a wheelchair for most of his life, and has become a rap artist, performing worldwide. He goes by the name King Montana. Mark feels that his son has far exceeded any of his athletic achievements on the track.

I have watched Mark give up most of his own athletic practice to help his son succeed. He will likely never run a 1:48 or even a 2:00 minute 800m again. In my eyes, and in those of many others, Mark will always be a "Champion."

Phil Romero and Mary Jane Deflice were Whittier students. Mary Jane moved here from Mexico, and was on my track and gymnastic teams. She told me this was a pivotal point in her life. We often go to the Frontier and reminisce about the old days. They want their daughter to experience athletics as they did.

Phil is a martial arts instructor, and brother of Delia Romero. He would come to Whittier to work with students. One day he came with a large case. You can imagine the students' eyes when he opened it and pulled out two gigantic Asian knives. Imagine being 3'8" tall, and a man rhythmically waving 4'-long swords in front of you, like ribbons in the wind. Every kid wanted to hold and swing one.

Mary Bolton was in fifth grade when she ran on my ATC team—always on her toes. In her 40s, she came into the gym with a guitar. After giving hugs and high-fives, she sang a song. The kids and I were spellbound with her Western ballad; it was like she had just won *American Idol*. I had no idea that she was a professional singer! Every kid from that day on wanted me to teach them how to sing. They figured if I taught her how to run, I must have done the same with her singing. At least it made for great motivation to get students to spring on their toes.

Jim Dudding was a counselor in the early '90s. He came from Ireland, with a tough brogue in his speech. The kids liked to listen to him talk. As a young lad he had played a lot of soccer. He would go out every recess and kick high-fly soccer balls. Even in his late 60s he could kick a ball so high you would lose it in the sunlight. He told me one day, "Coach, it makes my day to see these American kids get excited about catching soccer balls at recess." I could hardly understand a word he said. Jim was out there every recess, rain or shine.

Earl Lyon taught fifth grade in the early '70s. He started a chess club during recess. David Procter always gave him a touch match; I very seldom won. Somehow they always still found time to race a 50-yard dash before the bell rang. I could never beat Mr. Lyon in chess, or the race.

Kathy Johnston was a librarian in the '70s and '80s. She not only read to the kids but supported all their extra activities. She loved to watch the gymnastics team.

Ula Zimowsky was a nurse at Whittier for almost 20 years. She originally came from Poland, spoke seven languages, and sang opera. The kids were sometimes shocked to discover she could speak better Spanish than they could. When we needed a translation we would call on Ula.

Her husband, Kristopher Zimowsky, was in the NM Symphony Orchestra, and would sometimes play violin for the school. This was a great motivation for our kids to consider music. Ula's son Christian was on my gymnastics team.

Ula worked with Molly Foster, mother of Kip, Robbie, and Joe Koech (all outstanding role models). Molly was head nurse at Whittier for many years. She and Ula address the bruises and ailments that plague elementary students. Nurses are true angels, and often do not get the recognition they deserve.

Dwayne Norris began teaching fifth grade at Whittier in the '90s as a young man. He enrolled his daughter there for the early years. Her name was "Jelly" and we taught her how to jump-rope. She still remembers those early years and the importance of PE. Her dad supports our program to the hilt, and believes in multi-level age-grouping. If we need a fifth-grader to role model for the kindergarten class, he will send a student to lead for the day.

Dwayne understands the difference between a child who has been nurtured in the development years and a child who was missing that nurture, and appreciates what extracurricular activity can do for a kid's self-esteem. He believes that exercise and team-membership help cognitive development. I have seen him organize additional games during the school day, sometimes taking his class behind the gym to play kickball. He has told me, "Coach, I believe if a kid is involved in your program I will see the results in my classroom."

Brian Miner shares this philosophy. He was first assigned to Whittier to teach special education, and a few years later, third grade. As a former military man, he emphasizes self-discipline, walking students in a straight line between classes. If they cannot follow directions, he drills them like an army sergeant. He has learned to use his height—6'6"—as a motivator.

Mr. Miner also believes exercise is essential to releasing pent-up energy. There were many times when he would give up some of his prep time to observe a PE class. While there, he would also help with discipline, should the need arise. Many times

Brian would send an older student to help our younger students understand how to move in PE. The mentors he sent us also taught jump-rope skills.

As the years pass, I see Whittier classroom teachers cooperating. They realize the importance of fitness and the value of multi-level age-grouping. We have a special program for cooperative students: if they finish their homework and show respect, they now come to a PE class and work with young kindergarten classes. The demonstration of physical skill activities to young students by older student role models is the most productive technique of teaching. These classroom teachers who share their students are part of a generation that enables and empowers them in a unique and profound way.

THEN AND NOW

It would be impossible bring to light all the changes in education over the last 44 years. I will try to report the facts and refrain from judgment. From the late 1960s to 2012 these are some of the changes I have seen:

- Technology is available today in a way it was not in the late '60s. I didn't have CDs and boom-boxes back then, but in a PE class today, I will use a digital camera to show kids how to high-jump and jump-rope. I now use portable microphones to walk around the gym and talk to students hands-free. In track and field, I have light, adjustable hurdles, and in the high jump, we now have large, mobile, foam-filled pits. Starting blocks now are brightly-colored, easy to move and adjust and have small spikes that grab the all-weather surface. At a big track meet, the blocks have a speaker hooked up to each individual starting block. The starting blocks are Fully Automatic Timing (FAT) now, to signal each athlete to start exactly as the starter's pistol goes off—I used to use wooden blocks held together by a screw and a hand clasp. Stopwatches were different. If you had a three-face hand timer, you were advanced. Today I use digital watches with split times. A stopwatch today can time 40 or more runners, with splits for each.

- Many elementary schools today have a gym and modern equipment, such as folding mats, cones, markers, and poly spots to mark the floor. My first gymnastic rubber mats were one-piece, heavy and cumbersome. Coaches today have an office with a phone and internet-connected computer. In 1969, I had a broom closet I shared with the custodian. My supplies were two basketballs, two soccer balls, and a couple of baseball bats. We also had red playground balls that we would patch with latex, so they would last a few more days when they leaked. Physical education teachers in the 1960–70s were very creative, and were regular customers at warehouse and hardware stores. Today when something doesn't work, we just throw it away. Buying new is less expensive than fixing the old.

- Of course, one thing I know that will never change is the students' need to be noticed. The parent's eye has become the camera's eye; technology gives us faster, more efficient ways to learn, but the way we use it depletes quality time. The 21st Century alone has brought with it more changes in teaching and coaching than at any other time in history.

- In 1976, at Manzano, when kids came out for track and field, they were committed to our program only. They came daily, without fail. An athlete did what he was asked, and would never miss a meet for another athletic activity, nor would he leave early. Today, parents are always taking vacations and pulling kids early from practice or from a meet. Athletes (and parents) want to know why you are asking them to do a workout. It is not beyond the modern parent to want to know in advance which event his child will be participating in that day. Coaches are second-guessed daily on their strategies. Athletes go to personal fitness trainers and physical therapists for help even when we have school trainers available. Athletes attend camps around the country to improve their skills. If a student does not like the athletic program of their neighborhood school, they pick another.

- My workout-buddy Dan De La Cruz grew up in the Philippines. While in elementary school in the 1960s he remembers some of the disciple: one technique was to have students kneel down on a bed of lentil beans. They would hold their books in their hands with their arms extended for up to 30 minutes. Dan told me he never had to do this; after seeing others disciplined in this manner, he was always on good behavior. This policy is no longer used.

- In the 1930s corporal punishment was used extensively in the US and Canada. Punishments included spanking, tongue-burning (with hot peppers or sauce), washing the mouth with soap, and general striking. Many religious groups were in favor of corporal punishment and some religious conservative groups still practice it today. Benjamin Spock, a doctor renowned for his research on the psychological effects of spanking, was originally for it. He changed his mind in the 1980s, about the same time APS stopped the practice, as other districts continued. Today in Europe, Canada, and here, physical punishment of children is considered abuse.

- When I reported to my new position at Riverview Elementary School I wore a three-piece suit. Men wore ties and jackets. Women wore dresses. At Whittier I saw a female teacher sent home because her dress was too short (1" below the knee). Today some teachers wear blue jeans and T-shirts. In some schools you will see students with pajama bottoms or sweatpants. The dress code has changed drastically and varies from school to school. I, myself, wear a T-shirt, baseball cap, and blue jeans to class. I have seen other PE teachers in sweats and wind suits. Now at Whittier we have a student dress code of polo shirts and cotton pants.

- Men did not have long beards and mustaches. Facial hair as a whole was frowned-upon. One year I had a perm. For a couple of years I wore a short beard. I have seen other male teachers with long beards and ponytails.

- In 1968 we had class sizes of 40 in a sixth grade class (which was still considered elementary). Today we have a fifth grade class of 27. At the elementary level we now have kindergarten–fifth grade.

- In the '60s the junior high school was seventh–ninth grade. The mid-school now has sixth grade through the eighth grade. The junior highs had full athletic competition back in the '60s and '70s. Today the athletic competition is pared down for middle school students. High school was 10th–12th grade. Today high school is ninth–12th grade.

- In 1969 we had one elementary principal and secretary. In 2012 we have a principal, an assistant principal or dean of students, two secretaries, and two nurses.

- At most elementary schools there was either one full-time PE teacher or two schools shared a part-time teacher. Today, at some elementary schools there are three PE teachers.

- Some PE classes only had one or two balls for an entire class of 40 students. Every unit we teach today has an individual ball for each student. At first we had hard balls that hurt the students' fingers. We then had NERF and foam balls introduced that made it more enjoyable for students to learn passing and catching.

- Back in the '60s I used an overhead projector and a 8mm movie camera. I would write on my clipboard or use an indoor blackboard to present. I would use either a Polaroid camera or a 35mm slide/print camera to show kids a picture of their athletic skill. Now we have big-screen TVs, boom boxes, microphones, whiteboards, remote speakers, laptops, individual computers, projectors, cameras, cellphones with cameras, iPods and iPads, and other electronics. The young generation understands and embraces this way of working.

- There were not many elementary-level gyms. We taught PE outside, year-round. Many times we taught in the wind, light rain, or in cold weather. Playgrounds were mostly dirt, which the wind blew everywhere. On super-bad weather days we went into the cafeteria. Sometimes we would set up mats and tumble in the hallway. Our last choice was to hold PE in an actual classroom and push the students' desks to the side. Most times recess was outside, even on the snow. In exceptionally bad weather, recess was held in the hallways. Today, there are gyms at almost every elementary school and on bad weather days recess is held there. Students are not allowed outside when the temperature is below freezing. Some schools now have grass playgrounds, and share a shelter with the City Parks and Recreation Program. Most playgrounds now feature modern equipment.

- I used to carry small dumbbells in my car. We did chin-ups, pull-ups, and push-ups at parks for upper-body strength. We stepped onto cement park benches for lower-body workouts. Now high school weight rooms are as good as their college counterparts. Some highs schools even have two, with the latest equipment. Middle schools now have aerobics rooms, with modern stationary bicycles, stair climbers and elliptical equipment. High schools have athletic trainers, and a training room with up-to-date supplies, including ultrasounds, stationary bikes, whirlpools and computers.

- In the 1960s most schools had a dirt training track. Coaches would line the track with marble dust—which rain and wind would always erase. Supplies and equipment were archaic, and would constantly be lost or broken. We did not have separate areas for the throwing events.

- This all changed for the better in the '80s. All-weather tracks became standard. Newer shot and discus rings were added. The hurdles became lighter and safer. A second and more modern long jump pit was added at most schools. The pole vault area became safer and easier to set up. All high schools received new iron storage sheds to keep equipment close to the track.

- At Whittier I have fitness balls, aerobic steps, rubber bands, half-moon balance balls, fitness running ladders, gigantic hula hoops, 4-way tug-of-war ropes, every current size jump-rope, and small plastic hurdles. We even have a Dance, Dance, Revolution machine and a rock-climbing wall. Outside, we have a dedicated "wall ball" wall, and colorful and fun modern playground equipment: 4-Square and hop scotch areas painted on the ground, and Tether-Ball poles installed.

- Title IX introduced equal opportunity for females to compete in athletics, and equal sharing of supplies and facilities. This was an upgrade for all athletes.

- Whittier has a new library, and a new kindergarten building, both with modern equipment, and a new "Tech Lab," with the latest computers. New schools were designed with better facilities, while older schools were updated and remodeled. The buildings in APS are, for the most part, the best they have ever been.

- With all the changes in equipment and technology we also have changes in attitude and expectations. Students in both PE classes and on athletic teams are monitored more, and expected to pass a physical. They are not allowed to participate if they are sick, hurt, or dressed improperly. Teachers and coaches are made aware of students' health problems, which are strictly accommodated; many students will not be allowed to participate without a doctor's approval. High school physicals are mandatory; concussions are taken very seriously. The old 'run it off' or 'take a lap' is not acceptable anymore.

- Not all changes have been for the positive. Around the '90s, "clustered" feeder schools stopped coordinating. A cluster was a group of elementary and middle schools that fed a common high school. In some cases, the elementary teachers did not even know the names of their nearby middle school PE teachers, and this happened between middle-to-high school programs, also.

- "My way or the highway" is gone, maybe the result of helicopter-parenting. Students now assert themselves more and take charge of their own activities. Many times athletes are in simultaneous sports, and have to manage several coaches, and coaches, in turn, have to adjust their practice schedules. Students travel much more than they used to.

- College-required entrance exams are scheduled during the competition season. Student-athletes now visit colleges they may want to attend. I have prepared for track meets when five or six of my best athletes were out of town.

- Students do not have the listening skills their parents had. Many believe that American education has changed because American home life has changed. The media, movies, television, music industry, cell phones, and other technologies have a bigger influence on kids than the adults in their lives. Many students decide themselves what they will eat, what time they will go to bed, and when they will study. In all socioeconomic tiers of our society, the family unit is deteriorating, and the schools are reflecting that change. Within this environment, we have many families who try to hold on to old-time values, and we all must adjust. We teach all students, not only the ones who share our values.

- A PTA function in 1971 meant a packed cafeteria. 40+ years later, with kids performing in the gym, only some parents are in attendance. Parents are separated or divorced, busy with other kids, working several jobs to make ends meet, and/or perhaps unaware that an after-school function is scheduled. In 1971 when we had an open house we ran out of standing room in the cafeteria. At today's open houses, the teachers outnumber the parents.

- Educators are held more accountable for results than ever before. Schools are rated by their test scores. Coaches, in addition to "character building," are expected to boast "winning" programs. Back in the '90s a principal at the monthly faculty meetings would give out a stuffed giraffe. It went to the teacher who, "stuck her neck out," to help students. In the current school climate that same giraffe sits in the back of someone's closet. Now, if you stick your neck out, they cut it off.

While teacher salaries have improved, coaches of high school athletes have not made many advances. Most coaches are still doing it for the love of the game.

In my 44 years I have had to make changes. Most have been good. I have seen teachers retire instead of making the proper adjustments. Though I will not be around, I often wonder how coaching and teaching will change in the next 44 years? Will all this technology keep pace?

LETTERS OF SUPPORT

When I decided to write this book I asked former athletes and associates, knowing the book's themes, to contribute their stories. Following are some of the letters that did not fit other among the other stories.

> During my 36 years working for APS as teacher, coach, and as an administrator I had the privilege of working with several cadet teachers.
>
> I remember Jim Ciccarello having the potential to be an outstanding teacher. This has proven to be the case, as evidenced during his 44 years of teaching and coaching.
>
> I have observed his classes on many occasions and always enjoyed watching Jim work. He has great rapport with his students and athletes. He has the skills to motivate all young people to do their best. I have always admired Jim's creativity and the interest he takes in his job. He not only teaches skills, but encourages his students to pursue worthy goals and be good citizens.
>
> It was a distinct pleasure to witness Jim's recent induction into the Albuquerque/New Mexico Sports Hall Of Fame.

Sincerely,

Harold Cheeves

Cooperating UNM Student-teaching Supervisor

Thanks to the **Journal**'s Toby Smith for the delightful article on Coach Cicca-rello. Our weary world needs more teachers like him, who not only care about students—I think most teachers do—but have figured out a way to get them excited about themselves, and something physical and doable—jumping rope.

He has been doing this for over 40 years. When our five children went there, he had students tumbling all over the place and had a team for them when only private gyms were involved in this sport. Our family, which is all grown-up now, has great memories of Coach.

Catharine Stewart-Roache

Socorro, New Mexico

I first met Bob Martin at a basketball game in a three-on-three tournament. Bob grew up in Massachusetts, and played high school and college basketball. He moved to New Mexico and received a doctorate in education, working at several Albuquerque high schools. I was not only taken by his presence on the court, but his knowledge of education and his ability to help kids grow.

Having had the opportunity to be influenced greatly by so many coaches and physical educators throughout my life, it has given me the strong desire to coach/teach in the most contributory manner possible for leading young people. I believe it is the reason why so many of us take this incredible career path, which allows contributions to youth as they move forward in the maturation process... It has been a blessing to see and learn from so many great educators—and at the top of my personal inspiration list is Coach Ciccarello, who has maintained such a positive and unwavering enthusiasm for this profession. The numerous occasions on which we have shared stories and discussed methods in support of helping find ways to guide students has led to several intriguing personal stories, which we have shared. A recollection of a story regarding a student-athlete from a local high school several years ago is especially personal to me.

My relationship with this student did not start off well. When I met him in my first year teaching and coaching basketball, he was a sophomore who already was involved in several 'incidents'—including suspensions for smoking and fighting. He was classified as a special-education student due to learning disabilities which made it difficult for him to achieve and stay focused in the classroom… He was struggling greatly at this point.

There was one thing he could do well as anyone at that school, however, and it was shoot a basketball… He had started playing on the junior varsity team that year and I would watch him before our varsity games got underway. He was a player that season until an incident in one game where he lost control of his emotions and started swearing at the officials and crowd, then stormed off the court after being ejected from the game. Immediately, the athletic director told him to hand in his uniform—he was being kicked off the team for the remainder of the season. At that point there was also a real concern that this might be the end of his attending high school because basketball had been his declared reason for being enrolled in the first place.

Fortunately, he also happened to be in one of my PE classes and we had developed a relationship that was based on our mutual love for basketball. (Also, as the head varsity basketball coach, I think I had a position that gave me some extra influence with him.) We would talk often and I started to appreciate a kid who was trying to find a way to get things right in his world. These times also gave me a chance to share some advice with him regarding staying in school, and I offered him the chance next year to come out for basketball again, as long as he did well in academics and in the other aspects of his school life.

I basically told him that it was time for him to grow up.

To his credit, he wrote a letter of apology to the principal and also did better in his class work the rest of the school year. He also continued to improve his basketball skills—often playing during our collective lunch break in the school's gym. The following season, he came back out for the varsity team and became a valuable member. In fact, he played on two District Championship teams in his junior and senior years. His high school career came to an end when our team got beat in a regional playoff game in which he made seven 3-point baskets and finished as the game's leading scorer. Most importantly, later that year he went on to graduate. I took more pride in watching him walk across the stage than I have ever with any other student that I have taught.

He had grown up.

(The next year, I took a job as athletic director and coach at another high school. On the first day of my new position, I got a knock on my office door… it was this former student. He had enrolled at a junior-college and was doing well with his classes. He truly had grown up.)

The opportunity that physical educators and coaches have can be far-reaching and extremely worthwhile… This personal story—and the countless others that educators such as Jim Ciccarello have accumulated over the past 40+ years—helps make this such a unique profession. It's a great life!

Dr. Bob Martin
College Basketball Coach, High School Teacher

After suffering through a very frustrating first month of my teaching career I felt out of sorts and questioned if I had chosen the right path. A friend of mine suggested that we go and visit his elementary PE teacher to learn a few things and to lift our spirits. As we walked up to his gym I could hear children chanting, "I love PE! , I Love PE! I Love PE!" At this point, I didn't even love PE, let alone the hundreds of students that I felt I wasn't getting through to.

As I entered this magic gym I saw Coach Ciccarello with a duck puppet on his hand, his students chanting, everyone with a huge smile, excited and ready for some PE fun!

At that very moment I knew that my approach was all wrong. In my quest to fulfill my high expectations I had lost sight of the simple fact that PE is intrinsically fun and that I needed to foster this type of excitement.

After observing this day and many more over the next few years I greatly benefited from Coach's gifts: happy, lighthearted, focused and magical! He reminded my to love PE, and now, thousands of students later—they love PE too. All because Coach showed us how.

Joe Buck
PE Teacher, Alvarado Elementary

Coach Jim Ciccarello has easily been one of the most influential people in my life. Although I met him during the spring semester of my senior year of high school, I feel as if I have known him forever; his positive influence is profound.

With only one year to participate, most coaches would have given me little attention and focused instead on the younger athletes. Not Coach Ciccarello! An attribute of his that immediately stood out was his desire to help EVERYONE improve, not just those at the top. He gave me a fair chance in any event I wanted to attempt and always provided helpful insight and encouragement. His positive words could overcome even the most painful 300m workouts!

Coach Ciccarello motivates his athletes in a manner that does not instill fear of losing; it consists of putting in your best effort to achieve progress. Hard work pays off; this is evident in the vast number of successes of Coach's athletes, all motivated and empowered.

I am a third-year college student and still keep in touch with Coach. Whenever I am in Albuquerque, we meet up for a bagel and catch up. I enjoy hearing his exciting track stories, and especially value the wisdom he shares with me. Although I am no longer suiting up in a track outfit for his team, he continues to encourage and empower me; I feel like a million bucks whenever I spend time with him! Coach Ciccarello is a tremendous blessing and deserves all the best that this beautiful life has to offer. He has helped me more than he will ever realize.

Aubrey Hererra
Student at the University of Texas, Austin

Coach Ciccarello has had a significant impact in my life. His impact Coach has had on me extends beyond stories. Coach taught me the value of hard work, determination, and perseverance. Coach Ciccarello's workouts were difficult, to say the least, but he always encouraged each and every one of his athletes to strive for more and to challenge not only our bodies but also our minds. At the end of hard workouts Coach would always ask me if I wanted to go for a "cherry." That cherry is the pinnacle of the workout and the most important part—it separated the good from the great. The cherry rep came after your body was exhausted and your mind had already shut down. Physically and mentally drained, I learned to put those factors aside and push myself beyond my comfort zone in an effort to make myself the best I could be. Coach Ciccarello taught me to never give up and to never give in. When you think that you can't do one more rep, Coach would encourage you to get it done.

In life I have learned that it is important to always strive for the "cherry," to always push yourself to be the very best you can be in everything you do, to never hold yourself back, and to challenge yourself to become better and to do more than you think is possible. The lessons I learned from Coach Ciccarello extend far beyond the track, and are lessons that have shaped me into the person I am today and will be in the future. I have had many coaches in my high school and collegiate careers, but not one of those coaches have had as great an impact on my life as Coach Ciccarello. He is by far the greatest track coach I have ever run for and I look to him not only as a coach but a mentor and friend. I will never forget the great times I had with him and the lessons he taught me.

Yours truly,

Chad Clarke

UNM Student and Track Athlete

Hey Coach,

I don't know where to begin about stories for your book. They are so many. You inspired us—me, my brothers and sisters, my classmates—to work together, to strive for more and to not give up! Anyone who thinks about taking PE out of the curriculum for elementary kids should spend more time with you!

The gymnastics shows after school—and at the Pit! (I can't believe you got us that gig!) They were always great—something to look forward to. I think all the performances were so key to our development. We had to show up, be disciplined, and behave well. Thank you for being part of my life, and of course, my entire family's lives.

With love,

Chippie

AKA Liz Roache
AKA Roache—but all five of us went by Roache at one time or another
AKA Elizabeth McClain

As a child I was always involved with sports. I started off with gymnastics, then soccer, dance, and cross country. However, none of these sports reached out to me. I never enjoyed them. I never had a personal relationship with any of my coaches. So I never felt supported in my sport. This all changed my freshman year at La Cueva. Maddi and I were sitting in class and heard on the daily updates in class that pre-season for track was starting up soon. So Maddie and I thought, "What the heck, why not? Let's give it a try."

I have to admit, the first time I walked on the track and met Jim Ciccarello and all the other hurdlers, I was pretty intimidated. Most of those girls were either catching on quicker than me or had already been doing hurdles for two years. I remember on that first day after practice, I questioned if I could even really be a "hurdler." I thought I should just give up right then and there. At that very moment in the corner of my eye I saw Ciccarello come up to me and he said, "Mariah—right? I want to see you out here more often, as you have potential." He smiled and then walked away. I giggled and smiled thinking, huh; he actually cared to know my name. That had not happened before.

So I kept coming and found I had a love for track. I loved running hurdles, and most of all I loved how Coach Ciccarello cared to acknowledge all of us. He started talking to me more and more at practice and would spend extra time at the end of the day. He would always stay late to help me work on my hurdle form. He would say, "Mariah, you can't just be 'purty'—you got to be a 'purty' **hurdler**, too. I would always just laugh and say, "Yes, Coach." That's when it hit me, the name "Coach," really; I had never called anyone Coach. That's because no one ever really seemed like a coach before. However, this one guy was so different from any of my other instructors; he was, in my opinion, a REAL coach.

I had the pleasure of running for him for four full years. I cherished every moment of it. Even when he made us run the hard "repeats!" Good news was we always had Coach Sandy to rescue us when Coach Chic was on his trip.

Those four years I will never forget how much I loved running for La Cueva, but most of all, running for Coach Ciccarello. He did so much for me, and he never gave up on me. He is a true coach that will always remain in my memories and in my heart. Most people just think of their coaches as, well, a coach—however, Coach Ciccarello is so much more than a coach. He is a friend and I person I can always trust. There are always people you get blessed with in your life and Coach Ciccarello is most definitely one of them.

A blessing in disguise, he helped me with so much more than just track. He does not even know that I am the person I am because he taught me to not give up. I know that I will NEVER give up on what I want to do in my life. He always said, "Mariah, you can do anything if you just work hard. Dig down deep, all the way to your heart. Stop being a little dog, and instead run with the big dogs." By the way, those last few words were my coach's favorite saying. He was always about the "big dogs."

Today, I know that if it were not for his positive attitude and all that time in training, I would not have had the chance to run against some of the fastest hurdlers in New Mexico. He made all this possible for me and I couldn't repay him enough for this experience in my life. He is the one coach that never gave up on me when I felt like giving up. He was there with words of encouragement. So, thank you, Coach Ciccarello, for being the coach I can truly call 'Coach.' I will always remember you as the person who never gave up on me.

Mariah Rast
Former La Cueva Hurdler and Sprinter

When I look back on my collegiate and high school track career, Coach Ciccarello always comes to my mind. He was my track coach all four years in high school and is the perfect example of doing what it takes to push his athletes to be the best they can be. I cannot speak on everyone's behalf, but I can definitely take you into my life, Alexandra Darling.

The one experience I will never forget is the State Track Meet in 2007. La Cueva was favored to win that year, and being one of the leaders on that team, I felt a lot of pressure. I loved running and the rush of winning, but Coach stressed that it was about winning that team title. Although, I agreed completely, I knew that meant running more races, and being held accountable in each race I ran.

Earlier in the season, everything had been going really well, especially in the 300m hurdles. I specifically ran a 43.10 second 300m, which was also the State Record time. That record hadn't been broken since 1981. Being a senior, I knew that this was the only chance I was going to get at running that time. I told Coach after the City Meet that I was excited to go for it! He had more up his sleeve than I was aware of.

The week before State finally arrived my nerves were indescribable. I wanted to finish off my season well and I knew I was prepared. I had it in my head that I would be doing the following events at state: long jump, 100m and 300m hurdles, and the 4 x 400m. The Monday after our last hard workout of the season, Coach Ciccarello and Coach Sandy Beach came up to me and told me that I was going to be doing the following events at state: long jump, 100m and 300m hurdles, 4 x 400m, and the open 400m!!! DUN DUN DUNNNN…

I instantly threw a fit!! I told them in a very frustrated, freighted, and upset tone, "How can you do that to me? The 400m meters is only 15 minutes before the 300m hurdles, and I won't be able to get my record. What if I can't do it? What if I lose both races, and mess everything up for me?" I went on and on about why I thought it was the worst idea of all time. Even in tears I begged them to not make me do it. Coach Ciccarello and Sandy both stayed very calm and explained to me that after reviewing all the teams, the state title was going to be a lot harder to win than everyone thought. It was going to take everyone on the team to do things that they were not expecting and I needed to run both of the events back-to-back, and other races, to win a team State Championship. I barely listened to anything they had to say, and I remember leaving practice in an absolute panic.

Later that night, I received a phone call from none other than Curtis Beach. We had been friends through high school. And he was another great runner from Albuquerque. He called to say he had heard I was doing the 400m and the 300m hurdles at State, and wanted to let me know that I could do it! He said I was well-prepared, and to not be too nervous, because he was doing the exact same thing. After about 10 minutes, we both hung up, and I was completely changed. I knew what I had to do… Coach Sandy ended up being the one who mentioned to Curtis that I was having a hard time with the situation, and I am glad she did! The next day of practice arrived, and I went up to Coach Ciccarello and said I was ready and willing to do whatever the team needed of me.

The weekend of state came, and to make a long story short, I didn't get my New Mexico State Record; I instead got so much more… a coach who believed in me, individual state titles in the 400m, 100m, 300m, and the 4 x 400m relay, and most importantly, a TEAM title. What I took most out of my experiences in high school was that it is not about one person on a team. Although it is fun to shine as an individual, it was so much more rewarding to know that my achievements, along with my other teammates' and coaches', allowed us to share something special. I can still say that even though running in college a 4:26 in the 1500 meters or a 10:35 in the Steeplechase, the moment in May 2007 surpasses it all…

Thank you, Coach Ciccarello, for pushing me as an athlete and making me a better person in life! I look forward to our new chapter as coaches together. I hope I can do half the job you have!

Sincerely,

Alex Darling
La Cueva Girls' Track and Field Coach

I can't believe it has taken so long to write this letter. I planned on attending your induction ceremony into the Albuquerque/NM Hall Of Fame. Congratulations! What an honor and so well-deserved.

You have done so much for so many young people in our community. I know that you especially have a heart for the under-privileged, to whom you've offered your guidance and coaching with life lessons to include many opportunities for them.

These are opportunities they otherwise would not have had. On top of all that, you are a superb coach, as borne out by your many successes.

I am so glad that I can count you as a friend and that I have been able to learn so very much from you.

Thanks, Enjoy, Love,
Ann De Hart

I grew up in a tiny town in the Hudson Valley with a population of 150 people, and attended a one-room schoolhouse with one teacher and six grades. When we moved to the nearby city in fourth grade I had a hard time adjusting socially. I was a skinny backward boy, with no confidence and almost zero self-esteem. My grandmother bought me a YMCA membership. I hated going to the gym.

I didn't fit in and was teased by the other kids. I did want to learn to swim, though, so I started to take swimming lessons.

Before long I was getting swimming badges. I got my Life-Saving Certification and joined the swim team. I began to fit in and have more confidence, which allowed me to join the gymnastics team, and the wrestling and hockey teams. I was all-in. The support and encouragement from my coaches gave me much-needed confidence and made me want to excel. When I was 11 years old, I was top trophy-winner at the YMCA and was presented the trophies by Bob Mathias, the decathlon champion whose picture was on the Wheaties box. It changed my life. I was also invited to become a Leader at the Y, and was awarded a scholarship to their Leadership Camp at Lake George. My social life vastly improved, and my grades even got better.

These early experiences with great coaches like yourself helped me develop a "can-do" kind of attitude, and has taught me the importance of commitment, discipline and fair play in every area of my life. It has also given me the strength to face difficult situations. I also believe if one doesn't catch the importance of exercise early in life, it can be difficult to develop it later. I have been a gym rat for most of my life but after back problems and a hip replacement I stopped working out—and gained 50 pounds. I was diagnosed with diabetes and a fatty liver. My doctor told me he'd give me six weeks to loose weight before putting me on medications.

I immediately got back on the horse, or more specifically, the elliptical, and two months later, after my next round of labs, my doctor called and said, "All your labs are normal, I don't know how you did it." I told him, "I changed my way of eating and I work out five days a week." I'm sure this would not have been possible without developing a love of sports and the discipline that comes from training at an early age. I am forever grateful to all of my coaches and mentors, and to you, for your hard work. I can't wait to read the book.

Scott Sharot
Actor and Author

RESPECT

Perhaps it is appropriate that I end this story with a few words on *respect*. To effectively help people teachers and coaches must respect their students, and students and athletes must respect their leaders. We have come from a style of demanding to giving and taking, on both sides.

"My way or the highway" is over. If you truly want to help people you must listen to them. This is not to say there are no rules; we need to set boundaries, and consequences.

Circumstances sometimes dictate why a rule has been broken. A kid might be late to practice because the school had a "lockdown"— a foreign term in the old days. An athlete could be late because she had to submit a special report. Athletes sometimes have to run home before practice to address a family problem. Evaluate and adjust each rule, with each kid, as it relates to your overall mission.

In the '70s I had a kid miss an essential relay team practice. We were getting ready for a USA Age-Group Track Meet. Her parents had been fighting and would not take her to practice. I ran an alternate at the practice and worked her back into the rotation the next day. Some hard-core parents or coaches would have booted her off the relay. By my showing compassion, I developed a relationship with that athlete that lasted for many years. She went on to excel in track at every level.

When I am coaching high school kids today and someone tells me they cannot handle another repeat, I give them a break. Never do I say, "Everyone is doing it—so get in there and do it with them." When one shows respect for an athlete who is working hard, but hurting, he will work harder for you. He will try harder when he does recover, becoming a better athlete, which improves your team. At La Cueva track practice I have had many athletes show me and the program their respect. It behooves us as coaches, to respect our athletes.

Aubrey Herrera, even after an extra-hard workout, would come up to me out-of-breath and say, "Thanks for the workout, Coach." Carly Browning, when I asked her to change events would always say, "OK, Coach, whatever is good for the team." One day after a particularly hard workout I said to the kids, I apologized for working them so hard. No sooner did I say that when Maggie Sabik said, "Don't apologize, Coach. I know what I'm in for!"

That said, we teach fitness, not pain. Forty years ago I had never seen an inhaler. Nowadays, in a 10-class day I will have four or five kids who need to puff and take a break. Some kids are in better shape than others; many are overweight or sick. If a kid is sick or having a bad day, I just give him a break. We should never ask a child to humiliate himself. Equal competition for all is the true motivator.

I have heard stories of coaches who made athletes run when they were hurt, resulting in both further physical injury and damage to their relationship. If an athlete needs water or to use the rest room I excuse her immediately. If an athlete has a shin splint problem, or becomes emotional and needs time alone, I give her a break. Athletes come to practice after the day at home or school, and are not always on top of their game. We as adults have to recognize and respond to that. *Evaluate and adjust.*

I had a kid who blew up in a fourth grade PE class and started cussing. Immediately I pulled him aside and told him to take a walk and "cool off." 10 minutes later he returned and settled down. He needed the downtime to recover emotionally. Many years later he came back to me and told me he remembered my letting him go. It may be years before the significance of the lesson becomes clear to them, but by teaching them as young people, you prepare them for the rest of their lives.

Another keen aspect of earning respect is to recognize a student's performance. When a coach/teacher is at practice or in a PE class she must be looking at her students. When they do something good, verbalize it to them. Immediate reinforcement encourages excellence. They will try harder!

It is accepted that the family unit is breaking down. Many times the television is raising the child. Young kids will tell their parents what they will eat, or what time they want to go to bed. Kids are too young to know how to set their own boundaries, and they grow up not knowing how to distinguish right from wrong. They come to the classroom unfocused, with few social skills. They act out, and hurt others. Some do not like authority figures. They are trying to survive in a world that may not respect them. Teachers have to win back their respect. Once you earn it they will readily perform.

Let students contribute to their own learning. Often, I would have my entire class chant, "The fun starts here!" At Lowell Elementary I would study Mrs. LeCesne and other teachers, and I was amazed how often the students verbalized the important points of the lesson; I learned early the importance of "repeats." I firmly believe that having athletes repeat physical drills is the most effective way to learn a skill. This applies everywhere. Learning is learning.

Teachers, coaches and other adults helped us in return only for our respect. They were willing to help us when we were rank beginners. Earlier, I told you about an older woman who appreciated the fact that I did not give up, teaching her how to drive; kids and adults are not so different in this respect. People cherish the person who helped them when no one else could, or would.

Beverly Kanteena and Victor Martine have put four kids through the Whittier PE program: their son, Quirin, and three girls, Viktoryia, Orinda and Dyani. Two of them now attend NACA; Victor is of Navajo heritage while Beverly has roots in several Pueblo communities. This family has been very respectful all these years, supporting Whittier, and particular our PE program. Their kids are fine role models. This travels exclusively on the city bus. At times I have given rides to both kids and mom. Even without the means to join all field trips, they find a way. They remind me of my early years, in New Jersey.

Beverly wrote me a letter on 22 small index cards. She told me a story about her children at Whittier and the value of activities. I have condensed it for you to reflect on:

She told me how proud she was of her family. Her eldest son Quirin started in Kindergarten at Whittier. He used jump-rope to warm up for soccer practice and games. He has been such a great student he was flown to Washington DC for NACA graduation. Mission accomplished!

The girls *are* members of the jump-rope team. Beverly has expressed to me the value of all three being in the program; their self-image has improved performing in front of large audiences. The eldest, Viktoryia, has emphasized to her sisters and friends the value of practice and commitment, and has herself given up her recess to practice jump-rope. Beverly's children practice at home, parks, other schools, at NACA, and anywhere they can.

The parents of this family feel that their girls have developed courage and positive self-image, which will help them in their future years. They appreciate my efforts, and have expressed it many times, showing me and my program great respect. I certainly hope I have returned it.

When a Native American family like this, who has struggled in everyday life, achieves so much, I think the future looks bright all of us in education. They are role models of a rare caliber.

THE FUTURE

Education is about people. Teachers will deal with a different landscape many years from now.

Today economics determine how we educate our children. We are already expected to develop highly efficient, low-cost methods. Administrators and teachers will be asked to follow even more-difficult budgets. PE and athletics will reflect the climate, which itself will reflect the rest of the world. Technologies will dictate much of the change. Some time soon we may have groups of students being taught from a building nowhere near them.

I can guarantee one goal that will never change: we will motivate our children by spending time with them.

Human beings need approval. The human presence will always be important. Teachers will need to be available and ready to help students improve. Hands-on education will always be the most effective kind.

The schools will always be a sample of our daily lives. Respect for authority, parents, and teachers must be cultivated. We as adults will need to find ways to earn our students' respect, so that we can help them achieve. There is no other way.

There will always be highly-motivated students. Future educators will have to learn and develop new methods to encourage those students who lack motivation.

Just as we have had great athletes and fit kids in the past, so they will continue. Likewise, young people who physically inactive will continue to develop health problems.

Educated parents with the means to pay for extra activities will always enroll their children in them. They have learned through their own involvement how important these activities are to social, personal and academic growth. More-privileged children will flourish. We must work to see that the lower-income segments of our society do not fall further behind them.

It will behoove the schools to find ways to educate and provide PE and after-school activities for all children. The US has always been a world-leader in education; we literally cannot afford only to educate our elite. The schools must reach out and support all people, regardless of socioeconomic background.

How we educate all people will be our biggest challenge. We must not allow only the affluent to receive the benefits of physical activity, while the students on the lower end suffer its absence, and subsequent medical effects. *All children deserve, and stand to benefit from, physical activity.* The public schools in the past have served all children in this respect. Growing up in Jersey City, at PS # 23, I had a great physical education. PE and athletics saved my life.

I proclaim that we not only hold, serve and support—but that we increase these activities to include all children.

As I am fond of saying, the future is now. I am reaching the so called "Twilight Years." With luck, some of my love of teaching will continue to others. I am not sure of the day I will retire, but it is close. Now, the ones who follow will make their own path. Knowing some of the young educators and students I have met, I feel that the future is in good hands.

CONCLUSION

This has been a labor of love. Herein 44 years of teaching and coaching are represented. All of the above is truth, without embellishment. The people I have spoken about are real, as are their accomplishments.

When I first went into education my intent was to retire early, with visions of golf and travel. Four back operations, arthritis, prostate cancer, and some minor health problems would keep me from those particular dreams, but I achieved something else: I have helped people (it certainly wasn't money).

Never in my wildest imagination did I believe I would still be educating into my '70s. My motivation to write this book came from former students. Many would say, "Coach, I want to write a book about *you* someday." Finally, I decided to put a few stories on paper, and it grew. Anyway, who knows my story better than I do?

To those whom I neglected to mention, please forgive me. Among my 65,000 students over these precious years, you were all important to me. I will miss you all dearly as I fade into your memories.

The new generation will take over and new stories will be told. This time maybe you will be the one telling your story. Hopefully others in education, or elsewhere, will see value in these words. If I made an impact on some of you—mission accomplished!

I have but one request: pass the "love" on to those behind you.

15556970R00185

Made in the USA
Charleston, SC
09 November 2012